P9-EDY-708

Choosing and Using
MANAGEMENT CONSULTANTS

About the Author

Roger Bennett BA, MSc (Econ), PhD, currently a director of a leading UK management consultancy, has many years' experience of corporate and small business management consultancy, planning, lecturing and research. His main fields of concentration are strategic and human resource management, turnaround strategy, and the preparation of small business expansion plans. He is a well-known author in the management, business studies and human resources fields, having published several textbooks and numerous articles on management topics in academic journals and general interest magazines. In the past, Dr Bennett has lectured at London University and in various UK polytechnics. He has served on management-related advisory panels to government departments and is an external examiner to a number of professional bodies.

Choosing and Using

MANAGEMENT CONSULTANTS

Roger Bennett

KOGAN
PAGE

© Roger Bennett 1990
All rights reserved. No reproduction, copy, or transmission of this publication may be made without written permission.

No paragraph of this publication may be reproduced, copied or transmitted save with written permission or in accordance with the provisions of the Copyright Act 1956 (as amended), or under the terms of any licence permitting limited copying issued by the Copyright Licensing Agency, 7 Ridgmount Street, London WC1E 7AE.

Any person who does any unauthorised act in relation to this publication may be liable to criminal prosecution and civil claims for damages.

First published in 1990 by
Kogan Page Ltd,
120 Pentonville Rd, London N1 9JN

Printed and bound in Great Britain by
Richard Clay Ltd, Chaucer Press,
Bungay, Suffolk.
Typeset by The Castlefield Press Ltd,
Wellingborough, Northants

British Library Cataloguing in Publication Data
Bennett, Roger
   Choosing and Using Management Consultants.
   1. Management consultancy
   I. Title
   658.4'6

ISBN 0-7494-0045-5 (Pbk)

Contents

Preface   6

1   All About Management Consultancy   9

2   Choosing a Consultant   33

3   Strategy Consultants   51

4   Organisation Design and Development Consultants   73

5   Quality Management and Manufacturing Systems Consultants   89

6   Financial Management Consultants   107

7   Project Management Consultants   122

8   Computer and Information Technology Consultants   130

9   Personnel Management Consultants   155

10   Marketing Consultants   183

11   Design and Creativity Consultants   208

12   Transport Management Consultants   220

13   Property Management Consultants   229

14   1992 Consultants   242

15   Using a Consultant to Draft a Business Plan   268

16   Management Consultants, Professional Negligence and the Law   277

Index of Advertisers   296

Index   297

Preface

All sorts of organisations today employ management consultants: multinational enterprises, large private and public corporations, the civil service, local government, sporting and charitable organisations, education authorities and many others. And the DTI Enterprise Initiative has made consultancy services available to small and medium sized businesses that otherwise would never have contemplated using a management consultant.

Unfortunately, however, few of the managers who choose and use consultants know very much about management consultancy. They are not certain about the criteria to adopt when selecting consultants, about how to draft a consultancy contract, how to monitor consultants' work, or how to appraise consultants' performances. Indeed, there is much mystique and confusion where management consultancy is concerned.

My purpose in writing this book is to demystify management consultancy. I have tried to explain precisely who the consultants are; how they operate; how to control and get the very best out of them, and what to do if things go wrong. I describe the various types of management consultant, suggest where to look for a consultant suitable for your particular needs, and examine the consultant/client relationship from client briefing to submission and evaluation of the consultant's final report.

The last chapter includes a catalogue of common complaints about management consultants. I explain the causes of the difficulties that might arise and offer suggestions for overcoming problems. Often, disagreements between consultants and their clients are due merely to misunderstandings about the nature of consultancy work and/or to ignorance of consultants' motives and methods rather than to fundamental difficulties. This is unfortunate because a little planning and foresight can frequently pre-empt many of the problems and potential points of friction.

I have assumed that you know nothing at all about the subjects discussed in the various chapters. If you are a specialist in a certain area or are highly knowledgeable about consultancy work in a particular field please bear in mind that other readers will not possess your background. Thus, if you are an accountant you will find my descriptions of auditing, accounts packages, investment appraisal procedures, etc, tedious and simplistic. Equally, a marketing executive will *already* know all about advertising and public relations consultancies, telemarketing services, fulfilment houses and so on, and hence might be irritated to find in Chapter 10 a brief mention of the marketing concept and marketing mix. Please understand in these circumstances that people engage consultants precisely because they lack knowledge of particular functions and hence will be reading this book to obtain, from scratch, an outline of the issues and problems they involve; so please be patient if you know a great deal about an individual point.

My thanks are due to Rosalind Bailey who word-processed the entire manuscript and to Kogan Page for rapidly expediting the project. Sections of Chapters 6 and 8 are based on material that first appeared in my previous books *Organisation and Management* (1988) and *Small Business Survival* (1989), both published by Pitman Publishing. I am grateful to Pitman for their permission to use this material. Parts of Chapter 4 originated in my book, *Managing Activities and Resources*, published by Kogan Page in January 1989.

Roger Bennett
Autumn 1989

Chapter 1

All About Management Consultancy

Introduction — Development of management consultancy — What is management consultancy? — When to use a management consultant — Specialist versus full-service consultancies — Large and small consultancies — What do management consultants do? — Typical assignments — Diagnosis and objectivity — Consultants, agents and suppliers — Management auditing — Groupage — Facilities management — Locating management consultants — The Enterprise Initiative — Sources of information

After reading this chapter you should:

- appreciate the types and range of assignments undertaken by management consultants;
- understand what can and cannot be done under the DTI Enterprise Initiative and how the Enterprise Initiative works;
- know about current trends in management consultancy, especially in relation to linkages between the supply of equipment/services and the provision of consultancy advice;
- understand the differences between agents and suppliers;
- know the advantages and disadvantages of using outside consultants rather than in-house staff;
- be able to list suitable criteria for selecting a consultant;
- know where to look for consultants specialising in particular fields.

Introduction

Everyone has heard of management consultancy, yet hardly anybody knows what management consultants actually do! Interest in the subject has increased, of course, through the government's promotion of the DTI Enterprise Initiative (discussed presently) through which between 5 and 15 days of management consultancy is available to small and medium sized firms at a subsidised rate (assistance at half or two-thirds the cost are available, depending on the geographical location of the client firm). Most large companies use consultants at least occasionally, while local and national government, public corporations, the National Health Service and other public sector bodies all employ consultancy services from time to time. Even the armed forces now engage management consultants to advise on the administrative side of their work. It is surprising, therefore, that hardly anything has been written about management consultancy, and that so little is known about the consultant's role.

Development of management consultancy

Many of today's big general management consultancies began as offshoots from large accountancy practices. Accountants are frequently the first people to whom businesses turn for help and advice in difficult circumstances, so it was almost inevitable that the major accounting firms would become involved in widespread management consultancy. However, despite their expertise in financial and related areas most accountants lack knowledge of overall management practice; especially matters relating to organisational design, project management, marketing strategy and personnel management. Accordingly, accounting businesses set up divisions to deal with general management work. These became highly profitable and thus were converted into separate firms – within which financial management was but one of several constituent parts. Not surprisingly, accountants dominated these consultancies during their formative years, and accountancy has remained a dominant force in management consultancy to the present day.

The example in the 1950s and 60s of the success of United States non-accountancy based general management consultancies (which attracted large amounts of lucrative business in Britain as well as the US itself) encouraged UK firms to launch similar ventures. Around the same time there was a severe labour shortage in the UK which generated a boom in personnel management consultancy work. There was a proliferation of employment agencies, including many which dealt exclusively with managerial personnel. As these agencies acquired experience of recruitment consultancy, so too did they extend their activities into other aspects of personnel, diversifying into non-personnel activities as opportunities arose. The information technology revolution further boosted the demand for consultancy services, particularly from accounting firms.

Individuals initially employed by the large consultancy firms have set up their own consultancies, and there is now a vast range of small specialist consultancy firms. And as we shall see, many agents (commercial estate agents for instance) and equipment suppliers now provide consultancy services for their customers as part of a wider deal.

Specialist consultants normally possess a particular skill (information technology, electronics, knowledge about 1992, and so on) which is in heavy demand. There are, of course, management consultants who are as much entertainers as they are providers of useful services and advice, doing little more than appearing impressive and deliberately building up the egos of their clients. But they tend not to last long unless they have a tangible, worthwhile service to sell that will identifiably improve profitability within clients' firms.

Large consultancies employ qualified and experienced professionals plus younger people fresh from college. The latter are normally seeking general business experience prior to embarking on a long term career, usually within a large organisation. Consultancies have core staff on permanent contracts, plus numerous temporary consultants on short term contracts, engaged whenever there is sufficient demand. When dealing with a large consultancy it is essential that you establish *exactly* who is to do the work, and you should *always* expect to see that person's CV. Further information on the sorts of people who become consultants in various specialist areas is provided later in the text.

What is management consultancy?

It is not possible to define management consultancy with precision because of the enormous diversity of the field. The best definition perhaps, is that management consultancy is everything and anything that a management consultant might be called upon to do. This could include giving advice, conducting research, testing attitudes and opinions, suggesting solutions to problems and new methods for organising work, and actually *implementing* new procedures. Additionally, all sorts of agents (commercial estate agents, import agents, advertising and public relations agents, etc) provide important and wide-ranging advisory services.

Increasingly, manufacturers establish consultancy facilities for their customers, and equipment and materials suppliers frequently offer commissions to other businesses that will recommend their output to third parties and perhaps install equipment (a particular model of computer for example) on the supplier's behalf.

Contemporary management consultancy embraces anyone who gives significant help and advice to senior management. This can include suppliers and agents who offer advisory services as well as the 'pure' management consultant who does nothing more than give advice. And the provider of consultancy services need *not* be independent of materials or equipment supply.

When to use a management consultant

Management consultants thrive on inefficiency; wherever there is a need to increase output, enhance productivity and/or improve an organisation's rate of return, management consultants are likely to be found.

There is a wide variety of circumstances in which you might wish to engage a consultant. Nevertheless, certain situations make a consultant's contributions especially worth while, particularly the following instances.

- Where unusual difficulties are experienced for the first time and an outside expert can explain their true nature and how they have been overcome in other businesses.
- When existing staff have neither the time nor the knowledge to cope with a new project and it would not be cost-effective hiring someone to handle the project on a permanent full-time basis.
- When you are not entirely clear about the fundamental causes of the firm's problems.
- If you feel that an objective review of the company's operations is necessary to maintain your competitive edge.

The need to hire a consultant often results from senior managers becoming so tied up with day-to-day operations that they fail to realise the inevitability of change; and when change is forced upon them by external events they are unable either to predict its implications or to accommodate its effects. Typical indicators of inadequate performance include low productivity and rates of return, poor quality output, excessive stockholdings, late deliveries to customers, high levels of customer complaints, high labour turnover and low employee morale, and internal conflicts among the staff. All these lead eventually to declining profitability and market share; typical catalysts for asking external consultants to enter the firm.

In-house versus external consultancy services
In-house staff are obviously familiar with the business, its organisational structure, and (importantly) they know exactly where to look for information. The staff concerned are fully accountable for their actions in the long term, (consultants usually disappear immediately after an assignment finishes) and their careers within the organisation substantially depend on the success of their work. They are constantly and immediately available, and completely under management's control. Yet doing things in-house has several significant disadvantages.

- In-house specialists sometimes create 'little empires' around their specialisations. For example, many firms large enough to support in-house advertising departments choose to use outside agencies (see Chapter 10) because in-house advertising staff may become so obsessed with the advertising function that they forget the company's wider objectives. They confer with each other in jargon unintelligible to non-advertising colleagues; arrange numerous in-house meetings among themselves, set up specialist sections (eg, for media selection, copywriting, artwork, creativity, typesetting, promotions, merchandising, etc), and seem oblivious to the need to keep advertising expenditure under tight control. It is not unknown for (say) medium sized manufacturing companies with in-house advertising departments to become what are in effect advertising organisations with added-on manufacturing facilities!

- In-house staff are not subject to penetrating expert criticism from outside. Mistakes made by in-house employees through lack of specialist skills and knowledge might never be revealed.
- Internal employees usually have limited experience of other industries and firms.
- Security of tenure can lead to lack of effort and creativity.
- Parkinson's Law might apply. Employees may fill out their time to appear fully occupied throughout the year, even when this is not actually the case.
- Internal staff might be apathetic and lack the management skills and innovative attitudes needed to complete an unusual or exceptionally difficult project on schedule.

Outsiders
Outsiders are independent, objective and impartial where internal politics are concerned. They will not be afraid to ask penetrating (even embarrassing) questions of anyone in the organisation – right up to the very top. Indeed, senior executives may willingly discuss with an external consultant sensitive issues they would not discuss with their own subordinate staff.

Consultants' experience of similar problems in other firms and industries enables them to identify solutions quickly, and to appreciate all the options available and the difficulties involved. Few if any overheads are incurred – consultants only cost the value of the project to which they are assigned. Thus you are saved all the costs of training and developing a senior managerial employee – who possibly could not be kept fully employed on high level work all the time.

Other important advantages of using outsiders are their up-to-the-minute knowledge of specialist techniques; the commitment and motivation that comes from having to earn profits (rather than just earn an employee's salary); and their wide range of contacts with other experts and sub-contractors in their particular fields. Effectively, through using a consultant you are benefiting from other companies' mistakes, since work undertaken for other clients has enabled the consultant to acquire the experience and expertise needed to tackle the problems confronting your firm.

Nevertheless, consultants should always be used to *supplement* rather than replace in-house skills. If a consultant is used to relieve pressures on existing staff the work should be carefully dovetailed into the activities of the organisation overall. Importantly, if the consultant is engaged for an *ad hoc* project then it is essential that the company's internal staff *learn* from the assignment; if only by observing the consultant at work. An internal employee's attachment to an exercise supervised by an expert external consultant can be an extremely valuable medium for training the employee and a useful means for developing that person's career.

Justifying the use of an outside consultant to colleagues

If you are required to justify to your senior management colleagues the need for independent external advice you should proceed as follows. First, explain to them the existence and severity of the problem. Then state the precise objectives of the intended work, how and when targets will be achieved, and how the results can be evaluated. Outline the measures already undertaken to achieve internal solutions to the problem and why these have failed. Supply answers to the following questions.

- What internal resources and expertise does the company not possess in order to complete the project in-house and how much would it cost to purchase these?
- How will your competitive position be affected through *not* using a consultant?
- When will the project break-even and what long-run rate of return is expected?
- How much will company executives learn just by watching a top-class consultant undertaking the assignment?

Specialist versus full-service consultancies

Consultancies may be *specialist* or *full-service*. The latter offer a comprehensive range of services, including most of the specialisms discussed in this book. Full-service 'generalist', consultancies boast all-round experience and abilities, but are usually more expensive and thus might not be particularly interested in smaller clients that are looking for low-cost consultancy work. Also, assignments might take longer through a large consultancy on account of its bureaucracy and (possibly) lengthy periods between winning a contract and actually starting the work.

The advantages of using a full-service consultancy are that you can obtain all your requirements from a single source and that high quality general support services (advice and/or materials or equipment supplies not specifically or immediately related to the project) will be available whenever they are required. Because they employ consultants from a wide range of subject backgrounds they can usually supply one or more people especially suited to a client's particular needs. A major advantage is that should, regrettably, you have to sue the consultancy on account of its incompetence or professional negligence it will almost certainly have insurance and/ or substantial assets from which the resulting damages can be met.

Large and small consultancies

Creativity within large consultancies

Large consultancies are sometimes criticised for lacking innovation and creative ideas. The volume of work involved in undertaking hundreds of projects year after year has, so critics allege, caused them to apply dull, conventional and stereotyped solutions to diverse problems – each of which really requires an original approach. Clients might be expected to adapt their systems more to suit the administrative convenience of the consultancy undertaking the project than to suit the objective needs of their firms.

Maintaining innovation within a large consultancy is problematic for many reasons. First and foremost is the acute shortage of experienced, skilled and competent managerial talent that large consultancies need in order to staff their businesses. Individuals possessing managerial expertise in skills shortage areas are likely either to establish their own specialist consultancy firms, or to take highly paid permanent positions in large industrial/commercial organisations. The UK management education system will not be remotely capable of meeting the management skills shortfall for many years to come (if ever) and the shortage of suitable people will if anything become worse rather than better.

High salaries for top class consultants can create high staff turnover in the large consultancies (as they compete with each other for the limited talent currently available) possibly causing lack of continuity within the big consultancy firms. Moreover, the high cost of employing top class senior consultants encourages consultancies to economise on the number of experienced senior people they hire, leading perhaps to a reduction in the level of quality of their service.

Organisation of large consultancies

The large consultancies sometimes refer to their internal organisations as following either a '*honeycomb*' or '*motherhood*' structure. A honeycomb consultancy consists of a conglomeration of 'cells' each corresponding to some specialist area of expertise. Firms with honeycomb organisations recruit existing qualified expert staff in appropriate functional specialisations, creating additional cells whenever the firm undertakes new types of activity.

The advantage of a honeycomb system is that the consultancy can expand or contract its operations quickly and conveniently through hiring or firing the relevant experts. On the other hand, individual consultants engaged in this manner might feel little commitment to the firm (highly qualified and experienced experts can easily move on to other businesses) and labour turnover could be high.

Motherhood consultancies, conversely, seek to hire young, inexperienced but promising consultants and train them in *generalist* consultancy methods. Staff are then committed to their employing organisation, undertake a wide variety of assignments, and become steeped in the employer's culture and working practices. There is guaranteed continuity of operations within motherhood consultancies, but staff might lack the expertise of specialist outsiders – especially in narrow functional areas. Also, because of the long periods necessary to train new entrants, motherhood firms cannot expand or alter the scope of their operations as readily as honeycomb consultancies.

Small consultancies

These are run by one or just a few individuals and often specialise in a particular field. As some smaller consultancies specialise you can use different firms for different jobs and/or several consultants for various aspects of a single larger project. A problem with highly specialist consultancies is that the more technically specialised they are the less experience of general business problems they are likely to have had. Hence you may need to brief a small firm especially carefully and spend more time co-ordinating its work with that of your company than might be necessary using a full-service firm. Moreover, small consultancies might not enjoy the same access to ancillary services, business contacts and low cost sources of materials supply as their larger rivals. They cannot afford to employ their own specialist support staff and thus must call in supplementary services from outside as and when required.

Advantages of small consultancies

Small consultancies claim they provide personalised services specifically geared to client's specific needs. The owners of the consultancy will usually undertake all assignments personally, and clients can approach them immediately problems arise. There is little bureaucracy within their organisations, few overheads are carried, and compared to large consultancies they might be more flexible when negotiating an assignment price. Leadtimes between their accepting a project and starting the work may be lower than for bigger consultancies. Small firms insist that they are more responsive to customer requirements and more innovative than larger rivals. And they usually offer lower rates.

You can normally be sure that the person you engage will see the project through to its final completion (there is substantial staff turnover in some of the larger consultancies).

What do management consultants do?

Consultants engaged in general management consultancy will tell you that the same kinds of assignments arise time and again in consultancy work, typically involving one or more of the following problems:

- how to vary the size of a workforce; redundancy planning and implementation;
- deciding whether to decentralise, create divisions or establish completely independent and self-contained subsidiary units;
- structuring operations into sections that facilitate *auditing* and *appraisal* of staff and activities, and the easy introduction of new working methods;
- deciding whether to control operations tightly and comprehensively or simply to set overall targets, A variety of specialist services are also in demand. The main specialisms are described in later chapters of the book.

Typical assignments

To illustrate the diverse nature of a consultant's work consider the following (real life) examples of one week's assignments undertaken in a small (single-person) consultancy firm.

ASSIGNMENT ONE

Paul, Ray and Henry are three brothers who jointly own and control a profitable import business segmented into three divisions. Each brother manages one of the divisions of the firm. The business was founded by Henry, who at 36 is the oldest of the brothers. Paul is the youngest of the three and the least interested in the firm. Recently, Henry attended a one day course about 'performance appraisal' run by a well-known management training organisation. Henry's approach is extremely entrepreneural and he is constantly looking for new ways to improve the efficiency of the business, especially by cutting costs.

So impressed was Henry by the appraisal concepts and methods discussed during the course that he determines that from now on it shall be company policy to appraise all people and things. He proposes this to Ray and Paul, who agree with his view. Accordingly, the three brothers instruct their divisional managers (all divisions have two managers plus four other full-time employees) to conduct 'SWOTS' (ie, analyses of personal Strengths, Weaknesses, Opportunities, and Threats) on their staff.

The result is a disaster: divisional managers are incapable of expressing sensible opinions on subordinates' work, they begrudge having to spend time conducting appraisals, and are not really sure what is required in the first place. Subordinates bitterly resent the exercise and try to disrupt it whenever and wherever they can. There are angry meetings, arguments, hostile letters and resignation threats.

Ray suggests to Henry that the scheme be scrapped, but Henry is adamant that further appraisals be carried out. Paul, the youngest brother, seeks external advice.

ASSIGNMENT TWO

Alan is 27 and has completed four years' service with a food processing firm that has 20 employees. Three months ago Alan became a head of department, in charge of four full-time and three part-time staff. One of Alan's new subordinates is Helen, a 52 year old who has been with the firm for twelve years.

Helen is aggressive towards Alan. She is surly, frequently late for work, takes an excessive amount of sick leave and will do nothing unless she is told. Alan has no supervisory experience, has received no supervisory training and feels he cannot cope. Helen is making his life unpleasant and now his own superiors are beginning to complain about the low standard of the department's work. Helen's output is generally mediocre, but not so bad she can be fairly dismissed.

Alan's boss instructs him to seek advice from the firm's management consultant. Should he interview Helen and if so how? What actions short of dismissal could he take? Should he redesign Helen's job, supervise her more closely, leave her alone, allocate her to an alternative team, put her onto different duties, introduce a bonus system, or what?

ASSIGNMENT THREE

R & D Developments Limited is a small company wishing to expand into a lucrative new market but which lacks the resources and technical know-how required. The firm is approached by a larger company that already operates in the intended new market and invited to merge. The bidding company possesses substantial capital assets, a large amount of idle cash, first class employees, and premises large enough to accommodate R & D's equipment and staff.

However, the large company insists that R & D Developments must surrender its separate corporate identity and become a minority voting partner in the new concern.

Two of the company's principal shareholders seek advice on the following matters.

- What criteria should determine the decision whether to merge?
- How can the calibre of the bidding company be assessed?
- How should the new company be organised if the merger goes through?

The problems of being a consultant
Individuals go into management consultancy for many reasons: financial reward, the training and experience in general management that consultancy provides, loss of other jobs, or simply because of the innate interest and variety of consultancy work – consultants typically undertake many projects each year in widely differing commercial environments. Yet it remains uncommon for people to spend their entire careers as consultants, for a number of reasons.

- Clients are located throughout the country so much travelling and/or time spent away from home is required. Living in hotels becomes tedious after a while.
- The skills and experiences acquired through consultancy equip the individual with the all-round managerial competencies necessary for success in highly paid top management posts in large organisations. Consultants are constantly in touch with senior company executives in client firms, and many top-class consultants eventually receive offers they cannot refuse.
- Consultants work extremely hard. Clients want action and results. It is a high pressure existence that some people prefer not to live for too long.
- Consultants engaged on short term assignments rarely see the long term benefits of their work. Projects are necessarily *ad hoc* and do not allow the consultant the satisfaction of observing a business grow and prosper in the longer period.
- The demand for consultancy services varies according to the buoyancy of the national economy and, for industry-specific consultants, the health of the particular industry concerned. For example, a decline in manufacturing brings about a sharp

reduction in the demand for industrial designers, manufacturing systems consultants, industrial marketing consultants, and so on. And, if anything, clients seem to spend more on consultants when they are doing well than when they are doing badly (arguably the reverse should occur, with clients using consultants to revive the fortunes of ailing businesses). Depressions and industry reorganisations cause the collapse of many consultancy firms.

Diagnosis and objectivity

A consultant's major contribution may be the objective approach he or she brings to the analysis of a business. The solution to a problem may be obvious to an outsider, yet not recognised internally because senior executives are too close to day-to-day operations to be able to assess the situation objectively.

Diagnostic methods

When you are ill and go to the Doctor you expect the Doctor to diagnose the cause of your complaint. Doctors normally apply one of two approaches to diagnosis – inductive or deductive – depending on the available information and the seriousness of the complaint. The deductive approach involves asking general questions first and then narrowing down the range of possible origins of the problem as the consultation proceeds. Questions become increasingly specific until the reason for your illness is discovered. There are two difficulties with deductive questioning, the vast range of questions that might be asked, and the fact that asking a particular question can put an idea into the patient's mind – people asked whether they have been having headaches may suddenly decide that they have, even if this is not actually the case.

Inductive diagnosis means the Doctor takes one look at you and, from his or her many years of experience of treating similar illnesses, provisionally assumes a certain cause. Then you are asked questions to confirm or reject this opinion. The problem here is that the initial assessment may be incorrect so that the Doctor then pursues several wild goose chases before reaching the correct diagnosis.

Discovering what has gone wrong with a business is much the same. You may inwardly feel that you know the source of poor performance, yet be unable to establish conclusively the cause of the problem. Accordingly, a good consultant will help you enumerate all aspects of the company's policies and operations that might have gone wrong and then systematically narrow down the list.

The consultant will try to identify linkages between cause and effect. A good way to do this is by specifying the firm's objectives (see Chapter 3) and then working backwards through the entire organisation highlighting inefficiencies which have prevented the achievement of company aims. This requires thinking of businesses as systems, with inputs and outputs subject to managerial control.

Accordingly, a common approach to management consultancy is to define a theoretical perfectly functioning model of how a business *ought* to perform in a certain situation and then to compare this with actual events, noting all discrepancies and *how* and *why* they occur. Causes of problems and requirements for change can now be established and new systems, management structures, working methods, patterns of accountability and responsibility, changes in staffing levels, etc, may be imposed.

Directive versus non-directive consultancy styles
Consultants engaged in highly technical work (computer or manufacturing systems consultants for example) will typically instruct their clients about what they should do. Other types of consultant might see the consultancy role more in terms of helping clients define problems clearly, but leaving clients to determine appropriate solutions for themselves. In the latter case the consultant tries to make the client aware of possibilities and, thereafter, independently capable of initiating change. The assumptions behind the non-directive approach are that:

- only the client is truly capable of accurately defining the real reasons for the company's problems, so that (given the consultant's help) only the client can discover appropriate solutions to these problems;
- the fastest and most efficient way of getting to the heart of a problem is by self-discovery;
- there is no point in pushing a client towards implementation of a particular solution if he or she does not wholeheartedly accept the solution proposed.

Non-directive approaches can be highly effective in certain circumstances, but clients sometimes feel they are not receiving full value for money from consultants who adopt a non-directive style. Clients are paying large amounts of money to be asked questions the answers to which they must provide themselves, and many clients fail to perceive the value of such exercises and greatly prefer their consultants assertively to tell them what to do.

Directive consultancy involves the consultant taking the initiative in defining the problem, outlining the possible consequences of alternative causes of action, and recommending a specific solution. The client takes the final decision, but the consultant clearly charts out a path for the client to follow in deciding what to do.

Resource consultancy and process consultancy

Consultants themselves sometimes use the terms *resource* consultancy and *process* consultancy. By the former they mean the transfer of information from the consultant to the client. The aim is to increase the client's knowledge of a situation. It assumes that the more a client knows about a problem the better equipped the client will be to resolve the issue. Process consultancy, conversely, seeks to create in the client the capacity to solve problems independently by transferring to the client appropriate diagnostic and analytical skills.

Consultants, agents and suppliers

The trend in most fields of management consultancy is for consultants to become closely involved in the physical supply of the materials, components and services necessary to implement consultancy proposals. Consultants develop expert knowledge of particular types of assignment. They know the materials necessary, the best suppliers, keenest prices, maintenance costs, delivery leadtimes, etc, and it is thus only natural for them to use this expertise to produce or otherwise supply ancillary materials. For example, a marketing consultant (see Chapter 10) might be a part owner of a printing firm that creates, typesets and prints promotional literature (maildrops, point of sale displays, etc) for client firms. A vehicle fleet maintenance management consultant (see Chapter 12) may have a financial interest in the garages which service clients' vehicles, or a property management consultant (see Chapter 13) might have a stake in a building or property development firm.

This trend is not surprising considering how often satisfied clients will invite their consultant to participate in the implementation of the consultant's recommendations.

Sometimes the process is reversed – equipment and service suppliers may be asked by their customers for advice on general or administrative matters so frequently that they establish separate divisions or subsidiary companies devoted entirely to consultancy work. The services offered by these divisions/subsidiaries are usually concerned with how to install and utilise the suppliers' goods and not with choice among alternative sources of supply.

Further examples of diversification into consultancy are the large national car hire companies that have set up transport consultancy divisions, national chains of estate agents which have moved into general property management, and sales promotions fulfilment houses (see Chapter 10) and commercial television companies that nowadays offer extensive general marketing facilities and advice.

Legal differences

There are important legal differences between 'consultants', 'agents' and 'suppliers' even though in practice the individuals concerned may do essentially similar work. Technically, a 'consultant' is an independent businessperson who does nothing more than offer advice. A 'supplier' – in addition to giving advice – provides physical goods and/or services and *implements* recommended solutions. For example, a computer consultant (see Chapter 8) will conduct a systems analysis and suggest the client obtains particular types of software and equipment, and then may or may not be prepared physically to obtain and install the new system.

Agents

Agents undertake tasks on a client's behalf, usually by putting the client in touch with third parties. However, the agent then drops out of the situation so that resulting contracts are between the company and the third party, without further involvement of the agent. For instance, a commercial estate agent will put the owner of a property in touch with suitable tenants, but the contract that ensues is between landlord and tenant only. So that if, say, the tenant damages the property or fails to pay the rent then the agent is not liable for the consequent debt. Similarly an export agent finds foreign customers for a client's goods; but if the goods are defective, damaged or delivered late it is the company and not the agent who is liable to the overseas firm.

It is extremely important that the contract between the consultant and yourself clearly specifies the extent to which the consultant will act as an agent or a supplier. Consider for example a computer consultant hired by your company to install a new system. Assume you know nothing at all about information technology, and thus leave the choice of equipment, purchase of software, supply of consumables (printer, ribbons, disks, computer stationery, etc) to the consultancy firm. The consultancy will train your staff in computer procedures, and show how to transfer existing records onto computer files.

Your contract with this consultant should make clear whether he or she is to act as:

- an independent supplier of computer equipment, in which case you sue the consultant if the equipment supplied fails to work;
- an agent of a computer equipment manufacturer or importer, so that liability for faulty equipment lies with the supplying company and you have no redress against the consultant installing the system; or
- your own agent whom you employ to purchase equipment on your behalf, in which case you are *fully* liable for all the contracts for equipment and consumables that the consultant enters. If you do not like the equipment the consultant orders you still have to pay because under the law of agency the consultant has implicit authority (provided it is made clear to suppliers that he or she is an agent) to enter legally binding contracts on your behalf! Nevertheless, the law would expect the consultant to exercise 'ordinary skill and diligence' when selecting equipment, and if you can prove that he or she did not do so you can sue the consultant for consequential loss.

Matters relating to agency are further discussed in Chapter 16.

Management auditing

A major part of the general management consultant's work concerns management auditing of client's organisations. Management audits examine the adequacy of company policies and procedures for achieving the company's goals. Audits should be comprehensive – looking at all aspects of the firm's operations and not just some of them – and regular. As well as undertaking audits at predetermined intervals (say once every two or three years), audits are needed whenever external situations or internal circumstances unexpectedly change. Business environments are dynamic in nature – they evolve, generate new opportunities, and make irrelevant some existing activities. The purpose of a major audit is to reorganise resources – material, financial and human – and redirect effort towards the more efficient attainment of goals. Minor audits, taking one department at a time, might be completed between major analyses.

Two types of audit are needed: internal and external. External audits examine the general environments that surround the organisation – legal (the effects of changes in employment law for example), economic, market opportunities, behaviour of competitors, etc. Internal audits investigate operational systems within the enterprise. Often, they are conducted *via* checklists issued to department heads to gather information on the relevance of sectional activities, on the flow of work through sections, and on relationships between inputs and departmental productivity. A typical audit will examine such things as:

- management style and communications;
- whether organisation charts and job specifications are up to date;
- whether organisational and departmental objectives are understood by all department members;
- possible duplication of activities;
- operational efficiency within sections; and
- plant and/or office layout.

Groupage

Consultancies that provide services through outside organisations (eg, servicing and maintenance of vehicles at garages, property maintenance by building firms, cleaning services, or the physical transport of goods) typically operate groupage facilities whereby the work of small clients is combined with that of large clients (and other small clients) into a single bulk order to be placed with a third party supplier at a substantial bulk order discount on normal price. A vehicle fleet management consultant, for instance, might be able to give garages orders for servicing (say) several hundred vehicles at a time. In return the garages must offer attractive rates, and perhaps supply vehicle owners (ie, the consultancy's clients) with car batteries, tyres and other vehicle consumables at a special low price – substantially lower than the client could negotiate independently. These savings alone can justify a consultant's fee.

Facilities management

Consultants are increasingly involved in 'facilities management', meaning that the consultant takes over an *entire* function within the client's firm; managing it on the client's behalf, under the client's letterhead, and possibly using the client's equipment and employees.

In effect the client obtains an entire department at low overhead cost, and does not have to train and develop its own senior staff in a particular field. Facilities management is common in the export business, where 'export management companies' (sometimes known as 'combination export management consultants', see Chapter 14) might market and distribute a client firm's output overseas – handling all the documentation, customs clearances, marine and export credit insurances, delivery of the goods and collection of foreign currency debts that arise – but using the client firm's name.

The practice has spread to the management of computer systems, transport, and to the management of the land and buildings owned by large corporations. Facilities management consultants usually work for several clients simultaneously.

Locating management consultants

Advice on where to look for consultants specialising in specific areas is given in the relevant subject chapters. Otherwise, a number of trade associations of management consultants exist, and certain professional bodies maintain lists of consultants active in various fields.

Consultants registering with a professional body

The consultant may approach the relevant institute (the Institute of Marketing for example) and request registration, which (normally) is given only if certain minimum criteria are satisfied. These criteria relate to such matters as:

- requirements that the applicant has already operated as a consultant for a certain period (typically two years);
- qualifications and experience of staff;
- requirements that registered consultants carry adequate insurance against claims for professional negligence (see Chapter 16); and
- requirements that registered consultancies be sole traders or partnership without limited liability or that consultancies that are limited companies have some minimum paid up share capital (so that substantial resources are available to pay creditors or to meet court judgements if they are sued).

Additionally, consultancies which act as agents (eg, as advertising agents, property management agents or as agents of equipment manufacturers) and which might be involved in high value financial transactions through their agency work, may be required to provide detailed information about their internal finances (debt:equity ratios, net current assets, profitability) as a condition of entry to a professional body's 'approved' consultants list.

Registration costs perhaps two or three thousand pounds per year. In return, the professional body passes on to the consultancy any enquiries it receives which relate to the consultant's specialisation.

Potential clients approach the professional body in the first instance and are given a list of three or four registered consultants active in the client's line of work.

Contacting a professional institute is a useful way to begin your search for a consultant.

The Management Consultancies Association

Founded in 1956 by the then four largest UK consultancy firms (PA, P-E, Urwick Orr and Inbucon) the MCA today comprises 29 big consultancies, collectively undertaking about 65 per cent of all UK consultancy work measured in value terms. Aggregate annual fee income earned by MCA members is approaching £450 million, and they employ nearly 5000 individual consultants. On average, approximately a quarter of their work is for the public sector, although this proportion is much higher for certain firms. Information technology is the dominant activity, with total fee income for this being almost double the next highest category, which is finance and administration. Ninety-five per cent of MCA members' work is in the UK.

The Association's recent annual reports note the growing importance to MCA consultancies of the provision of hands-on help in the implementation of agreed strategies, especially where IT (Information Technology) is concerned.

Members must be independent of equipment suppliers or other outside interests – although they are expected to be able to assist clients to implement consultancy recommendations, which obviously involves liaison with third parties - and they must employ qualified consultants. Ninety per cent of the latter must hold degrees or equivalent professional qualifications and there must exist within the member firm a documented and established programme for training both new entrants and existing personnel. These are important matters, since some unqualified non-MCA consultants pass themselves off as being professionally qualified by joining one of the several professional institutes that allow individuals to become members simply on the basis of experience, without the applicant having to study the subject seriously or take examinations. Then they put the institute's letters after their names to imply that they are expert in a certain field. When dealing with an MCA firm, you can at least be sure that its staff possess genuine and appropriate qualifications.

Specific experience requirements apply to MCA members. Firms must have existed for at least five years, with at least three of their senior consultants each having a minimum of ten years' management consultancy experience. At least a quarter of the firm's entire consulting staff must have been with the consultancy for five years, and the average length of service of employed consultants must be at least three years. These criteria apply to 'full' members of the MCA. The Association offers 'associate' membership to firms that satisfy all other requirements but which either (i) have not been trading for five years, or (ii) are highly specialised in a specific area and are thus unable to provide general 'across-the-board' advice.

The Association operates a *Code of Professional Conduct* which requires members:

- to regard all information received from clients as totally confidential;
- not to enter into arrangements that would detract from the objectivity and impartiality of the advice they give; and
- not to pay commissions to outsiders for introducing clients to the consultancy (so that clients know who they are actually dealing with right from the outset of an exercise and to ensure that clients select the best consultant for their requirements).

Note (importantly) that the MCA code forbids members to accept fees based on payments by results (see Chapter 2). Remunerations must be calculated as fixed or time-based fees agreed in advance. The MCA provides a client information service to provide details of member firms capable of undertaking various kinds of assignment. Also it offers a complaints and arbitration procedure for use by dissatisfied customers.

The Institute of Management Consultants
The Institute of Management Consultants is a professional institution comprising about 3300 individuals engaged in management consultancy. It began in 1962 as an offshoot of the MCA, sharing MCA premises for some years. The Institute provides:

- a free client advisory service;
- a complaints procedure should, unhappily, an assignment undertaken by a member go badly wrong; and
- general advice on selecting management consultants.

Another useful source of information on the location of various types of consultant is The Management Consultancy Information Service, which operates in association with the Confederation of British Industry and which offers (free) lists of management consultants who have registered with the service. A *Directory of Management Consultants in the UK* is published by TFPL

Publishing. This directory lists consultants both by specialism and by the industries in which they mainly operate.

The Enterprise Initiative

Consultants normally prefer to work for large rather than small businesses. Big clients offer longer assignments, higher fees, and a good chance of repeat business. Also the executives of a large organisation are likely to have experience of dealing with consultants and know how to brief them in a clear and precise way (owners of small businesses sometimes do not know what they actually want from their consultants).

In order to put management consultancy within the grasp of small and medium-sized businesses the Department of Trade and Industry (DTI) in January 1988 initiated a scheme for subsidising the cost of smaller business consultancy work. Initially the scope of the scheme was limited to consultancy help with marketing (both home and export), design, quality management and manufacturing, but this was revised in April 1988 and extended to include business planning and financial and information systems. Details of the scheme as they relate to each of these functions are given in appropriate chapters. Firms are entitled to apply for help in any two of the above-mentioned areas. To qualify for assistance you must employ less than 500 workers or be a member of a group of companies employing fewer than 500 worldwide.

First, you telephone the DTI Regional Office which deals with the scheme in your area (telephone numbers are listed in the EI brochure which you obtain from DTI). A DTI 'Enterprise Counsellor' (an experienced business person) then visits your firm to discuss your perceived problems and whether the scheme can help. DTI has appointed certain professional bodies and other organisations to oversee and control the quality of the provision of consultancy services provided through the Initiative. The Institute of Marketing, for instance, is the 'contractor' for the marketing element of the scheme; the Design Council is the contractor for design. On receipt of an application approved by an Enterprise Counsellor the contractor matches the client with a mutually agreed consultant. Clients pay half the cost of between five and fifteen days of consultancy work (one-third if your firm is in a designated Assisted Area or Urban Programme Area) and DTI pays the rest. Consultants are forbidden to invoice clients for (say) 14 days work while actually doing and charging for seven (so that the client would obtain the consultant's services entirely free).

The aim of the Enterprise Initiative is to provide access to expert consultants who will help you look at your business at the strategic level rather than actually undertake nitty-gritty work; the scheme does not normally cover particular aspects of functions independent of an overall strategy. Accordingly, EI consultancy is not available solely for such activities as:

- advertising/public relations campaigns;
- market research projects;
- development of pricing, sales and distribution policies;
- redesign of sales literature;
- advice on production inspection methods;
- training of staff;
- assistance with raising finance; and
- software programming or computer systems installation.

However, some of these elements can be covered in projects which take a wider, strategic view of a company's operations. The most comprehensive EI help is available under the manufacturing systems part of the scheme, through which advice on certain practical activities is permitted. Yet even here the stated purpose is that EI 'encourage' managers to *review* production operations as part of a *business strategy*' (my emphasis).

DTI has imposed a ceiling on the amount payable to consultants hired under the scheme. At the time of writing this is £300-400 per day (you need to ask the DTI for current details). This is not much for top class consultancy work, so if you engage a 'big name' consultancy for an EI assisted project make sure it does not use your business merely as a training ground for its junior staff.

In principle, this should not happen because DTI operates tight quality control over the consultancy services provided under the scheme. Quality control includes (i) the vetting of consultancies undertaking EI work (since 1988 they need to have been established for at least two years and to provide four references plus examples of recently completed projects), and (ii) the requirement that each client report be copied to the Scheme Contractor (for example, the Institute of Marketing) for appraisal. The client is not obliged to pay the consultant until the quality of the final report is confirmed by the Scheme Contractor. Thus, the work has to be fully up to scratch, even if it has been undertaken by relatively junior consultancy staff.

Further problems with EI
The major problem with the Enterprise Initiative, perhaps, is that it does not go far enough. For most of its constituent elements the emphasis is on strategy rather than implementation. You have to pay

extra if you decide to use the consultant to implement his or her proposals. You should discuss the procedures for implementing the consultant's proposals with your Enterprise Counsellor.

A consultant might tell you that the EI subsidy provides everything up to and including a strategy, but that additional payments are necessary for further aspects of the work (research, negotiating with third parties, arranging supplies and so on). This may be fair enough; no-one should be expected to work for nothing – yet it would clearly be improper for the EI scheme to be used simply as a vehicle for advertising and promoting consultants' services at the taxpayers' expense! The Scheme Contractor will of course seek to avoid any possibility of consultants deliberately providing incomplete treatment of a client's problems in the hope of then – having persuaded the client of the need for change – attracting further contracts to finish the job. In particular, EI rules specify that each completed consultancy assignment *must* be accompanied by a viable and reasonable action plan.

Using the Enterprise Initiative effectively

To get the best from the Enterprise Initiative you need to dovetail the consultancy project into the overall development of operations within your firm. Plan the consultant's contribution carefully, making sure it will represent a useful contribution to your total corporate plans and strategies. This means you must organise the assignment in such a way that:

- it is self-contained in the sense that if all you get is a strategy then the strategy offered is not dependent for its success on further work undertaken by the consultant who devised the strategy;
- the exercise is one of several building blocks for improving the performance of your business;
- additional work to implement the strategy can be done in-house or by another firm (if the consultant wishes to tender afresh for extra work he or she is quite free to do so).

Objectives for the exercise, and criteria for establishing whether it has been a success, will be drafted jointly by the consultant and the client, who agree the terms of reference of the project. When the project is completed the Scheme Contractor will check the final report against these agreed terms of reference to ensure the work has been completed in full.

The EI boasts that the independent experts engaged under the scheme are to 'help firms beat the competition', and that is exactly what you are entitled to expect from the scheme. Your business should be better equipped to beat its competitors the day the consultant leaves than the day he or she started.

Sources of information

British Institute of Management
Management House
Cottingham Road
Corby
Northants NN17 7TT
0536 204222

Confederation of British Industry
Centre Point
New Oxford Street
London WC1A 4DD
01-379 7400

Department of Trade and Industry
Contact points are spread throughout the country. You can obtain their addresses and telephone numbers by ringing 01-215 5000

Directory of Management Consultants in the UK
TFPL Publishing
76 Park Road
London NW1 4SH
01-258 3740

Institute of Directors
116 Pall Mall
London SW19 5ED
01-839 1233

Institute of Management Consultants
5th Floor
32/33 Hatton Garden
London EC1N 8DL
01-242 2140

Management Consultancies Association
11 West Halkin Street
London SW1X 8JL
01-235 3897

Management Consultancy Information Service
38 Blenheim Avenue
Gants Hill
Ilford
Essex IG2 6JO
01-554 4695

Chapter 2

Choosing a Consultant

Introduction — Narrowing the field — Fees — Consultancy contracts — Briefing a consultant — Monitoring a project — Evaluating a consultant's contributions

After reading this chapter you should:

- be able to specify objectives for a consultancy exercise;
- know what to look for in a consultant's proposal;
- be able to select a consultant through a logical process using relevant and objective criteria;
- understand how consultants compute their fees and know how to negotiate in order to minimise your fee obligations; and
- appreciate the problems and pitfalls associated with consultancy contracts.

Introduction

Your choice of consultant will depend crucially on your initial definition of the problems your company faces; yet you may need a consultant's help to define the company's problems accurately in the first place! For example, is a breakdown in the firm's financial information system an accounting problem or an information technology problem – should you simply contact your accountant for help and advice on this matter, or do you need to see a proper computer consultant? Suppose you have a problem with vehicle maintenance bills, should you go to a vehicle fleet management consultant (see Chapter 12) or someone who is expert in general cost control? Your initial specification of the problem will determine where you look for assistance, and an incorrect assessment of the nature of your difficulties can lead to an unsuitable choice of consultant.

An advantage of approaching a large full-service consultancy is that they employ a wide range of specialists in many functional areas (marketing, personnel, accounting, IT, etc) so your problems can be passed around the consultancy's various departments until an appropriate consultant is located. And a large full-service consultancy has no incentive to mislead you about the fundamental nature of the problems your firm confronts – unlike a small specialist consultancy which stands to lose the assignment if you change your mind about the type of consultant appropriate for the job.

Narrowing the field

The first task is to collect lists of consultancies specialising in the relevant field. This you can do *via* the bodies and publications mentioned in the last and subsequent chapters and, if possible, through personal contacts with other companies that have already used management consultants. From these lists select seven or eight promising candidates and write or phone, briefly outlining the nature of the assignment you have in mind and asking for details of their work.* In reply, you will normally receive from consultants loose-leaf brochures which state their areas of specialisation, the sorts of assignment they undertake, outline curricula vitae of owners and/or senior staff, and examples of the clients for whom they have previously worked. From these brochures you should reduce the short list to (say) three or four firms, and for each one telephone two of their past clients and request a reference. When speaking to a previous client do not simply ask for an overall impression: standards in some companies are lower than elsewhere. Rather, ask whether the project was completed on time; whether the initial budget was adhered to (and if not why not); and what specific benefits resulted from the consultant's work. How did the previous client's staff get on with the consultant? How detailed was the consultant's final report? Has the firm subsequently discovered available options not mentioned by the consultant? Has there been any genuine lasting change resulting from the consultant's visit? What criteria did the company use to evaluate the consultant's work? Do they intend rehiring the consultant?

Next, suggest a brief meeting with remaining candidates and that each submit an outline proposal. Many consultants will do this free, but you should be prepared to pay a small amount to cover the consultant's time, travelling and secretarial costs attached to drafting the short proposal.

Do not be too alarmed if one or more of the consultants still on your shortlist do not belong to any of the consultants' trade associations and/or do not appear on the list of consultants provided by a

---

*If you are using the Enterprise Initiative (see Chapter 1) the procedure is rather different. The Enterprise Counsellor will put you in touch with the appropriate contractor who then supplies you with a short list of approved consultancies.

particular professional body. Some registers exclude consultancies that have not been established for a certain number of years (even though their staff might have vast experience of successful consultancy work), or which have limited liability, or are not resident in the UK, or which are prepared to work on a payments by results basis. Indeed, a first class consultancy may simply feel that the (substantial) cost of registration is not financially worthwhile.

Nor should you refuse to consider a proposal from a consultant who undertakes assignments for one of your competitors. A competent consultant who provides excellent service and is expert in his or her field is bound to attract offers from firms in the same industry. That the consultant is in great demand should be seen as a strength and not a weakness. The answer here may be to impose a strict confidentially requirement on the consultant's contract, with explicit provision for the payment of substantial damages if the confidentiality clause is breached.

Need for experience
A common reason for using a consultant is the client firm's inexperience of a particular function or issue. Look for experience in candidate consultancies, but remember that experience should be up-to-date and relevant to your requirements – it is no substitute for top class technical ability and professional expertise. Experience, by definition, relates to the past whereas current decisions affect the future. Abraham Lincoln is reputed to have said that very often, people claiming 20 years' experience of something should really say they have one year's experience – repeated 20 times!

Nevertheless, genuinely experienced consultants undoubtedly bring a breadth of knowledge and background information to their advisory roles not possessed by others. This is especially valuable when the client firm does not really know what it wants. Experienced consultants should understand the client's problem and are usually better equipped to define the fundamental *essence* of a situation than the rest. They are ideal for giving a second opinion to managers who feel uneasy about committing extensive resources to new types of project they have not previously encountered.

Requesting estimates and proposals
Candidates remaining after the initial meetings should now be asked to submit estimates or quotations and a formal proposal for the assignment outlining expected costs, activities, methods of approach, time required, etc.

Specify the assignment in as much detail as possible and make sure each consultant quotes for exactly the same things (otherwise you will not be able to compare like with like when evaluating quotations). Prospective consultants need to know exactly what you want them to do, and your expectations regarding the extent, accuracy and quality of their efforts. State how much data you will provide in-house, and how much the consultant is required to gather.

A consultant's proposal will normally include (i) a statement of the consultant's perception of the problem that needs to be solved, (ii) how the consultant will approach the job, (iii) a schedule of intended work, (iv) details of duties/research to be performed by the consultant (and by the client), (v) materials and equipment to be supplied and (vi) who will provide secretarial and other assistance. A proposed starting date will be specified, plus a price for the job and a schedule for payment. Review points during the exercise may or may not be suggested (impose them if they are not mentioned).

Many consultants append to their proposals a draft contract for the work, stating their standard terms and conditions. Read this *very carefully indeed* to ensure it corresponds with what you want done, and that it will not affect your rights to compensation (see Chapter 16) if the consultant is incompetent or negligent.

Look for originality in the proposal and willingness to submit regular and comprehensive reports on the progress of the project. Now ask yourself the following questions in respect of each proposal.

- Is the consultant addressing your specific needs?
- Has the consultant volunteered outline criteria for measuring his or her performance and for assessing the value of intended contributions?
- Has the consultant's intended work schedule been split up into clearly defined stages?
- Does the consultant specify the degree of risk attached to the success of the project?
- If sub-contracting is involved, how will the consultant monitor the quality of sub-contracted duties?
- Will the consultant be working only on your assignment throughout the duration of the project or will he or she be simultaneously involved in other projects? In the latter case, to what extent will collateral activities interfere with work done for your firm?
- Has the consultant considered the motivation and ability levels of your staff and the need to train them to implement recommended solutions?

- How much post-implementation help and advice is offered?
- Is the proposed timetable for the assignment realistic?
- Has the consultancy demonstrated that it possesses the resources and facilities to do the job?
- What proven experience of your particular industry and type of business does the consultant possess?
- Will the consultancy guarantee that the individuals with whom you negotiate the fee shall be the people who actually complete the assignment or will junior consultancy staff be involved? Larger consultancies often employ 'practice development officers' whose only function is to sell the consultancy to prospective clients. Such people put an attractive face on the consultancy, but may mislead you about the quality of its work. Always insist on meeting the staff who will execute the assignment prior to signing the contract.
- Has the consultant taken the trouble to identify selling points which distinguish his or her services from those of other firms?
- Is the consultant willing to discuss previous non-confidential assignments of a type similar to that proposed for your firm?

Whether the distinction between a consultant who is genuinely and totally independent and one who has financial links with third party suppliers is important depends on the circumstances of the situation. Independents are not *necessarily* better than the rest, but it is essential that you know when outside interests are involved. An advantage of dealing with MCA or IMC consultancies (see Chapter 1) is that you know exactly where you stand in this respect: complete independence is a prerequisite for membership of these bodies.

Make sure that candidate consultancies have included the analysis of *identical* options in their proposals. To illustrate the need for this, consider the case of (say) a financial systems consultant who suggests that ten days work will be necessary to investigate existing accounting procedures and install a new system. Another candidate may insist that only five days' work is required. But the latter might be ignoring the need to investigate the feasibilities of more complex systems which, if installed, might be far superior in the longer period!

Another consideration is whether you are engaging a consultant to support your current employees or deliberately to antagonise them. The latter may be a good reason for using consultants, since a consultant's presence can sometimes shock apathetic employees into greater effort. However, the answer to this question will (or should) affect your choice of consultant because you need to determine whether you require a consultant who will quickly establish smooth and amicable relations with your staff, or one who will cause annoyance.

To summarise, you need to consider the following factors when selecting a consultant:

- experience
- track record
- specialist knowledge
- innovative and creative ability
- availability and how soon he or she can begin work
- cost
- interest in the project
- capacity to understand and analyse your problem
- ease of control and evaluation
- willingness to guarantee achievement of certain objectives
- ability to guarantee that particular people will work on the project
- research competence
- communication ability *vis-à-vis* yourself and your company's staff.

Now make your choice and write to unsuccessful candidates thanking them for their interest and briefly explaining why they were rejected – perhaps enclosing a cheque to cover their expenses. It is only fair to give reasons for rejection, considering the effort put into preparing outline proposals and to enable unsuccessful applicants to learn from the experience.

Fees

Consultancies must cover their overheads and the cost of the time directly absorbed by particular jobs. The costs of physical goods and ancillary services supplied to clients will be passed on, usually with the addition of a (negotiable) commission to cover the administrative expense involved. Travelling and other incidental disbursements are normally invoiced on a separate bill.

A consultancy's overheads are typically low compared to other types of business. They include premises, secretarial and research support, stationery and other office expenses, promotion costs (publicity, advertising, printing of brochures and so on) and the costs of providing free initial outline proposals. A consultancy will be looking for a 15 to 20 per cent pre-tax profit.

Most consultants price their work at an hourly or daily rate. This overcomes the cash flow problems otherwise created if certain jobs unexpectedly overrun their schedules, and it makes allocating expenditures to particular assignments an easier task. If a client company insists on a fixed fee in order to facilitate its internal budgeting, the consultant will simply estimate the length of time required for the job and convert this into a lump sum, adding an appropriate allowance (eg, 10 per cent) for contingencies.

However time based systems are not appropriate for every case. Consultants who supply large amounts of equipment or materials to their clients sometimes operate mostly through commissions received from materials or equipment producers. Computer and property management consultants occasionally function in this way. Advertising agencies (which provide much advice to their clients) have for many years worked on commissions received from media owners (see Chapter 10).

Some consultants charge flat rate fixed fees for their services. Certain vehicle fleet management consultants, for example, charge a fixed standard amount for each of the vehicles they manage. Clients are willing to pay this in view of the large discounts they receive on the costs of servicing, vehicle repairs, and the costs of vehicle consumables (batteries, tyres, etc).

Fee structures

Members of the Management Consultancies Association and certain other consultancy bodies will not accept assignments based on payments by results, arguing that to do so would encourage consultants only to suggest to their clients measures guaranteed to yield immediate short term benefits, while ignoring important long run considerations.

For example, the best advice might be to shut down a subsidiary, merge divisions, or have a function that is currently undertaken in-house (advertising for instance) performed by an outside agency. Yet a consultant who is locked into a payments by results system might be extremely reluctant to give such advice, choosing instead to recommend quickly and easily implemented policies for attaining readily achievable short run targets and hence maximising his or her reward. The correct strategies might take several months to implement and their beneficial effects might not be felt for long periods.

Implementation of payments by results

Payments by results (PBR) might be calculated as, say, a percentage of costs saved or of higher outputs or profit. A variation on PBR used by at least a couple of major consultancies is for the consultant to submit several invoices at the termination of an assignment, leaving the client to choose which one to pay. A client who is delighted with the consultant's services and who can relate outcomes to predetermined quantitative targets will, the consultant hopes, pay the highest valued invoice; clients who feel that none of their initial objectives have been met might select the lowest amount.

Without doubt, PBR is appropriate for certain types of assignment, especially where the installation of a system; or the successful introduction of new products, processes or technologies; the creation of new designs or the investment of substantial financial resources are concerned. PBR provides incentives to the consultant, while ensuring that the client firm can be reasonably sure the consultant's fee will be fully earned.

Consultants prepared to work on PBR tend to be more entrepreneural and innovative than the rest and, if the project succeeds, more expensive. A consultant on PBR gets little if the project fails, but will expect a high reward – much higher than would be expected by a fixed fee consultant – if it is successful.

Disbursements
You will probably be invoiced separately for out-of-pocket expenses for travel, living expenses, telephone calls, and perhaps also for secretarial services. To avoid subsequent arguments you should clarify your obligations in these respects at the outset of the exercise, and impose a ceiling on disbursement expenditure. Unfortunately, this might encourage the consultant to spend the ceiling amount specified – regardless of circumstances. Accordingly, you should insist that all significant disbursements be justified and authorised prior to spending the money.

Management consultants normally claim to travel first class, although this is negotiable. All incidental expenses (for which you should ask to see receipts) should of course be charged at cost without the addition of a percentage commission.

What a consultant will charge
Expect to pay between £250 and £800 a day (at 1990 prices), possibly more but rarely less. A 'day' means about six client contact hours (all the back up work not directly observed is included in the daily rate). When you telephone two or three of the consultant's previous clients to ask for references tell them the price you have been quoted and compare this amount with what they paid. Bigger firms tend to charge higher prices, justified perhaps by their larger overheads and more extensive provision of ancillary services. Long term assignments are usually charged at a discount rate.

Be prepared to offer a fee sufficient to attract good calibre applicants for the assignment and thereafter to motivate the consultant selected to do a good job. The agreed formula for computing fees should be clear and understandable and relate the consultant's reward to the quantity and quality of his or her work. It should offer the consultant a minimum fallback return if the project is a disaster, provided of course that the failure is not the consultant's fault. The consultant should not be expected to attain impossibly demanding targets in order to justify a reasonable reward.

Some consultancy assignments need to be split into constituent parts, possibly including a separate diagnostic component. For this you engage a consultant just to analyse your situation and report on what needs to be done. There is no implication that the same consultant will then be hired to carry out his or her recommendations.

Sources of disagreement

Disputes sometimes arise over contingency allowances specified in initial estimates or quotations. It is conventional for consultants to add (say) a 10 per cent contingency allowance to cover unanticipated expenditures. Suppose, for example, that the various parts of an estimate add up to 20 days at £500 per day, onto which a two day contingency allowance is added. If everything goes to plan and the project is completed in 20 days, are you liable for the extra £1,000 in respect of the two days not utilised? Clarify this matter at the start of the exercise.

Beware also of 'optional extras' included in the quote. Some consultants incorporate these in order to make the basic price for a job appear cheap. In fact, the 'extras' may be crucially important for the project's success, though you do not realise this until you are fully committed to the exercise and by then it is too late to engage someone else to complete the assignment.

Commission versus fixed fees

Certain types of consultancy are able to claim commissions from equipment, materials and ancillary service suppliers based on a percentage of the value of the client's order that results from the consultant's recommendations. These commissions are not normally available directly to client firms. Equipment and materials suppliers cover the cost of the commissions they pay by increasing the average price of their output. Such commissions, arguably, are the best way of rewarding consultants who supply large amounts of equipment/materials to big spending businesses. The consultancy services attached to the equipment can then be provided cheaply (possibly free) and the discipline of having to operate within a predetermined margin encourages consulting firms to reduce operating costs to the minimum. But there are several problems with commissions.

Because of the nature of their business some clients require large amounts of attention and highly specialist advice even though the value of their final equipment/materials orders will be low. Consider for instance a small firm seeking to computerise its accounting system. Much analysis of existing procedures will be necessary prior to selecting the equipment, though only a cheap desktop system may actually be purchased. A consultant taking commission from a system manufacturer will not be interested in such an assignment – unless you agree to pay an additional time based or lump sum fee. This means in effect that you are paying twice for the same service because the implicit cost of the consultant's advice will already have been built-in to the commission allowed by the equipment manufacturer, which will of course increase its equipment sale prices to cover this expense.

In contrast, high spend projects give the consultant a high return, possibly far in excess of that warranted by his or her actual contribution. (Remember you are paying for this *via* higher equipment prices.) Were you to have paid the consultant a lump sum or time based rate instead of having to pay the higher equipment price created by the commission then the consultant's services might have been much cheaper. Effectively, big spend clients are subsidising smaller assignments; which is fine for small businesses yet unfair to larger clients.

Also, suppose a manufacturer's commission is not sufficient for the consultant to be able to provide a first class service but that clients bitterly resent having to pay extra fees. Rather than upset customers by demanding additional payment the consultant might provide a substandard service in order to keep his or her expenditures within the limits imposed by the manufacturer's commission.

A final problem is where consultants are encouraged to direct their clients towards those materials and equipment which offer the highest commissions. The consultant loses his or her objectivity, and might suggest that clients spend more than is really necessary (eg, on excessively sophisticated computing equipment, or unnecessarily luxuriant promotional materials). Another argument against consultancies being paid through commission is that it becomes difficult to compare the calibre of various consultants. With time based or fixed fee systems, if one consultancy firm offers to complete a specific project to a predetermined level of quality at a lower cost than others this indicates a higher level of efficiency within that consultancy. Commission based systems deprive clients of this simple criterion, forcing them to examine other aspects of applicant consultancies' services which they may not be competent to evaluate.

A serious problem with fixed fees is that they encourage consultants to overestimate the time and effort necessary to complete assignments. You still have to pay the full amount if the consultant completes the job early. Time rates, conversely, encourage consultants to prolong the time spent on each assignment. Accordingly, you should always specify an upper limit on the amount of time you are willing to allow for the job.

Alternative fee structures
Time or fixed fee systems are not the only payment methods available. Alternative fee structures include the following methods of charge.

Quarterly or semi-annually negotiated fixed fees for ongoing consultancy services.
Here the fee is based on the consultant's historical experience of the time, effort and incidental expenses attached to working for that or a similar client. A clearly defined programme of work is agreed between the client and consultant. Clients are invoiced (usually monthly) in arrear.

Retainer, basic service plus supplementary charges.
Some consultancies, especially smaller consultancies operating within a limited geographical area, offer low-cost packages of services based on client commitment to the consultancy firm. One such consultancy that I know offers the following service and payment system.

The client (normally a small business) pays a lump sum of £2,500 per year (invoiced quarterly) in return for:
- three days per annum 'dedicated' advice involving the consultant visiting the clients' premises.
  - Once the client's three days' dedicated assistance is used up the client is entitled to one and a half days further work at two thirds the consultant's normal rate, and an additional one and a half days at three quarters the normal rate;
- up to ten hours per year telephone advice as and when it is needed.

— Telephone advice in excess of the ten hours already paid for is charged at the (low) rate of £20 per hour;
- a guarantee of further attention (paid for separately) within 48 hours of a client's call for extra services; and
- a quarterly newsletter containing useful information on local business conditions, local authority procurement programmes, market trends, investment opportunities, etc.

A 'team' rate

Here the consultancy firm recognises it cannot guarantee to supply a client with the personal services of any one of its consultants (especially 'big name' consultants) all the time and thus computes an hourly or daily 'team rate' which assumes (i) that a senior consultant will be engaged on the project for a certain proportion of its duration, (ii) that junior consultants will do a certain part of the work, (iii) that certain ancillary inputs will be needed, and (iv) that a certain amount of secretarial/administrative support will be required. The proportions might be based on experience of similar past projects or may be computed separately for each assignment.

Mixtures of the above

For example a basic fee plus an hourly team rate that comes into operation when the initial payment has been spent, plus a provision for the consultancy to pass on to you part of the commissions/ discounts it receives from its provision of equipment or materials.

Invoicing procedures differ, although for larger clients the commonest practice is to bill monthly in arrear. Smaller businesses are typically (and reasonably) required to pay an initial deposit, but this should not exceed 25 per cent in normal circumstances.

You should not even consider making substantial advance payments without experiencing the consultant's services. And even for a small advance payment you need to make sure the consultant's firm possesses assets you can sequestrate if he or she fails to turn up for the assignment.

Negotiating the fee

Try negotiating the consultant's estimated fee. Consultants are rarely willing to reduce their daily or hourly rates, arguing that they need to cover their overheads. But often you can knock down their original price by offering to reduce their work load and expenses through providing additional company services – use of a company car for travelling, office facilities, company-based research assistants, etc.

Costing a consultancy project

The true cost of a consultant's services includes not only his or her fees and disbursements but also the time of your own executives absorbed by briefing and assisting the consultant. Against this should be set the financial benefits of the project and (importantly) the learning effects of observing the consultant operate – simply watching an expert consultant at work can teach you how to tackle major problems independently.

Consultancy project costs should not normally be set against the budget of any particular department because the benefits of the exercise should eventually be felt right through the organisation. Rather, the expenditure should be treated as a company-wide expense, analogous (say) to the salary of a managing director.

Control over project expenditures should be exercised through regular reports and client briefings which compare planned and actual costs and achievements at certain predetermined review points during the assignment (every two or three days for short projects). Causes of difficulties, delays and unanticipated expenditures can be analysed at these meetings, and corrective action implemented. Each review needs to specify (i) work done and expenditures incurred, (ii) commitments entered for future expenditure and, where appropriate, (iii) revised estimates of the final cost.

Consultancy contracts

A written contract is essential to avoid misunderstandings and to provide firm evidence about what the consultant *should* have done if you subsequently need to complain. The problem with drafting a consultancy contract is that there is no such thing as a 'standard' consultancy assignment: each job is to some extent unique so that standardised documents applicable to any situation are extremely difficult to create. The contract might conveniently be embodied in an exchange of letters commissioning and accepting the assignment at a given price. It need not be excessively legalistic, but *must* clearly state exactly what is to be done; the criteria for accepting the consultant's finished work (eg, expectations regarding what his or her final report should contain); the time allowed; constraints on expenditure; and whether the consultant is to be a supplier or agent (see Chapters 1 and 16) as well as giving advice. If agency work is involved it is essential that the extent of the consultant's contractual powers be specified.

When drafting the contract look ahead and ask yourself what could go wrong and what would then be necessary to remedy the situation. A good way to do this is to assume that the project will fail and that in consequence you have to sue the consultant for incompetence or negligence (see Chapter 16). What would be the grounds for the action and which elements of the contract could you point to as evidence of the consultant having demonstrably failed to provide what was initially agreed?

Take care at the contract stage to ensure that the consultant does not add to the activities set out in his or her original estimate without your explicit consent. List and briefly describe all the products and materials the consultant will supply, when they are to be delivered and your expectations regarding their quality. Then you need paragraphs stating:

- the consultant's fee and how it is to be computed;
- who is to do the work and whether delegation and/or sub-contracting is to be allowed;
- when and how the consultant is to be paid;
- that the consultant will be liable for careless or otherwise inadequate work (defined by reference to previously agreed criteria);
- liability for the consultant's clerical costs, travelling, subsistence and other incidental expenses;
- the extent to which the consultant can use your facilities (e.g., for research or secretarial support);
- the length of the contract and the circumstances in which it can be changed or terminated;
- that both parties to the agreement will work deligently towards completion of the assignment and that each will co-operate fully with the other side;
- that you will make available to the consultant all the information needed to complete the assignment;
- date of submission of the final report and what it should contain;
- that work done for you is to be regarded as strictly confidential;
- penalty clauses for late submission of work (where appropriate);
- arbitration procedures in the event of a dispute; and
- who ultimately is to be liable for defects in equipment and/or materials supplied by the consultant.

The consultant might (reasonably) insist that a clause be inserted absolving the consultant of all liability for the consequences of events beyond his or her control. For certain assignments (design projects for instance) it may be necessary to specify who will own the copyright/patent rights to any materials generated via the project.

If the consultant absolutely insists on inserting a disclaimer or exemption clause that you find unacceptable, consider suggesting a compromise whereby the consultant changes the disclaimer to a clause restricting his or her liability for damages to some mutually acceptable amount. This creates an incentive for the consultant to do a good job because he or she is still liable for damages caused by negligence or incompetence, while you retain the ability to obtain partial redress if things go wrong. Actually, you might be able to sue for more than this amount in certain circumstances, since restriction of liability clauses are in practice extremely difficult to enforce.

Briefing a consultant

Consultant and client need to agree targets and to establish firm criteria against which the success or failure of the exercise may be evaluated. Together you should draft a plan to guide the consultant's work, clearly indicating intermediate objectives along the way. Then determine the information that is needed and who will be responsible for its collection. Disputes over this matter, (data gathering and research can be extremely time consuming and expensive) are not uncommon, so clarify your expectations at the start of the project.

Present your perceptions of the company's problems and ask for the consultant's views. What is the true purpose of the exercise? The more clearly you specify this the more obvious will be the solutions to your difficulties.

You should expect the consultant to be an expert in his or her particular field and to know something about your industry *before* beginning the assignment. Thus you ought not to be paying consultants simply to learn about your line of work; they should be at least familiar with this before they begin the assignment and if they are not they should find out at their own expense and inconvenience. The initial meeting between client and consultant prior to signing the contract is the appropriate place and time for the consultant to learn about your business.

It is important to distinguish clearly between strategic, tactical and operational aspects of the exercise. Do you expect little more than general advice concerning the overall direction of your business (or one of its functions); or are you looking for detailed expert implementation of new systems? Your interpretation of the situation may be that strategy selection is just the start of the assignment – occupying no more than a couple of hours – prior to moving on to other matters. The consultant, conversely, might be under the impression that he or she will spend several days investigating strategic issues.

Specify priorities making sure the consultant will spend the bulk of his or her time dealing with the most pressing and serious problems. Advise the consultant of any environmental changes that might occur during the period of the assignment (entry or exit of a competitor for instance and how these may affect the project).

Assure the consultant that the assignment is fully supported by top management, and that he or she will be given all information and resources reasonably necessary. Identify to the consultant the person to whom he or she should report (normally the firm's chief executive) and introduce the consultant to all members of your staff involved in the project. Outline the scope and nature of the final report you expect the consultant to produce.

By now you should be fully aware of any potential problems in your relationship with the consultant. Indeed, it may be that you conclude at this stage that you do not really need a consultant's services (equally the consultant may wish to withdraw). But the exercise will still have been beneficial through helping you clarify the nature and existence (or non-existence) of problems.

Beware of the consultant who at this late stage suggests sub-contracting part of the project to other more specialist consultants (it could mean the consultant has lost interest in the job, yet wishes to retain the revenue). And be particularly vigilant against consultants attempting to redefine the extent and character of the assignment.

Monitoring the project

Although you must regularly liaise with the consultant during the assignment to check progress and to ensure that all expenditures are justified, you should not pester the consultant with petty queries, complaints, or demands for information. Nevertheless, make it clear that you are following his or her work with great interest.

Arrange for a substantial meeting when a third of the work has been done. At this meeting determine whether the original brief needs to be altered, and seek assurances that the objectives of the assignment will be attained on schedule.

Avoid involving a consultant with domestic company politics. And do not use a consultant simply to justify unpopular decisions on matters relating to plant closures or redundancies that you have already decided to implement.

Few senior executives are capable of viewing their own companies dispassionately, especially if the firm has taken years of hard work to build up. They are too close to day-to-day operations to see the wider significance of their activities and the overall direction the business should take. A good consultant will be distant enough to see the situation clearly and objectively yet still be able to discuss the firm's problems with sympathy and tact.

Be prepared to listen attentively to the consultant's comments and be willing to admit you may have made mistakes. Consultants for their part must be totally committed to improving your firm, and not concerned merely with criticism and finding petty faults.

Evaluating a consultant's contributions

Detailed advice on the appraisal of various types of specialist consultant is given in appropriate chapters of the book. In general, however, you need to look carefully at the calibre of the consultant's final report and consider:

- whether it lives up to the consultant's initial proposal;
- how long it took to prepare;
- its depth, insights and clarity of presentation.

Does the report tell you anything you did not already know, and if not why not? Do not pay the consultant's fee if the report contains only trivial information. (See Chapter 16 for details of how to deal with negligent or incompetent consultants).

Did the consultant work harmoniously with your staff (assuming you wanted this) and if not who was to blame? Beware of consultants who try to impose on your business 'standard solutions' to problems regardless of circumstances. This saves the consultant time; but stereotyped policies drawn from a stack of ready made solutions held in the consultant's word-processor might be entirely inappropriate for the needs of your firm.

A good consultant will leave you feeling competent to implement recommended policies, and be willing to provide a reasonable amount of low-cost post assignment advice and assistance. Is this the case, or did your consultant disappear immediately the assignment ended?

Examine your operating costs before and after the project. Have practical benefits been achieved in direct consequence of the consultant's work? If not, are they visible on the immediate horizon, and if not why not? Have you learned anything just through observing the consultant at work?

Was the consultant easy to approach during the exercise; was he or she readily available, or was the consultant simultaneously concerned with other clients' problems more than your own?

Solutions offered should be realistic, well thought out and (importantly) easily implemented. Academic solutions drawn from textbooks are rarely acceptable; you need sound, level headed and down to earth practical advice.

Chapter 3

Strategy Consultants

Introduction — Why use a strategy consultant? — Managing external change — Who are strategy consultants? — Corporate planning — What strategy consultants do — The tools of strategic analysis — Positioning — Portfolio analysis — Competitive analysis — Acquisition strategies — Analytical frameworks the consultant might use — The consultant's report — Problems and pitfalls — Appraising a strategy consultant's work

After reading this chapter you should:

- know the meaning of business strategy and what strategy consultants do;
- understand the concepts of (i) product/company positioning, (ii) product portfolios, (iii) the analysis of strengths, weaknesses, opportunities and threats, (iv) competitive strategy;
- be aware of standard methods of strategy analysis: POISE, APACS, DPA, etc;
- identify circumstances in which you might want to use a strategy consultant;
- appreciate the frequency with which most firms need to introduce new products, change prices, enter new markets and alter distribution channels;
- know what to expect in a strategy consultant's report and the questions to ask about its recommendations;
- understand the major problems of strategy consulting; and
- be able to appraise the work of a strategy consultant.

Introduction

The larger consultancies typically regard strategy consulting as the *blue ribband* component of their general advisory work, as it embraces all aspects of business policy, planning, control and organisation. A corporate strategy is a sort of route map for guiding the overall direction of the firm. It concerns such issues as the products the firm should offer for sale, the markets (overseas as well as domestic) and market segments in which it should operate, organisation structure, pricing policy, and where and how the company should finance its activities. Merger and acquisition policies are crucially important here, and many strategy assignments involve the critical analysis of intended takeovers. Examples of strategy consulting tasks are:

- helping a firm choose new ways of utilising existing physical and labour resources following technical developments that have rendered some of its existing products obsolete;
- advising on how to switch a product from a saturated and unprofitable low-price bottom-end market location to the top-end high-price sector of the same market;
- locating opportunities for profitable diversification;
- evaluating the likely consequences of intended large scale capital expenditures and/or major reorganisations of a company; and
- assessing the possibilities created by changing a firm's legal and/ or financial structure, eg, becoming a PLC, moving from debt to equity financing, or entering the unlisted securities market.

A firm with a coherent strategy will experience improved co-ordination between its divisions and subsidiaries and more effective allocation of resources. And it will be able to monitor the efficiency of its working methods and rate of growth against predetermined standards.

Firms engage strategy consultants either as part of their overall corporate development programmes, or – more commonly – following a particular catastrophic event (loss of major customers, failure to penetrate a lucrative market, collapse of an important project) which indicates that the company's basic philosophy, structures and activities are not suitable for its present needs.

Why use a strategy consultant?

Senior managers sometimes overrate the strengths and underrate the weaknesses of their firms. They see opportunities that are not really there, while not noticing threats that are obvious to a dispassionate outsider.

One stimulus for calling in a strategy consultant is the realisation that in fact a company has no strategy! Another is the awareness that different senior managers perceive the firm's base objectives in entirely different ways. (Such problems often arise following the transfer of ownership of a business, or on the retirement of a dominant senior executive – usually the founder of the firm – who previously took sole responsibility for all strategic matters.)

A further reason for hiring a consultant is the inexperience in strategic affairs of so many middle (and some senior) managers.

Existing management might only have experienced one firm and may lack the wider perspective a consultant can bring to bear. Too often, firms become locked into a particular type of business without realising the existence of alternative and more lucrative possibilities.

Managing external change

A change in the business environment can be devastating. Consider, for instance, the changeover from conventional typewriting to word processing. Firms producing ordinary typewriters were, in a limited sense, in the same industry as the manufacturers of WP's (ie, the creation of letters, memoranda, reports and other 'hard copy' documents) but the skills of their employees and their processes of manufacture had an essential 'mechanical' orientation. They made and assembled typing keys, carriage returns, roller bars, etc, and were not in a position to transfer these engineering skills to the computer based technologies that word processing involves (microelectronics, computer programming, software design, and so on). Even the materials from which WP's are constructed (circuit boards, microchips, plastic keyboard) are different from those in typewriters.

An important aspect of a strategist's work, therefore, is to identify key variables particularly relevant to a specific company. These variables will normally concern:

- how the firm's current and intended markets are expected to develop; whether competitors might enter, and if so how new competitors are likely to behave;
- major influences on consumer demand for products, including anticipated changes in consumer taste and behaviour; and
- laws that affect the firm.

Consultants usually apply one of two methods when analysing external change. They can either

- predict the external changes that might occur and then suggest how these would affect the firm, or
- specify all the client firm's major functions and *then* list the factors that may affect each function.

The second option is easier and thus more common than the first, although important variables might be overlooked in the process. Make sure that possibilities for change in the business environment have been thoroughly investigated if your consultant opts for the second approach.

Who are strategy consultants?

Strategy consulting is difficult, requiring not only a comprehensive grasp of management principles and practice but also the ability to tell senior managers things which, frankly, they should already know. Most strategy specialists begin in some other form of consultancy (usually finance or marketing) and then move into strategy work. So look for a recognised accountancy or marketing qualification (see Chapters 6 and 10) in the consultant's CV; and look for a good track record evidenced by successful previous strategy assignments.

A *bona fide* strategist will be pleased to give you a list of recent clients; though it would obviously be improper to ask the consultant for confidential details of the work he or she did for those businesses.

Younger strategy consultants might have a Master of Business Administration degree (MBA), but in this case make sure it is from a properly accredited business school as there are numerous easy-to-acquire low quality MBA degrees on the market. A reasonably comprehensive and up-to-date list of institutions awarding academically respectable MBAs is contained in the book *Guide to Business Schools,* edited by S Paliwoda and A C Harrison (Pitman), which is published in collaboration with the UK Association of MBAs.

Strategy specialists may belong to big consultancy organisations or be small independent consultancy firms. Normally the consultant will be interested in designing and implementing solutions as well as in providing strategic advice. To find a strategy consultant look in the *Directory of Management Consultants in the UK,* or contact the Management Consultancies Association or Institute of Management Consultants (see Chapter 1).

The rise of the strategy consultant

There are perhaps three dominant reasons for the advance of strategy consulting during the 1980s, (i) the escalating cost to companies of providing corporate planning facilities in-house, (ii) the enormous increase in mergers and acquisitions that has occurred in recent years, and (iii) the need for firms to rethink their fundamental strategic philosophies in preparation for 1992 (see Chapter 14).

Corporate planning

It can be cheaper to purchase strategic planning facilities from outside consultants, as and when they are needed, than to use your own (possibly inexperienced) staff. Corporate plans are statements about *how* the company intends achieving its strategic objectives, specifying how the firm's *total* resources are to be deployed. They describe the activities and resources necessary for intended future operations, identify possible new technology, identify activities which should be discontinued and state whether existing organisation structures should remain undisturbed.

Firms recognise the benefits of corporate planning: readiness for future events, avoiding having to take important decisions in chaotic unforeseen conditions, sidestepping foreseeable pitfalls, discovery of profitable new opportunities not previously recognised, and so on; yet are (rightly) horrified by the costs involved. Corporate planning (indeed any sort of planning) is highly expensive in terms of the management time it absorbs (meetings, perusal of data, research, conducting interviews, secretarial support, the effort attached to becoming familiar with strategy principles, etc).

Strategy consultants, conversely, spend much time working on the corporate plans of various enterprises and thus can achieve considerable economies of scale when drafting plans. They will know from experience the sorts of planning problem likely to affect your type of business and can refer to previous assignments when suggesting strategies. Accordingly the consultant might be able to produce a more comprehensive yet detailed corporate plan within a given budget than could ever be created in-house.

Questions to ask

If your consultant drafts a corporate plan, evaluate its calibre by asking the following questions.

- Does it cover all aspects of the work of the firm: personnel, finance, production, organisation, marketing? If not, what are the implications of the changes recommended in the areas covered by the plan for the activities it does not mention?
- Are the tactics needed to implement the plan obvious from suggested strategies? If not, what tactical options are available and how are they to be implemented?
- Does the plan include guidelines and criteria against which the company's future performance can be appraised?
- What are the consultant's assumptions about (i) the market, (ii) technological and legal environments affecting the firm and (iii) the firm's ability to operate in the future as efficiently as it has in the past. In particular what assumptions has the consultant made regarding:
  — the future stability of consumer tastes and incomes (new taxes that reduce consumer incomes can destroy the markets for certain goods);

> — the likely behaviour of competitors (especially new foreign competitors after 1992) including their price, promotion and product policies, and
>
> — the possibility of entirely new production or distribution technologies rendering the firm's existing production or marketing methods obsolete.

- Does the plan consider *all* courses of action available (not just some of them), and have all the side effects and implications of the consultant's recommendations been fully considered?
- Are suggested targets reasonable? There is a little point in setting ridiculously optimistic objectives since this only leads to cynicism and disillusionment when they are not achieved.
- Has the consultant detailed the resources, authority and information that key employees will need to implement recommendations?
- Is the plan concrete? Does it establish clear targets for market shares, rates of return on investments, specified percentage reductions in the labour force, greater efficiency in the use of working capital, etc?
- Does it compare the financial, technical and other resources actually available with those necessary to achieve strategic objectives and then state how deficiencies will be made up?
- Is it obvious from the plan what the consultant considers the business should be doing, how and in what markets, four or five years from today?
- How many of the company's strengths, weaknesses, opportunities and threats that you were not aware of previously has the consultant discovered through the plan?

What strategy consultants do

The consultant will seek to identify your current objectives, assess their value, possibly present you with fresh objectives, and suggest an action plan for attaining specific goals. Sometimes, owners of businesses do not really know what their objectives are – they may think that their aim is to maximise short-term profit whereas in reality they are committed to long-term security irrespective of immediate rates of return. And they will not welcome advice to initiate high-risk high-return activities in this case.

Your business will be put under the microscope, focussing on the sources of your competitive advantage (see below), on openings for new products, the existence of new market segments, and on the adequacy of your organisation for coping with change.

Two approaches are possible. With the first, the company supplies information about itself to the consultant who, given that information, then recommends a strategy for the firm. Under the second, it is the consultant who assembles, analyses and interprets information – listing available options and presenting these in a form that the company's senior management can easily understand.

There is a big difference between the approaches. The latter says to the consultant, 'You go and find out about my situation, so I can decide what to do about it'. Conversely, the former states, 'Here is my situation; what should I do?' Make sure from the outset that your consultant fully understands your perception of his or her role. Otherwise you might be disappointed by the final report, and you will not have precise criteria against which to complain about its quality.

Relations with company staff

Existing staff will have to implement at least some of the chosen strategies, and it is thus essential that they are fully aware of the consultant's work. Utilise the skills and experience of your employees; brief them *before* the consultant arrives and offer them every opportunity to express their views. Note that an employee may be more willing to speak frankly about work to an outsider than to you, since no internal consequences will follow from the employee's critical yet confidential comments about the firm.

The tools of strategic analysis

There are certain well-established techniques that a strategy consultant might apply and which you can expect to see discussed in the final report. The main ones are competitive analysis, portfolio analysis, and product and/or company positioning. Also relevant are a variety of impressive sounding algorithms (SWOTS, DPA, POISE, the 7-S system) that consultants use to guide and structure their work.

Of course, each consultant has his or her own particular method that differentiates his or her own work from that of other consultancy firms, but this will almost certainly be derived from one or more of the techniques outlined below.

Positioning

Positioning can relate either to a company or to one or more of its outputs. Product positioning means finding out how customers

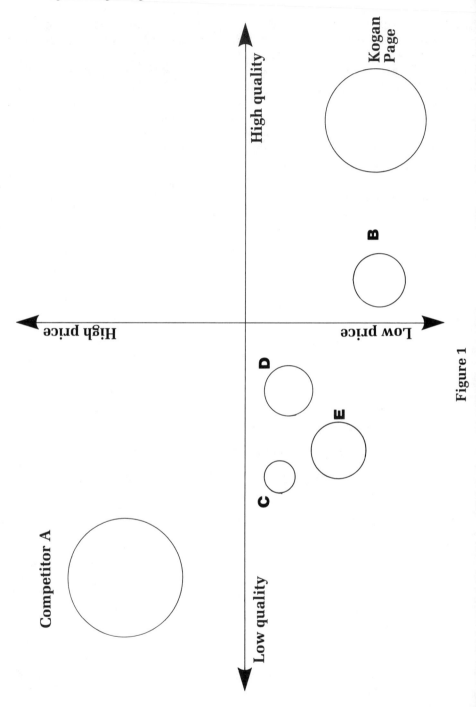

Figure 1

think about your product in relation to competing products, with a view either to modifying the product (plus associated advertising and other publicity) to make it fit in with these perceptions, or to changing the product's position in consumers' minds. A product's position is its 'personality', as seen by consumers. To illustrate, consider the market for books on management consultancy, and suppose that consumers evaluate these by just two variables: quality and price.

Quality might be judged by the design of a book's cover, by its contents pages and the potential reader's first impression of the overall layout of the text. Hopefully the customer will regard the book you are currently reading as high quality at a low price. A competitor might be seen by consumers as of similar quality, but expensive; while another may be regarded as low quality yet cheap. The various texts may be located in appropriate positions on a *perceptual map*, as shown in Figure 1.

Here, this book's major competitor, text A, is seen by potential readers as expensive but not very good. Text A's position is shown as a circle bigger than that surrounding the high-quality low-price position of this Kogan Page text, indicating that despite text A's disadvantages it currently enjoys higher sales (perhaps it was published earlier when there was little competition in the field, was aggressively marketed and/or has an exceptionally attractive cover). Another (low selling) text is available in the low-price high-quality sector, and there is a cluster of competitors (C, D & E) which are cheap but not very good. Obviously there is a gap in the market for a high-price high-quality book.

There are two aspects to positioning:

- deciding what variables to put on the axes of the perceptual map (the consultant may present several maps each using different pairs of variables); and
- actually measuring consumers' perceptions.

The latter might require marketing research (see Chapters 10 and 14), and the consultant may refer you to a suitable research agency for this. Otherwise the consultant might use his or her own judgement to interpret consumers' thoughts about your products and/or firm, using *ad hoc* subjective methods. Thus, he or she may ask questions of a few representative customers, talk to colleagues, read your promotional literature from the consumer's point of view, and so on. The desired outcome is a concise statement of how consumers perceive the firm and its products. Also, opportunities for new activities could be revealed.

What determines a product's position?
Positions depend on the nature of (i) the product, (ii) competing products, and on how consumers see themselves (the lifestyles to which they aspire, role models etc). A good consultant will identify the ideal position for your output, define the characteristics that your products need to possess in order to occupy this position and suggest policies to effect the change. If the consultant suggests entering a new market segment, ask:

- why he or she feels it is big enough to be profitable;
- whether the firm has the resources to serve the new market effectively; and
- why competitors have not already moved in to fill the gap? Note that fresh competition might be attracted if you are seen to be interested in the new market.

Portfolio analysis

A company which offers several products has a 'portfolio' of activities, each with a particular combination of risk and return. Accordingly, products may be categorised as:

- *declining products*, which contribute little to company profits because of (say) reduced demand, intensification of competition, increased production costs or low rate of market growth;
- *safe products*, upon which the business depends for a steady cash flow;
- *developing products*, ie, those which are increasing their market share in rapidly expanding markets.

Normally the firm will expect a product to begin in the last category, then become 'safe', eventually moving into decline – though note that product modifications or improved marketing might halt a product's loss of sales.

Businesses need balanced portfolios of activities, avoiding having too many high risk and/or declining products. Observe how the concept can be applied to the subsidiaries of a holding company, to the divisions of a firm, or to individual departments engaged in a particular line of work. Each self-contained collection of operations (a division for example) is called a 'strategic business unit' and the firm is regarded as a collection of independent SBUs.

The firm requires an even balance of units/products in order to ensure (i) a continuous inflow of cash, (ii) that new products are available to take over from those in decline, and (iii) that all the company's activities are not exceptionally risky.

Methods of portfolio analysis

The problem is deciding whether to develop or abandon specific products, since heavy expenditures on a product which sells in a low growth market sector can drain the company of cash. One of the earliest analyses of the issue was by the Boston Consulting Group, which classified products according to two variables: the product's share of its total market, and the rate of the market's growth. The best products, obviously, were those with high market shares of buoyant markets experiencing high rates of growth, and the firm's strategy should be directed, therefore, to promoting these.

A development of this approach, the 'Business Screen' method, uses *market attractiveness* and *organisational strength* to categorise products and activities. Market attractiveness depends on the size, growth rate, profitability and competitive intensity of the market and on how easily it can be served. Organisational strength involves the quality of the firm's product, the firm's efficiency and the effectiveness of its marketing.

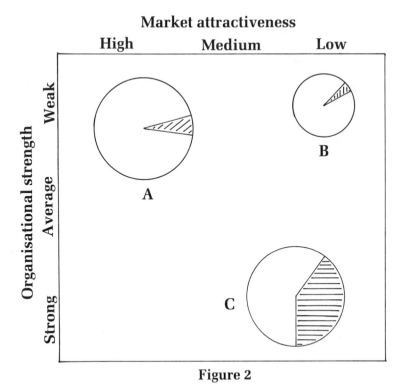

Figure 2

Your consultant may evaluate these factors subjectively and incorporate a diagram similar to that shown in Figure 2 into the final report. Figure 2 shows a firm with three products, A, B, and C. The areas of the circles indicate the relative sizes of the markets for each product, while the wedges in each circle show the firm's share of that particular market. We see that although the market for product A is large and highly attractive, the company is weak in its ability to serve this potentially lucrative segment, implying the need for further investment in this field.

Product B should probably be discarded, while product C presents a 'question mark' about how to proceed. There is a large market for product C, the firm can supply it easily, and the company already has a large market share. But the market for C is stagnant and profit margins are low. Detailed justifications of the consultant's choice of position for each product should be included in the main body of the report.

A further variant is the 'Directional Policy Matrix' approach which classifies products according to *market profitability* on one axis and *competitive capacity* on the other (see the section on competitive analysis below).

Problems with portfolio analysis

The main limitation of portfolio analysis is its concentration on the *composition* of the firm's activities rather than on *how* the firm should be run. Other problems include the measurement of market size and how to define market segments (a broad definition of a market will give the firm a relatively low market share and *vice versa*). Also, the list of factors potentially contributing to 'organisational strength' and to 'market attraction' is extremely long, so great skill is needed to sort out which are important in any given situation.

Competitive strategy

Your competitive position depends on your market share, product quality, brand and corporate images (see Chapter 10), distribution arrangements, and on your ability to expand or contract operations at short notice. The guru of competitive analysis is Michael Porter, who asserts that successful corporate strategies *must* contain measures for achieving at least one of the following.

- Cost leadership resulting from superefficient organisation and/or production methods or from the economies made possible by producing on a massive scale.

- Making the firm's output appear different and superior to that of competitors.
- Finding profitable niches not serviced by other firms.*

Market conditions usually determine the particular strategies that businesses adopt. A firm in a newly established industry, for instance, will probably be most concerned with product differentiation, whereas companies in older industries might be more interested in cutting costs. Firms in highly competitive markets may embark on a trail of acquisitions to eliminate competition and/or establish a large organisation able to obtain economies of scale; while firms in declining industries will probably want to disinvest and concentrate on profitable market niches.

A consultant using the Porter framework will report on a number of factors, as listed below.

How easily competitors can enter the industry
This depends on (i) how much an entrant will need to spend in order to establish operations in the industry, (ii) how readily the entrant can establish a favourable brand image, and (iii) the entrant's access to distribution channels (eg, whether it will have to purchase its own warehouses or retail outlets, set up a franchise system, etc). Other relevant factors include access to raw materials, lack of experience of the industry and, where relevant, the need to obtain a government licence.

The bargaining power of customers and suppliers
Customers are powerful if they are few in number, if they know all about the product and about competitors' prices, and if they can quickly switch between supplying firms. Suppliers have power when their output is unique and the purchasing company must design its own production system to accommodate the product supplied.

Availability of substitutes
If many substitute products are available the firm loses its ability to raise its prices by significant amounts since a price increase will merely cause consumers to switch to other brands.

Porter asserts that the following general principles of inter-firm competition normally apply.

- Rivalry between companies increases as the market shares of existing firms become more equal. Severe competition is unlikely in 'market-leader market-follower' situations.

---

*Porter, M., *Competitive Strategy* (Macmillan, New York, 1980).

- Competition intensifies as the rate of expansion of the market as a whole slows down.
- Since goods which are difficult to store or are perishable must be sold quickly, there will be great competition in the industries supplying such goods.
- Firms will compete more aggressively when they have much to lose from the activities of competing businesses (eg, because of extremely large investments in plant and equipment).
- Competition becomes fierce when competing products acquire more and more similar characteristics, and is greatest in industries supplying products which are virtually the same.

Acquisition strategies

The quest for profitable yet low-risk diversification is perhaps the main strategic reason for taking over other firms; although *technical* factors might also be important. Technical motives might involve such matters as:

- economies of scale (cost reductions made possible by integration of processes, bulk buying, etc) possibly available through more extensive operations;
- control over outlets or supplies;
- tax considerations eg, the carryover of past trading losses of the acquired firm to the books of the predator company;
- fullest use of production capacity and idle cash;
- an increase in the capacity to borrow funds; and
- greater financial and other resources, including increased capacity to undertake research.

Strategic motives usually relate to the competitive position of the firm. Apart from the desire to acquire businesses already trading in certain markets and/or possessing certain specialist employees, equipment and skills, strategic reasons for takeovers might include:

- possibilities for expert use of resources, eg, if one firm possesses large amounts of land and buildings and the other is exceptionally skilled in property management; and
- reduction of the likelihood of company failure through spreading risks over a wider range of activities, including operations overseas.

Acquiring European companies
Foreign acquisitions enable the firm to avoid total reliance on the economic prosperity of a single country for its sales since a decline in the fortunes of one country might be offset by high market growth elsewhere.

European acquisitions are enormously important in the run up to 1992. British companies need European partners to assist with (i) selling and distribution in the single market, (ii) the procurement of low cost supplies from other EC nations, (iii) the ability to tender effectively for European public works contracts, and so on. Also it may be necessary to knock out potential European competitors before the full consequences of the single market are felt (see Chapter 14 for further discussion of these matters).

If you seek a consultant's advice on an intended acquisition, make sure your consultant covers the following points.

- All the legal implications of the takeover *vis-à-vis* UK and EC company and monopoly law.
- The alternatives to a straight takeover that exist. Consortia or *ad hoc* joint ventures might be more cost effective in the longer run.
- The cheapest way of financing the takeover (cash, shares, loans, etc) and the financial implications of the suggested method. If you buy another firm for cash your own business becomes short of liquid funds, whereas if you pay for the acquisition in shares (eg, two shares in your company for one share in the other) then short-term earnings per share for existing shareholders might fall. How will shareholders react if this occurs?
- Whether your current organisation will be able to handle the new technologies and/or management methods that the acquisition will bring to the firm.
- The implications of the acquisition for cash flow and for return on capital employed under several different sets of assumptions regarding:
  — market demand after the takeover; and
  — entry of new competitors to the market (attracted perhaps by publicity surrounding the takeover itself).
- Control problems attached to a larger and more diverse organisa-tion, including appraisal systems, performance criteria for newly created divisions and departments, new management information requirements and how the information will be provided.
- The compatibility of working methods in the two companies and what changes are necessary to remove divergences in these. How exactly is the acquired business to be integrated into your organisational system?
- Whether the target company is critically dependent on key employees who might quit following the takeover. Also, what compensation payments will you be obliged to pay to managers in the firm to be acquired who turn out not to be worth employing in the larger company?

- In the case of a foreign acquisition, will the economic factors that affect market growth in that country (interest rates, inflation, taxes, etc) move in parallel with similar factors here in the UK? If so, a damaging economic depression in Britain will probably be matched by a depression in the other country, which means double trouble for the parent firm.
- Whether the management of the target company is concealing anything about its past performance, specific weaknesses (carefully analysed under headings for marketing, finance, operations, and personnel) percentage market share of its primary market, or vulnerabilities to particular environmental circumstances.
- How the images and reputations and market standing of both businesses will be affected by the takeover.

Analytical frameworks the consultant might use

All sorts of algorithms and mnemonics have been used to assist consultants analyse strategy issues. The traditional frameworks are outlined below, though obviously all strategy consultants devise their own schemes in order to differentiate their services from those of competing consulting firms. Nevertheless, what follows will help you understand how a strategy consultant's mind works.

Specifying objectives

The common approach is to begin by asking three fundamental questions: what business is the firm in; what business should it be in; and what does it need to do to get to where it wants to be? Suppose you are a motor vehicle manufacturer. Are you in the engineering business, and hence need to focus all your attention on producing and selling engines and car bodies, or are you in the transport business generally and thus interested in diversifying into any form of transport – air and sea transport, electric and solar powered vehicles, etc – regardless of its form or of technical engineering considerations? If you are an academic book publisher, should you be interested in educational software, in instructional training packages, in generating distance learning materials, or in magazine and non-academic publishing as well as your existing lines of work? Is a short-course management training centre in the education business, or it is really in the hospitality business (trainees often remember a management training course as much for quality of its cuisine as for the course they attended)? Critical analysis of these issues should reveal the core objectives of the firm.

SWOTS
The most straightforward way to begin the analysis is, quite simply, to list all the firm's strengths and weaknesses, its opportunities, and the threats it confronts. Typically, strengths and weaknesses exist internally, relating to such things as equipment availability, labour skills and utilisation and access to finance and material supplies. Opportunities are usually found outside the firm – in possibilities for mergers and acquisitions, cost cutting programmes, fresh relations with suppliers and/or distributors, and so on. Threats might arise from competitors, from impending legislation that could damage the firm, from dangers of technical obsolescence or from sudden changes in public taste.

APACS
This stands for 'Adaptive Planning and Control System', which is a simple yet useful procedure for roughing out a corporate plan. Eight steps are involved:

* statement of objectives;
* appraisal of internal strengths, weaknesses and the external environment;
* specification of activities necessary to achieve objectives;
* evaluation of the consequences of alternative courses of action;
* prediction of results to actions chosen;
* the issue of orders to ensure implementation of plans;
* assessment of results; and
* if necessary, modification of the plan.

POISE
The 'Philosophy, Organisation, Information, Strategy and Efficiency' analysis technique begins by drafting a 'mission statement', which is a concise specification of the organisation's purpose, of why it exists and the broad direction it should take. Once these are established strategies may be devised depending on the firm's:

* *environmental circumstances* – problems and opportunities available in the outside world;
* *resources* – what it has and what it needs; and
* *competencies* – what it is good at; its strengths and weaknesses.

Then the consultant examines the internal organisation, asking such questions as:

* Are the firm's management information systems, forecasting pro-

cedures, means of co-ordinating activity, and general administration capable of supporting the policies needed to implement plans; and if not, why not?

- How adequate are marketing and product research for the specified tasks?
- Does the firm possess a reliable materials procurement system?
- What measures exist for ascertaining when existing products have reached the ends of their life cycles?
- Has the firm an organisation development programme capable of effecting structural change, and if so how long will structural alterations take to implement?
- What mechanisms exist for controlling expenditures?
- How adequate is the company's human resource plan?

Marketing plans should be examined in relation to product, price, promotional and distribution policies. Products, in particular will be scrutinised *vis-à-vis* their consumer appeal, production cost and quality (decisions to vary the quality of output have many strategic implications). The firm's ability to finance its intended future operations obviously needs investigation. Thus, trends in working capital and in key financial ratios, (profits to sales, the current ratio, stock turnover, debtors to creditors, etc) must be examined. On the manufacturing side, plant productivity, machine and warehouse capacities, the availabilities of skilled labour and the efficiency of existing scheduling procedures must be analysed. The effectiveness of the company's administrative methods and the calibre of its management should also be studied. Next the consultant seeks to identify the activities the business already performs (or could perform) really well, plus the existence of any new opportunities in completely different fields.

DPA

The 'Diagnosis – Prognosis – Action' technique reduces to asking a series of questions. Pick the right questions and the answers to them will necessarily determine the correct corporate strategy for the firm. Questions might include:

- What does the company need to do in order to beat its rivals in the technical field (eg, initiate product and market research, establish a system for monitoring economic and other trends)?
- How does the company's output differ from that of competitors and what must it do to take full advantage of such differences?
- Are relations with suppliers and major customers satisfactory? What can be done to improve such relations?

The business must consider whether *really* radical changes are required, asking not so much 'How can we improve current operations', but rather 'What else can we do to maximise profits and/ or growth'? Answers might suggest a diversification strategy, the adoption of new technologies, disinvestment in unprofitable activities, or the consolidation of an existing market share.

The 7-S System
This framework results from the work of the McKinsey management consultancy company and is increasingly discussed in the sorts of book read by strategy consultants.*
The Ss stand for:

- *Strategy —*
  The company's mission statement and corporate plan.
- *Structure —*
  How the firm is organised, line and staff relationships, degree of decentralisation, etc.
- *Systems —*
  Internal communications, the management information system, budgetary control and project management methods.
- *Style —*
  How senior managers relate to subordinates (autocratic or participative management styles), authority and supervision systems. The state of interpersonal relations within the firm.
- *Staff —*
  The adequacy of recruitment, induction, training and promotion methods. Analysis of the culture of the enterprise.
- *Shared values —*
  Morale within the firm; whether all employees are working towards the same corporate objectives; whether staff share common views on important issues.
- *Skills —*
  The strengths and weaknesses of the firm taken as a whole, its opportunities and the threats it faces.

---

* For details of the original system and its application see Waterman, R.H., Peters, T.J., and Phillips. R., 'Structure Is Not Organisation', *Business Horizons,* June 1980, and Peter. T.J., and Waterman. R.H., *In Search of Excellence: Lessons from America's Best Run Companies,* Harper and Row, New York, 1982. The framework is explained and discussed in, for example, the texts by Kotler. R., *Marketing Management: Analysis, Planning, Implementation and Control,* 6th edn., Prentice Hall, New Jersey, 1988; by Koontz, H., and Weirhrich, H., *Management,* 9th edn., McGraw Hill, New York, 1988; and by Hax, A.C. and Majluf, N.S., *Strategic Management: An Integrative Perspective,* Prentice Hall, New Jersey, 1984.

The consultant's report

Typically, the final report will open with a general introduction briefly outlining the background to the investigation and (importantly) where, when and why problems first arose – you need to know exactly what went wrong before you can even begin to consider remedial action.

The report should comment on the adequacy of your product range; relations between the risks and returns of current activities; and on pricing strategies and choice of markets. There will be extensive discussion of strategic aims, since the more concrete are the company's objectives the more obvious are the policies that are needed.

Strategic targets should then be broken down into specific objectives stating who is to achieve each target and when. Make sure the recommended objectives do not conflict (look particularly at intended advertising and production activities here – you do not want a massive promotional campaign for a new product if the firm's ability to produce it in sufficient quantity is in doubt). And insist that the consultant arranges objectives into a clear hierarchy with the most general and crucial at the top and the least important at the base. Priorities should be clearly stated.

Recommendations might include measures for co-ordinating and integrating diverse activities, for avoiding duplicated effort and for eliminating waste. The relevance of your present organisation structure (organisation charts, departmental divisions, authority and responsibility structures) for achieving the suggested strategic objectives must also be considered.

Although it is generally unwise to set unrealistically optimistic targets, there are certain circumstances in which a consultant might recommend you adopt objectives you cannot possibly achieve. For instance, complete domination of a certain market might be impossible given EC competition law and the company's current and foreseeable resource base, yet the *attempt* to dominate the market could itself be highly worthwhile eg, through the experience, synergy and introduction of new management and marketing methods that the effort will involve.

Problems and pitfalls

A strategy consultant's advice needs to be specific, detailed and plausible. The consultant must be observed to have identified key strategic problems and to offer *practical* policies for their resolution. Accordingly, the consultant's final report will normally be highly prescriptive, outlining precise measures for implementing the suggested corporate plan.

Unfortunately, the consultant's desire to be seen to be earning his or her fee and hence to suggest immediately applicable solutions might override his or her responsibility to report on *all* aspects of a difficult situation, perhaps even to recommend solutions to problems that actually have no hope of solution in the first place.

One frequent complaint is that consultants' reports are 'mass-produced', comprising little more than reworked standard paragraphs lifted from previous reports stored in their secretaries' word-processors! This should not happen, however, if you brief your consultant properly and make absolutely clear your expectations of the depth and scope of the report.

Another common criticism is that a 'big name' strategy consultant is contracted, only to find that the person who actually turns up to do the work is a relatively inexperienced junior employee of the consulting firm. You are being used as a training ground for the consultant's staff – which might be perfectly acceptable *provided* the junior consultant does a good job and you are not expected to pay top rates applicable to the consultancy firm's top staff. Prior to work commencing you should ask the consultancy firm precisely who will do the work, and for copies of their curricula vitae.

Appraising a consultant's work

Your evaluation of whether a consultant has done a good job will depend in part on your initial expectations, which should be clearly specified at the outset of the investigation. Also, you need to be fully aware of your own ultimate aspirations! If, for example you want your business to survive indefinitely – albeit earning only moderate returns – then you will not appreciate a consultant who recommends your adopting high-risk high-return strategies. Inform your consultant of your attitude towards the balance of risk and return at the beginning of the exercise.

After the investigation you should be better informed about the environments in which your business operates and better equipped to take strategic decisions. Ask yourself the following questions.

- Are the insights into the firm's strategic situation provided by the consultant's report more extensive than those you would have probably experienced yourself had you not hired the consultant?
- Does the report contain a *clear* diagnosis of the company's strategic problems and then directly relate recommended actions to their solution?

- Has a reasonably wide range of alternative scenarios been investigated?
- Have you learned from the analysis anything that you might be able to apply to other problems, ie, can you *transfer* what you have learned to other fields? Quite often, a strategy consultant's fee is worth paying just to learn how the consultant sets about his or her work. Then you can apply the methods you have observed to the solution of the next strategy issue that arises.
- Has the consultant indicated when improvements are likely to occur? Has the time horizon specified been adequately justified?

Appraisal is difficult because the effects of strategy changes might not be felt for several years, and it is unreasonable to expect the consultant to foresee every possible change in circumstances. Nevertheless, predicting change – including changes that will render unworkable the consultant's recommendations – is an important part of strategy determination. Thus, you are fully justified in insisting that several 'what if' projections be undertaken in order to account for all plausible changes in the wider situation.

A common complaint is that although the use of a strategy consultant (i) causes management to *feel* better about the direction of the organisation, and (ii) generates greatly enhanced awareness of the strategic problems and opportunities that it faces; profitability remains exactly the same as before!

This is not necessarily a fair criticism, because the consultant might have pointed out strategic errors which – had they not been corrected – would have ruined the firm, so the fact that profits have not increased might not be relevant.

Similar comments apply to inaccuracies in a consultant's forecasts. A forecast of the consequences of a particular course of action may be objectively correct, but then – armed with this information – the firm initiates activities which alter the total situation. Hence, forecasted events are *prevented* from happening. Forecasts can never be accurate in these circumstances.

Chapter 4

Organisation Design and Development Consultants

Introduction — Selecting an organisation design and development (ODD) consultant — What an ODD consultant will do — Basic issues in organisational design — Management by objectives — Recent developments in ODD: Managing a flexible workforce; Management of professionally qualified staff — Evaluating an ODD consultant

After reading this chapter you should:

- be aware of the types of problem that cause managements to engage ODD consultants;
- know what to look for in an ODD consultant;
- be able to specify objectives for the outcomes to an ODD exercise;
- understand the elements of organisation design (decentralisation, departmentation, spans of control, specialisation versus flexibility, etc); and
- appreciate the special problems attached to devising organisation structures suitable for flexible workforces and for the management of professionally qualified staff.

Introduction

Organisations can be designed and developed just like products. Many factors cause the need for organisational restructuring – rapid expansion, changes in production and other technologies, the death or retirement of the founder of a firm, labour shortages, and so on. Organisation design and development (ODD) consultants specialise in altering the makeups – the configurations – of organisations in order to improve their efficiency. Typical problems causing businesses to engage ODD consultants are:

- management's inability to appraise the efficiencies of certain activities because of numerous complex interrelationships within the company;
- staff not knowing the organisation's true objectives;
- absence of procedures for interdepartmental consultation and/or joint departmental decision taking;

- a single favoured department dominating others, even to the extent that other departments feel they need its permission to undertake certain actions;
- conflicts between individual and organisational objectives, including the pursuit of personal rather than company goals; and
- slow and ineffective decision taking within the organisation.

ODD consultants might be human resource management consultants (see Chapter 9), strategy consultants (see Chapter 3) or specialists in the theory of organisation. The consultant will advise your company on such matters as:

- whether you should have departments (i) for particular functions (marketing and personnel departments for example), (ii) for products (each of the company's products representing a cost centre in its own right), (iii) for geographical regions, or (iv) for teams of individuals concerned with specific projects;
- the best organisation structure for the firm in terms of the number of levels of authority in its hierarchy and how many immediate subordinates each line manager should personally control;
- whether each member of the organisation should specialise in and be responsible for, a single function or whether duties and responsibilities should overlap;
- how individuals, sections and departments are to be appraised and controlled;
- whether employees should be closely supervised, or left alone to complete broadly defined tasks; and
- how activities are to be co-ordinated (communication systems, the extent of delegation of work to lower levels) and by whom.

Selecting an ODD consultant

Many consultants who specialise in this area have academic backgrounds, especially in occupational psychology, organisational behaviour, and other aspects of behavioural science. Beware, therefore, of the possibility that a consultant might present you with a theoretically perfect organisational model which in reality is so impractical that it can never work. Consultants may be impartial and objective; but they do not have to live permanently with the organisational structures they create! Significant hands-on experience of industrial/commercial management is a quality greatly to be admired in an ODD consultant.

In making the selection remember that the consultant needs to be capable not only of impressing senior managerial staff but also of influencing and persuading lower level employees to accept his or her recommendations. Ask the following questions in respect of each candidate.

- Will this person/firm inspire confidence among subordinate staff?
- What practical experience of industrial or commercial management does the consultant possess?
- Has the consultant a good track record of reorganising other companies?
- Will this consultant be able to communicate with your employees in language they can understand?
- Has the consultant *justified* as well as explained his or her general approach to ODD?
- How precisely is the consultant willing to predict the outcomes of the intended exercise?

What an ODD consultant will do

The purposes of ODD are (i) to improve employees' morale and motivation by increasing their involvement with the organisation, (ii) to enhance decision making and information flows, (iii) to make it easier for individuals, sections and department to communicate, and (iv) to improve staff appraisal and control.

To achieve these aims the consultant needs to know the aims of your business (see Chapter 3) and the short, medium and long term problems it faces. Then he or she will require detailed information on existing organisation structures and on company personnel – especially their training, adaptability and willingness to accept change. The consultant will examine:

- internal decision making procedures;
- interpersonal relations within the company and senior executives' management styles;
- external threats; and
- the *culture* of the business.

A firm's *culture* consists of customs and shared attitudes among its employees. Organisational cultures evolve gradually, and members of organisations may not even be aware that cultures exist. Yet culture is important because it helps define how workers *feel* about their jobs. A culture will have arisen within a specific environmental context and be related to particular organisational needs. The problem is that an organisation's needs and activities necessarily alter, while its underlying culture remains unchanged. Culture involves common assumptions about how work should be performed and about appropriate objectives for the organisation, for departments within it and for individual employees. Changing an organisation's culture may be the most pressing of the consultant's tasks.

Next the consultant will decide which of the firm's activities belong together, and how the efforts of the new groupings can be co-ordinated in order to achieve the organisation's goals. Then an outline organisation structure will be drafted and the duties and responsibilities of the various positions within it carefully defined. A scheme for implementing the intended structure, including plans for informing/consulting your staff (and perhaps for initiating redundancies) must then be devised.

Usually, the consultant will begin by interviewing senior executives and studying the firm's current organisation chart. Then a questionnaire might be drafted for distribution to lower level employees, asking them to comment on their work and how they feel about the organisation and its aims. The consultant will be particularly interested in points of contact between various managers and will try to establish the nature and quality of communications between them. It is likely that the consultant will then want to interview various subordinate staff.

The consultant's report

The report will analyse the causes of deficiencies in the existing structure and recommend improvements. A new organisation chart might be drafted, and a manual submitted outlining intended job descriptions for key personnel in the new scheme. A good report will specify:

- how employees perceive the firm's objectives;
- measures necessary to create correct understanding of company objectives among employees;
- the barriers to communication between individuals and departments that are preventing the efficient transmission of information needed to run the business and how these can be removed (eg, the transfer of a manager who is failing to pass on essential information); and
- measures for grouping work logically and in a manner enabling easily appraisal and control.

Implementation

Organisation structures have to be adapted to fit the talents and degree of enthusiasm of those who work within them. Sophisticated communication and participative management systems, project teams, management by objectives programmes and so on are doomed to failure if the personnel involved do not possess the levels of skill and commitment required. Autocratic structures with close supervision and much division of labour may be more appropriate here.

Implementation could mean employees having to change job or take on new and/or additional duties. Spans of control (see below) may be widened or narrowed; decentralised units might be created or wound up. Responsibility for taking key decisions may be shifted, upwards or downwards, to different personnel.

Certain employees might require training in management and decision taking in order to perform effectively in their new roles. This is frequently the case when previously the firm (a family business for instance) was run by one or two dominant individuals who have now retired or died – leaving a decision taking void at the top of the company.

Basic issues in organisational design

ODD is about who does what, how, and with which other people. In the past certain ODD consultants have argued that there exists a handful of fundamental principles of organisation that should always be applied regardless of the nature of the firm or the industry within which it operates. Nowadays, however, few analysts would adopt so dogmatic an approach, so it is today more appropriate to ask a set of questions about any given organisational situation rather than to seek to impose predetermined solutions. The questions are as follows.

Should managers have wide or narrow spans of control?

A manager's span of control is the number of immediate subordinates who report directly to that person. Narrow spans involve just two or three subordinates; wide spans have perhaps twelve or fifteen subordinate employees. Most analysts suggest that any more than six or seven subordinates represents too wide a span of control because of the complex relationships and competing demands on the controlling manager's time that result. Four factors are relevant to the choice of a span of control: organisational diversity, complexity of work and the calibres of the manager and his or her subordinates.

Organisational diversity affects the efficiency of internal communications. If face to face contacts between manager and subordinates are impossible, communication depends on telephone calls, letters, memoranda and similar indirect means. Interruptions in information flows and other communications breakdowns cause loss of effective control, especially if people and departments are geographically separated. Complex work means that managers need time to assess the reports and suggestions of subordinates and they ought not to be overburdened with minor problems arising from lower levels. A narrow span of control is appropriate in this case. Note however that the imposition of narrow spans of control throughout the organisation necessarily creates many more levels of authority than in 'flatter' structures, resulting perhaps in long channels of communication and in important information not being passed up and down the chain of command. Top management may lose touch with what happens at lower levels within the organisation.

Some managers are better able to handle large numbers of subordinates than others, depending on their training, experience and personal qualities. The degree of authority given the manager is also relevant here. Similarly, well-trained enthusiastic and competent subordinates need less control and supervision than others, so that wide span of control may then be applied.

Narrow spans of control recognise that an individual's capacity to supervise others is limited and it is better to deal with a small number of subordinates properly than to have contact with many subordinates but only in casual ways. However, wide spans also offer advantages – they force managers to delegate (so that subordinates acquire experience of higher levels of work), subordinates may experience a higher degree of job satisfaction, and the cost of supervision is low. On the other hand, co-ordination of subordinates' activities may be poor. Communication between subordinates of equal rank could be inadequate and lead to much duplication of effort.

Should the principle of 'unity of command' be applied?
Unity of command means 'one person one boss', ie, that nobody should report to more than one superior. Its justification is that if a subordinate is accountable to several superiors then conflicting orders might be issued from different sources and the subordinate might not know which order to obey. Practical application of this principle is difficult because of the strong influences that informal authority systems can sometimes exert. A person might in theory be responsible to a single superior, but in reality behave according to standards determined by someone else. Moreover, the principle cannot normally be applied to individuals who belong to several project teams (see below).

To what extent should managers specialise in a specific field?
The advantages of a conventional line and staff system, with narrow spans of control and carefully delineated authority and responsibility structures, are (i) that specialist skills develop among managers (who acquire extensive knowledge of specific functions), (ii) that they are logical, coherent and easy to understand, and (iii) that a clear line of authority runs from the top of the organisation to its base. Unfortunately, however, communication in line and staff systems can be slow, and they might not be able to accommodate change.

Accordingly, firms which operate in fast moving market and technical environments sometimes prefer to organise their activities through project teams which cut across orthodox line and staff structures and traditional departmental divisions. This is sometimes known as 'matrix organisation'. Individuals from various disciplines (accountants, production engineers, market researchers, etc) are put into each of several project teams as and when they are needed.

Matrix structures are particularly appropriate when the firm is involved in many technically complex and interrelated projects requiring interdepartmental co-operation and highly specialised functional skills. The method is commonly used where several departments performing related duties are grouped together into a division. In this way, interdepartmental communications are enhanced and duplication of effort avoided. Note that matrix structures do not show authority systems, which makes them especially suitable for joint activities that involve colleagues of equal rank. Each team will need a leader/facilitator responsible for (i) publicising its aims, (ii) securing agreement on the tasks that must be completed, (iii) determining policies and accountability, and (iv) obtaining resources from outside. Project work involves much co-ordination and planning, resulting in many meetings and much committee work.

Matrix structures violate the principle that everyone should have just a single superior, since individuals are equally responsible to each of the leaders of several project teams as well as to a functional boss (an advertising manager might be under the firm's marketing director, for example).

Flexible versus formal structures.
An organisation operating within a rapidly changing environment may have to alter its organisation at short notice and for all aspects of its work. Consider for instance a computer manufacturing company which finds that a competitor has introduced a cheaper and superior model. This business must completely reorganise its design, production, marketing and administration systems almost at

once. Thus, it should adopt flexible organisation structures possessing total labour mobility, overlapping responsibilities, and fragile and transitory departmental structures that can be altered at will. The employees of such a company must be capable of taking on different types of work at short notice, and be culturally attuned to accepting change.

Conversely, organisations in relatively stable environments, or which employ poorly educated and/or apathetic staff, or which are concerned with routine assembly line or equally mundane activities that cannot be made more interesting, may opt for rigid, formal and bureaucratic organisational forms. Rules will exist covering every aspect of the firm's work. There will be clear divisions of work and close supervision. All procedures will be standardised and stated in writing; workers will not be allowed discretion in how they undertake their tasks. Relationships are extremely formal in such a system; everyone knows their place and exactly what they are expected to do.

Such measures relieve employees of the burden of having to think for themselves, and there is certainty that work will be completed on time. But individual initiative is stifled and this type of organisation is not remotely capable of accommodating change: people 'pass the buck' whenever they are confronted by new ideas.

How should departments be structured?

The first and possibly most important decision in designing the organisation of a business (or other) enterprise concerns the structuring of departments. A 'department' is a set of activities under a particular manager's control. Departments may be defined in product, function, market or personal terms.

With product departmentation each department deals with a single product or service. Departmental staff control all activities associated with the good, including purchase of raw materials, administration of processing and the sale and distribution of the final product. Senior departmental managers acquire a wide range of general managerial skills. They become experts in the problems associated with their own product. This specialised knowledge might be essential if the firm produces technically complicated goods.

An advantage of product departmentation is that co-ordination between relevant functions and stages of production is easily achieved. Performance appraisal is relatively straightforward in product department systems, since profit and cost centre are easily defined. Managers' performances can be measured against the costs, revenues and output levels of a product.

Market departmentation occurs when departments are constructed around geographical regions or particular customer types (regional sales offices, or a separate department to deal with wholesale customers, for example). It may be cheaper to locate a department near to customers; local factors may then be taken into account when deciding policy. Similarly, market departmentation could relate to customer size (eg, special facilities for large buyers), or to various distribution channels, export or home markets etc. Problems of co-ordination may ensue, and some loss of central control will be experienced. As with product departmentation, this method necessarily involves the duplication of activities. To avoid this, many organisations establish departments to cover specific functional areas – production, accounts, transport, administration and so on. The major functional departments contain sections, so that an advertising department for example, might be sub-divided into sections for media selection, sales promotion, package design and other promotional activities. The responsibilities of functional departments follow logically and naturally from the work of the organisation and will parallel occupational distinctions. Everyone concerned with selling will be in the marketing department, all who are involved in manufacture will be in production, and so on.

Functional departmentation is easy to understand but may encourage narrow and introspective attitudes. Departments with wider responsibilities might provide staff with challenging environments that stimulate effort and initiative. Another problem here is that functional specialists (production managers for instance) often develop patterns of thought and behaviour related more to their specialisms than to the well-being of the organisation as a whole. It is essential therefore that staff within a single functional department be regularly exposed to, and preferably involved with, the work of other departments.

In small family businesses it is common for departments to be created around specific people. As new functional needs arise they are allocated according to the interests of the family members. Eventually, each department controls a variety of unrelated activities. A partner in a small firm might for example be interested in finance and advertising. Thus, all things concerned with these functions will be dealt with in that partner's department.

To what extent should a company decentralise its activities?
Decentralisation is an important feature of many large companies; indeed, all organisations are 'decentralised' to a greater or lesser extent. Note that decentralisation is not the same as delegation, since

an organisation may be divided into regional, industrial, product or other divisions without any one division becoming subservient to the rest. Nevertheless, all decentralised structures require some control and the issue is how much 'regional' autonomy the central control should allow. Three factors are particularly important here: the calibre of the personnel in charge of divisions; the communication systems linking divisions to the centre; and the quality of information flow.

The aims of decentralisation are improved efficiency, less red tape, better divisional decision taking and faster response to environmental change. In a loosely controlled system, decisions are taken by local (though not necessarily geographically disparate) managers with expert knowledge of local conditions, within budgetary constraints imposed by the centre. Typically, divisional heads are given targets by the centre in the context of an overall corporate plan, but are then left to achieve objectives in their own ways.

The advantages of decentralisation include motivation of divisional managers who can use their own initiative in solving problems, its value in training local managers for more senior central posts and the relative ease with which divisional activities can be integrated by the central control. Disadvantages are the duplication of effort involved, losses of economies of scale and specialisation and the possibility of divisions regarding themselves as independent bodies with objectives different from those of the parent organisation. Rivalries between divisions may emerge, with divisions vying for attention and additional resources.

Appraising divisions
An important task when creating divisions is to ensure that their performances can be easily measured and appraised, since sometimes one division subsidises others – without anyone being aware of the fact! The problems involved here include:

- whether each division is to be regarded as a cost centre in its own right ('buying in' materials and services from other divisions);
- choice of criteria for measuring profitability (absolute money values, rates of return on capital employed, etc);
- deciding whether divisions should manage their own idle cash balances or turn them over to a central treasury for investment outside the division; and
- how to establish an efficient system for setting divisional targets and budgets, ie, how to inaugurate a divisional management by objectives scheme.

Management by objectives (MBO)

Most large and medium sized companies now operate systems for determining individual, departmental, divisional and company-wide objectives. Devising and implementing MBO programmes is a major ODD consultancy task. With MBO, corporate objectives are segmented into departmental targets and then into objectives for individual employees. Superiors and subordinates meet and jointly agree subordinates' job specifications and goals, preferably in quantitative terms. MBO supposedly motivates employees through involving them in the determination of objectives, and should help them develop their individual careers. Subordinates who exceed their targets will experience a sense of satisfaction in their achievements. Causes of success can be isolated, analysed and applied elsewhere. MBO imposes disciplined and logical approaches to decision taking. It forces managers to consider carefully the nature of their objectives, the factors affecting attainment of objectives, possible barriers and all the alternatives available. Moreover, MBO forces subordinates to think hard about their roles and personal objectives, about why tasks are necessary and how best to get things done. Also:

- targets are clarified and mechanisms are created for monitoring performances;
- crucial elements are identified in each job (this information is useful for determining training and recruitment needs);
- personal achievements of subordinates are recognised and rewarded;
- superiors and subordinates are obliged to communicate, so that superiors can quickly identify which subordinates are ready for promotion and the help they will need in preparing themselves for this;
- performance is appraised against quantified targets, not subjective criteria; and
- there is forced co-ordination of activities; between departments, between junior and senior management, and between short and long term goals.

Of course, many problems attach to MBO, so if you engage a consultant to set up an MBO programme, ask what he or she intends doing in order to:-

- prevent individuals concentrating exclusively on personal targets at the expense of helping attain wider organisational goals;
- avoid meaningless attempts to quantify activities that cannot be properly measured in numerical terms;

- discourage myopic emphasis on immediately attainable objectives and encourage concern with important longer-term targets;
- ensure that all participants are given the information, resources or authority necessary for completion of tasks allocated to them;
- prevent senior managers paying more attention to subordinates' personal qualities than to the work they do; and
- control the time spent on consultations between higher and lower executives. A dictatorial system whereby superiors simply impose targets on subordinates without consultation might be more efficient. Moreover, firms operating in highly uncertain, rapidly changing market environments may need to alter their objectives so frequently that MBO procedures become impractical.

Recent developments in ODD

Two current issues are increasingly important in ODD; flexible workforces, and the management of highly trained and specialist professionally qualified staff.

Managing a flexible workforce
The magnitude of the part-time, casual and contract labour force has expanded enormously in recent years. Three major factors explain this trend.

- Firms often find that their permanent full-time employees are not fully utilised throughout the year (sometimes not even through an entire working week) so that contract labour hired for short periods and/or to undertake specific assignments can be much cheaper than employing permanent staff.
- The size of the firm's labour force can be varied at will.
- Widespread redundancies and unprecedented high unemployment in the 1980s has released a large supply of workers willing, through choice or economic necessity, to work casually.

Clearly, new work patterns demand fresh approaches to labour management and organisational design. The common approach is to distinguish between *core* and *peripheral* workers. Core workers comprise full-time permanent employees who plan, take decisions and organise the work of casuals. They are superannuated, have security of tenure, receive training, and enjoy numerous fringe benefits. In return, however, their contracts of employment demand total job flexibility, ie, they must stand ready to do whatever work is available, irrespective of occupational divisions, at any time. Core workers have no job description other than to complete whatever tasks need doing.

Peripheral workers, conversely, are hired on short term and/or part-time contracts whenever labour is required. They exercise little discretion over how they perform their work and (generally) do not have 'careers'. Peripheral staff might include job sharers, agency employees, self-employed consultants and sub-contract labour as well as casuals and part-timers – indeed, anyone who can be hired and fired quickly and easily as market conditions change.

ODD consultants are increasingly involved in helping firms maximise the efficiency of their flexible workers, essentially through creating for peripheral workers opportunities for satisfying and meaningful jobs. Examples are homeworking (usually linked to a central control through a computer), job sharing, and formal career-break systems. Such schemes:

- enhance the morale of flexible workers, who are made to feel wanted and of real value to the organisation;
- enable individuals to choose how and when they do their work;
- help employers of flexible labour to retain their best peripheral workers; and
- help overcome problems of low commitment, poor communication and shoddy work among casually employed staff.

Control difficulties
Special management problems apply to the management of a flexible workforce, including:

- how to appraise the performances of peripheral workers;
- monitoring the output of home based employees;
- achieving the wholehearted participation of peripheral workers in the meetings, committees, etc, necessary for effective decision taking within the firm;
- securing adequate representation of peripheral workers in management/union negotiations, on health and safety committees, etc;
- preventing permanent employees resenting 'special' treatment afforded to flexible staff (eg, if common grading and promotion systems apply to both core and peripheral workers);
- controlling the quality of recruitment of peripheral workers; and
- arranging for the supervision of peripheral employees and deciding whether this should be done by other peripheral workers in a higher grade or by core employees. Note that flexible

workers are not usually capable to handling crises or sudden influxes of extra work since they lack the resources, information, experience and authority necessary for this – leading perhaps to overwork among core staff.

Profit sharing, holiday and sick pay and paid time off for training are among the many strategies that might be employed to overcome some of these difficulties. Further devices include:

- paying peripheral workers to attend general discussions about the firm's objectives;
- making peripheral workers responsible for the quality of their outputs, and generally broadening the scope of their jobs;
- offering fringe benefits such as company cars and superannuation to peripheral employees;
- providing contractually binding guarantees of re-entry to jobs after a break in continuity of service; and
- devising grievance and appeals procedures, consultation systems, etc, suitable for casually employed staff.

Induction of flexible workers into existing work groups is especially important, as it is essential that peripheral workers be made to feel part of the team and be introduced to the wider aspect of the organisation.

Note that UK employment law does not normally protect flexible workers, most of whom are excluded from the 1978 Employment Protection (Consolidation) Act (see Chapter 9) which requires that workers be *continuously* employed before acquiring rights to redundancy pay, maternity leave, redress for unfair dismissal, etc. Also, various aspects of health and safety and other employment legislation do not apply to casual workers. Indeed protections have been withdrawn from several categories of part-time staff in recent years.

Management of professionally qualified staff

Within organisations, professionals need to be able to practise their profession without coming into conflict with, or undermining, the formal authority systems of the employing firm. Numerous possibilities for conflict exist. Professionally qualified employees often complain that their talents are not fully utilised by employing companies; that they are asked to undertake mundane duties for which professional qualifications are not really required, and that the extent to which they are expected to exercise 'professional' judgement is not clearly defined. Thus, for instance, a qualified accountant might be asked simply to 'do the books' and not be involved in the (many) broader management functions for which he or she has been trained, or a solicitor may be expected to handle routine paperwork that could easily be dealt with by a solicitor's clerk. How much independent discretion should a professionally qualified employee be allowed? To what extent do professional staff require or deserve special facilities to enable them to practise their professional skills? And how, in general, can they be conveniently fitted into existing organisation structures?

Professionals are encountered most frequently when the organisation's work is complex. Yet tensions can easily arise between professional and line management staff. Either the professionally qualified employee must adapt his or her perspectives and working methods to fit in with the bureaucracy of the organisation, or the organisation itself must change its ways. The former option is perhaps the more likely, for whereas the professional contributes a particular function which *partially* satisfies the organisation's needs, the line management system is necessary for *all* the organisation's work. Thus, most firms will choose to subordinate their professional staff to the requirements of the existing system. Though note that certain organisations (universities, colleges or research centres for example) are necessarily dominated by professionally qualified employees. Typically, such institutions adopt 'federal' organisation structures whereby individuals enjoy great personal autonomy in how they undertake their work, but have separate administrations to perform routine management tasks. In effect, two distinct organisations operate simultaneously and side by side.

Unfortunately, the separation of the professional from the normal line of command can undermine the authority of the central administration. Note, particularly how professional immunity from the ordinary rules of superior/subordinate relationships will be closely observed by non-professional staff, who may question why they too should not be allowed to innovate, take important decisions, and not fear adverse criticism from higher authority about the decisions they take. Nevertheless, conventional line and staff systems might not be suitable when large numbers of professionals are employed because:

- line managers may become overwhelmed with requests for decisions on professional matters which they do not really understand;
- overworked line managers might ignore important advice offered by professionals;
- professionals find they are increasingly involved in the mundane administration needed to implement professional decisions;

- many issues cannot be unambiguously assigned to 'administrative' or 'professional' categories, since they require research and administrative action as well as professional discretion.

Line systems exist to control, to supervise, and to appraise subordinates' performances. Yet professional work is often free of direct 'control'. A lawyer, for instance, is not controlled by a line supervisor when preparing legal advice for a line manager's consideration; a company medical officer is not supervised by other managers while conducting medical examinations. The management of professionally qualified staff should therefore involve less direct control, but greater co-ordination of activities and dovetailing of the professional's role into the needs of the organisation. This might to achieved through having special support services for professional activities.

Evaluating an ODD consultant

At best, an ODD consultant's intervention will revitalise the organisation and create increased efficiency and profits for the firm. Unfortunately, the consultant will not normally be around when the major long term effects of an ODD exercise begin to be felt. In the immediate short term, therefore, ask yourself the following questions.

- Do you feel you now *understand* the root causes of past organisational problems better than before?
- What have you learned about the practical mechanics of organisational design and development just through watching the consultant at work? Do you now feel competent independently to undertake the next ODD exercise your company requires?
- Did the consultant explain to various individuals precisely *how* they would be affected by an organisational change, or did the consultant expect company managers to undertake this task?
- Did the consultant attempt to secure acceptance of proposed changes among the staff by briefing sessions, consultation and grievance procedures (see Chapter 9), explanatory leaflets for distribution to employees, counselling services, and so on?
- Are your staff now more committed to the organisation than when the consultant arrived?

Chapter 5

Quality Management and Manufacturing Systems Consultants

Introduction — Quality assurance — BS 5750 — Who are quality management consultants? — Briefing a quality consultant — What a quality consultant will do — Quality circles — Manufacturing systems — Productivity consultants — Current issues in manufacturing management: Technical standards after 1992; Robotics and flexible manufacturing systems; Optimised production technology; Just-in-time stock control procedures — Evaluating a manufacturing management consultant — Sources of information

After reading this chapter you should:

- appreciate the difference between quality management and statistical quality control;
- know about Quality circles;
- possess an outline knowledge of BS 5750;
- appreciate the range of quality management consultancy services available; and
- understand the work of manufacturing management consultants and their role in installing optimised production technology systems, just-in-time inventory control procedures, flexible manufacturing systems and so on.

Introduction

Mention *quality* to most British managers and they normally think first of statistical quality control – of tolerance and other specifications, acceptability ratios, sampling, probability calculations and so on. Traditionally, British industry has tended to adopt 'scientific' approaches to quality management, involving close supervision of employees, specialisation and the division of labour, narrow job and output specifications, and the frequent checking of work. Even so, the quality of output in UK companies applying such measures is often no better, and sometimes worse, than elsewhere. Indeed, by the 1980s the quality of output of very many UK companies had acquired an unenviable reputation for being (at best) second rate. Not surprisingly, therefore, those concerned with quality matters have looked abroad for fresh ideas regarding quality management, finding particularly impressive examples in Japan.

There, inspection and quality control are viewed not as independent functions, but as integral and inseparable components of the *total* production system, intimately intertwined with all other aspects of work. Production operatives assume personal responsibility for quality control and no clear distinction exists between production and inspection staff. Indeed, some large Japanese firms have dispensed entirely with specialist quality control departments and have all but abolished goods inwards inspection. Instead, they assume that suppliers will furnish high quality inputs not through fear of inspection, but as a matter of course and they issue to suppliers deliberately vague component specifications, arguing that the very act of laying down precise acceptance criteria itself implies that some defective input is acceptable provided the predetermined minimum standards are met. Excellence is taken for granted, so that inspections are seen not as a means for improving quality, but as an insult to the workers concerned. Quality management, therefore, is seen as a *philosophy* of excellence rather than a set of specific inspection techniques!

Quality management in Britain

An increasing number of management consultants specialise in quality management, due substantially to the fact that in 1987 the British Standards Institute published a specification (BS 5750 '*Quality Systems*' – briefly described below) for quality management which the government, local authorities and many big businesses have been quick to insist that their suppliers observe – even to the point of making supplying firms' adherence to BS 5750 a condition for awarding contracts for supplies. BS 5750 has many direct overlaps with a wider-based international standard (ISO 9000) which you will see referred to at many points in the BS 5750 text. There is additionally a European standard (which is essentially the same as BS 5750) called EN 29000. All these standards are for 'quality assurance' schemes.

Quality assurance

Quality assurance (QA) is more than quality control. It concerns the total system (including the management system) needed to assure customers that their quality requirements will be met. BS 5750 provides a recognised quality management standard the strict observance of which entitles the company to BSI certification that particular quality control procedures are followed within the firm. HMSO publishes a *Register of Quality Assessed UK Companies* which lists all certificated firms. This certification can be a powerful selling point for supplying companies when seeking orders, because customers are assured that the supplier is taking positive measures to guarantee the quality of its supplies.

QA programmes cover every aspect of the work of the firm, including the motivation (as well as the abilities) of employees, their training, experience, suitability for various tasks, and so on. QA standards (such as BS 5750) require firms to implement definite procedures for ensuring that specific quality environments will be maintained (for example that tools used on certain jobs be of a particular type, and that only qualified and certificated staff be employed on certain projects).

A QA system, moreover, might invite supplying firms to *improve* as well as provide contracted items and themselves to initiate alterations in the appearance, design or durability of requisitioned products. The quality of a product involves its fitness for the purpose for which it is intended as well as its physical condition on despatch. Suppliers need therefore to know the *purposes* of the articles they are invited to produce and the operational circumstances of their use. Hence, a clear statement of the purpose of the item, leaving technical details (including perhaps the choice of input materials) to the discretion of the supplying firm, might have greater long term value than precise and detailed specifications of weights, sizes, machine tolerances, etc.

Often QA is implemented through checklists issued to various departments asking them to scrutinise their procedures and confirm that certain measures have been undertaken. Typically, a checklist question will ask, 'What have you done to ensure that . . . ?' and then ask the respondent to detail the measures taken.

BS 5750

The aim of BS 5750 is to provide suppliers with a means for obtaining BSI certificated approval that their quality management systems are up to scratch. Customers may then have confidence in a company's ability (i) to deliver goods of a prespecified quality and (ii) to maintain the quality of its output at a consistent level. You will find that most quality management consultants offer assistance to companies in raising their quality procedures to the standards necessary for BS 5750 recognition.

BS5750 is a detailed and extensive document with several parts and appendices. It requires the supplier to *demonstrate* its ability to design and supply products in predetermined ways. Apart from design procedures, the specification covers the supplier's own procurement systems: its inspection and testing methods, the means by which customers may verify its claimed quality systems, how customers can check the supplier's records and other documents relating to quality procedures, and how customers may confirm the nature and extent of quality related training given to the supplier's staff. Examples of particular requirements are as follows.

- The firm must produce a quality assurance manual, with written procedures detailing:
  - internal allocations of responsibility for various aspects of quality;
  - quality control procedures, methods and work instructions; and
  - testing, inspection and audit programmes.
- Staff responsibilities for verifying quality management procedures must be (demonstrably) independent of other functions.
- Effective control over the quality of output of sub-contractors must be guaranteed.
- Design staff must possess appropriate qualifications.
- Certain quality control records must be maintained and made available to customers.
- The firm must ensure that proper testing equipment is used.
- All the resources needed to guarantee maintenance of good quality must be identified.
- The firm must ensure that its handling, storing and packaging procedures prevent damage to or the deterioration of goods.
- Open access to customers' representatives must be provided, and customers must be given all the inspection and other facilities necessary to verify the supplier's quality procedures.

Appendices to some of the parts of the BS 5750 contain sample questions that could be asked in order to ascertain whether a system is up to BS 5750. Examples are listed below.

- How frequently does the company conduct quality audits and how extensive are these?
- Has the firm clearly identified the staff responsible for quality control?
- Are customers' representatives given free and adequate access to inspect the supplier's quality systems?
- How are goods received inspected?
- Is the firm's test equipment up-to-date?

FOR EVERY TOP LINE COMPANY WHICH WANTS TO IMPROVE

ITS BOTTOM LINE

The Doctus Management Consultancy's systematic approach to improved productivity and profit performance – against a fixed cost and time scale – has resulted in substantial benefits for our client companies.

This formula has worked successfully for companies such as British Caledonian Airways, Severn Trent Water Authority, British Nuclear Fuels plc and North of Scotland Hydro – Electric Board.

If you are a key decision maker – contact Laura Cooper at the address below.

DOCTUS

Bringing futures into being

DOCTUS MANAGEMENT
CONSULTANCY LIMITED
Windsor House, 2 Pepper Street, Chester CH1 1DF.
Tel: (0244) 351935. Fax: (0244) 319294.

A MEMBER OF THE MANAGEMENT
CONSULTANCIES ASSOCIATION

A DOCTUS PLC GROUP COMPANY

- How quickly are faults in the company's quality management system corrected?
- Are the firm's quality control records and work instruction documents adequate?
- Do the company's design procedures consider relevant aspects of reliability, safety, ease of maintenance, etc?
- Are crates, boxes and containers suitable for the goods?

Who are quality management consultants?

Most quality consultants have an engineering background, reflecting the subject's close relations with production control. Many are heavily involved in helping firms prepare for 1992, and 1992 literature (including the publications of the DTI) is a good source of information for locating consultancies. Some quality consultants act as contractors for various schemes run by the British Standards Institute – details of these schemes (normally concerning BS 5750) and of individual contractors are available direct from the BSI, otherwise look in the *Directory of Management Consultants in the UK* (see Chapter 1).

Help with the installation of a quality management system is available *via* the DTI Enterprise Initiative (see Chapter 1), particularly for the preparation of quality control documentation (including manuals) and for advice on how to meet BS 5750. However the Enterprise Initiative does *not* cover specific product inspection methods or anything to do with quality training.

Briefing a quality consultant

First you must discuss with the consultant your customers' quality needs and expectations. Outline all the quality deficiencies you have noticed and specify your *precise* requirements: do you want to improve the quality of a specific product, a set of quality assurance procedures, or an entire quality management scheme? Enormous differences attach to the work (and cost) involved in each possibility.

What a quality consultant will do

Quality is a nebulous concept. It concerns not only the reliability, durability and physical characteristics of goods but also certain intangible attributes derived from their advertising and general presentation: consumers might *feel* a product is of good quality even if physically it is not. Isolating exactly what your customers mean by the quality of your products is a major element in the quality consultant's task.

The consultant will identify and measure the costs of deficiencies in your existing quality system and suggest how weaknesses might be overcome. Also, he or she should assess the implications for sales of your present quality levels and predict by how much sales will increase following improvements in the quality of your goods. Other important quality consultancy duties are:

- writing clear and precise quality control instructions and manuals;
- representing your firm when your customers inspect your premises to see your quality control procedures for themselves; and
- arranging for staff to be trained in quality management.

A major function is to develop *quality performance measurement indices* (QPMIs) for client firms. This requires reviewing current and desired performance standards and (importantly) securing the co-operation of all the employees – including shop floor workers – who will be involved in the intended quality improvement programme. QPMI formulation requires close examination not only of production methods but also of employees' *attitudes* towards quality. To improve the latter the consultant might arrange seminars, quality workshops, briefing sessions, etc. Personal counselling of certain key employees might also be required.

The consultant will seek to discover the root causes of defective production. This can result from random variations in processes or from systematic deficiencies. Non-random variations can be due to operator or management inadequacy, or to environmental problems. Some possible causes of non-random quality deficiencies are listed below.

- Operator inadequacy
  - carelessness or undue haste
  - inexperience or lack of training
  - physical inabilities; for instance, insufficient strength for lifting weights, poor eyesight, low tolerance to stress
  - misunderstanding instructions, drawings or specifications
  - tiredness, lack of concentration
- Management inadequacy
  - lack of supervision
  - complex procedures, incorrect instructions, unclear job specifications
  - provision of badly worn machines, processing faults, low quality tools and materials
  - poor design
  - inadequate training of operatives, inappropriate selection of operatives for particular jobs
- Environmental problems
  - poor lighting
  - excessive noise
  - badly designed furniture, poor workplace layout.

External inspections of suppliers' premises
Large financial savings are available through insisting that your suppliers adhere to predetermined quality procedures (eg, BS 5750) because:

- internal production flows can be speeded up in consequence of greater reliability of input materials;

- less stocks of inputs need be held since you can rely on fresh supplies arriving on time;
- less inspection of incoming supplies will be required;
- less working capital is needed; and
- inputs will be safer to use.

This presupposes, of course, that suppliers are willing to conform to your procedural requirements and to submit to outside inspections. Increasingly however suppliers realise they must satisfy customers' requirements in this regard.

A quality consultant will inspect suppliers on your behalf and report on the calibre of their quality management procedures.

Make or buy decisions
A further role for a quality consultant is to advise on 'make or buy' decisions in relation to input components. If you produce your own components you enjoy complete control over their specification, design, quality and time of delivery. Also, there is no profit margin as with supplies purchased from outside. External suppliers however will normally have produced far more units of output than those delivered to the individual purchasing firm, and thus experience scale economies (and hence lower costs) not possible in firms producing their own components. Moreover, internal production of supplies often requires additional investments in manufacturing plant, and extra labour might have to be employed. A firm could invest heavily in plant and equipment needed for component manufacture only to find that outside firms offer these components for sale at prices lower than internal production costs. A consultant will analyse all the costs and benefits involved (direct costs, overheads, extra supervision, reliability of supplies, consequences of the acquisition of additional skills, etc) and submit a report.

Quality circles

Frequently, the major barrier preventing better quality production is the apathy of employees towards quality matters. It then becomes necessary to change workers' attitudes towards quality control. One device for achieving better attitudes is the establishment of *quality circles*.

Japanese industry has not always enjoyed its current reputation for high quality. This was especially true in the 1950s when Japanese products were frequently regarded as cheap and unreliable imitations of existing western goods. Thus, great effort was expended on improving quality in Japanese firms, and the technique of the quality circle was one important result. The first recorded circle was formed in 1963 in the Nippon Telegraph and Telephone Corporation, though the idea quickly spread and soon there were many tens of thousands of quality circles operating throughout Japan.

A quality circle is a departmental workers' discussion group that meets regularly to consider, analyse, investigate and resolve production and quality problems. The group is trained in problem solving techniques and, importantly, is given resources and (limited) authority to implement decisions. Circle leadership might be assumed by an existing departmental supervisor, or by someone directly elected from the group. In their western form, circles meet during working hours (though in Japan they initially met outside the firm's time) and participation may or may not be compulsory. If membership is 'voluntary' management might encourage participation by group bonuses, generous payments of expenses, hints of promotion for enthusiastic members, overt managerial disapproval of those who do not take part, etc. Circle leaders are specially trained in the techniques of group motivation and control and are made responsible for generating interest in the circle's work among fellow employees. Circles normally concentrate on mundane, practical (rather than organisational) problems and solve them using ideas and methods developed by circle members. Typically, circle activities are initiated by the circle, although management might occasionally refer problems to the circle for analysis and resolution.

Many large UK companies now have quality circles, though not always under this name (other titles for quality circles are 'quality improvement teams', 'corrective action teams', 'customer care teams' and 'customer focus groups'). And certain quality management consultants today specialise in the installation of quality circles in client firms.

Problems with quality circles

Often, circles succeed in the short run, but fail in the longer term. Morale improves initially as workers become involved (often for the first time) in decision taking, and as participants are brought together to discuss quality and productivity issues. Workers begin to take an interest in company affairs and to apply their personal knowledge, skills and experiences to the solution of quality problems. Since circle decisions are taken by those responsible for their implementation they are almost certain to be carried out.

Eventually, however, apathy sets in as employees begin to feel they are undertaking (unpaid) extra duties the benefits of which will accrue entirely to the firm and not to circle members. Improved performances might not be adequately rewarded and frustrations may arise from the circle's inability to solve problems the sources of which are beyond its control. Antagonisms develop between circle leaders and other managers about how particular difficulties should be overcome and over the extent of the resources and executive authority the circle should command. Within the group, friction may occur as low status, low paid employees offer more and better solutions to problems than do appointed supervisors and other higher paid departmental managers.

The circle acquires experience of participative decision making and may wish to apply this to other areas of the organisation's work (industrial relations or welfare for example), even though management might oppose employee participation apart from quality circles. Members then regard the circle's terms of reference as unduly restrictive and feel that their efforts are being thwarted by higher management or others outside the group. Attendance at circle meetings falls and meeting themselves are held less frequently. The circle has then effectively collapsed. True, productivity and quality have improved, but one suspects that similar results might have been achieved through some other type of initiative.

Why circles fail

Were it simply the case that quality improvement *via* quality circles has been prevented through management techniques not keeping pace with modern production methods, the situation could easily be remedied through altering organisational structures and techniques of management control. Unfortunately, far deeper problems are involved. Note first that Japanese companies take complete responsibility for their employees' careers. There is a total job security, much training and job rotation and employee participation in decision making is accepted as the general norm (activities are centred on groups rather than individuals – tasks are assigned to teams).

In Japan, pay and promotion depend on length of service, so that new recruits are virtually guaranteed steady progression within the firm. Since promotion opportunities are necessarily limited, lateral transfers of workers to other departments and jobs regularly occur. Workers thus obtain a bird's-eye view of the entire organisation and are then able to relate quality problems in one section to the operations of the firm as a whole. Employees identify with the corporate personalities of their firms – all grades of worker (including managers) dress alike, eat in the same canteen and are employed under similar conditions of service. There is a single 'company union' representing all employees. Open communication between management and workers is encouraged. Much consultation between management and labour occurs and worker participation in decision taking is common. Continuous training, job rotation and acquisition of experience plus guaranteed life-long employment develops in employees a great sense of loyalty to the firm, its profitability and survival. Individuals construct their long-term career plans around the assumption they will progress within the organisation.

Installing a quality circle

Few (if any) UK businesses operate in the manner previously outlined (even Japanese companies that have set up in Britain, which tend to adopt local UK employment practices – albeit with modifications) so great care is needed when seeking to transfer the quality circle concept to British firms, which increasingly employ part-time and casual labour and where workers only rarely feel a long-term commitment to their employing companies.

If you use a consultant to set up a quality circle in your company, make sure that:

- a mechanism is created whereby all relevant information needed by the circle to operate effectively is actually provided;
- circle leaders are properly trained;
- the circle is fully integrated into the wider aspects of the company's work;
- the consultant provides contingency plans for reviving the circle if key personnel lose enthusiasm or leave the firm;
- documents are created for recording circle activities and the assignment of duties and for detailing whether objectives are attained; and
- specific action plans accompany recommended circle activities.

Audit circle activities periodically. How many of its recommendations have been implemented? What is the state of morale within the group? Are subordinates more interested in their day-to-day activities than before? How has management reacted to circle proposals? Has output quality actually improved?

Be aware that no consultant can install a successful quality circle unless all the firm's employees recognise a responsibility for the quality of the company's products and accept the principle that they should actively participate in production and quality decisions. Note, moreover, that in many cases the establishment of a quality circle is a management's first ever attempt at employee participation, so that is has no experience of the difficulties that arise from participative management techniques. Too often, circles are established as *ad hoc* devices for improving quality and departmental efficiency rather than as a long term attempt to alter management style.

Manufacturing systems

If yours is a manufacturing business then you will know already the major sources of technical assistance for improving your particular type of production system. Nevertheless, management consultants can contribute to the analysis of manufacturing systems in a number of ways. For example they could:

- arrange for the orderly conduct of production systems feasibility studies and present the results in a logical manner;
- assess the implications of intended production operations for the strategy of the firm (see Chapter 3);
- suggest organisational structures appropriate for fast changing technical environments (see Chapter 4).

A common problem in high-tech industries is that management techniques do not evolve quickly enough to accommodate new production methods. Accordingly, consultancy advice might be needed regarding how best to attune employees to the organisational structures and managerial styles appropriate for new situations.

Manufacturing management consultants

Assistance with manufacturing management problems is available through the DTI Enterprise Initiative. The 'Manufacturing Systems' component of this covers such matters as production planning, standardisation, plant utilisation, energy management, robotics, and computer assisted production. Moreover, help with introducing specific production techniques is included in the scheme: casting, welding and fabrication, moulding, finishing, assembly, and so on. The only major exclusions are assignments relating to wage and bonus systems, industrial relations, direct health and safety issues, and anything to do with sub-contract work.

This aspect of the Enterprise Initiative is administered on behalf of the DTI by the Production Engineering Research Association. Other sources of information about engineering consultants are the Institutions of Production Engineers and Mechanical Engineers, and individual entries in Yellow Pages under 'Engineering consultants'.

Productivity consultants

Some of the largest and most prestigious of today's full service management consultancies arose from work study (time and motion) consultancy firms. Work study involves method study (how work is performed), work measurement (assessing the time taken to complete tasks), and motion study (the breakdown of jobs into standard human body movements). Traditionally the aim was to simplify work, eliminate unnecessary tasks, avoid duplication of effort and hence cut operating costs. At first, work study techniques followed the precepts of specialisation and the division of labour, and thus experienced all the human problems – boredom, frustration, alienation – that application of the division of labour necessarily entails.

Nowadays however, traditional work study has given way to more general 'productivity analysis', which – as well as being concerned with analysing work procedures ('organisation and methods' for example) – also recognises the need to provide employees with variety, satisfaction and interest in their work. Productivity analysis normally begins with a productivity audit.

Productivity audits

This examines the firm's productivity situation under four main headings: workers, resources, jobs, and the environments in which the business operates.

Environmental factors cannot be controlled, but they can at least be recognised and their likely consequences assessed. Resource factors include plant and equipment, capacity utilisation, use of stocks, and production planning and control. Employee related factors concern incentive schemes, training arrangements, workers' attitudes and the overall culture of the enterprise. Job factors involve job design, performance standards, supervision arrangements, etc.

The consultant's role

A consultant undertaking a productivity audit on your behalf will examine these (and perhaps other) variables and then devise various indices – usually in the form of ratios of outputs to appropriate inputs and activities – to measure productivity within various departments. Productivity will be measured per worker, section, unit of equipment and unit of capital employed. Values added at each stage in the production process will be carefully evaluated.

To appraise the calibre of a consultant's contributions to a productivity audit, ask yourself the following questions.

- Has the consultant successfully combined different types of input and output into a common denominator that can be used to compare the productivities of various sections and activities within the firm?
- Have the relationships between inputs and outputs been clearly defined?
- Are the productivity measures devised by the consultant properly understood by those who use them?
- Have particular examples of low productivity and general underperformance been exposed?
- Does the analysis suggest definite techniques for *controlling* productivity?

Current issues in manufacturing management

Key issues in manufacturing technology management currently include the effects of harmonisation of technical standards following 1992, robotics and flexible manufacturing systems, and the ever increasing interest shown by British firms in optimised production technology and related techniques. Consultants are available to help in all these fields.

Technical standards following 1992

Product standards are being harmonised across all European community countries in preparation for 1992. On the one hand this means that products will be subject to fewer country-specific regulations; equally however it means that many new (legally binding) European standards will be created as new common standards are reached. Two sources of help and information are available in these respects.

For straightforward enquiries, the 'Exports to Europe' branch of the DTI, will give general advice on existing regulations, standards and technical requirements in particular EC countries. Whereas for more detailed information on safety regulations, product modification requirements, accreditation procedures and so on, the 'Technical Help for Exporters' (THE) service run on behalf of the DTI by the British Standards Institute may be approached.

THE offers the following:

- A consultancy service whereby THE engineers will examine your output to ensure it meets relevant foreign requirements. If it does not then THE will specify the modifications necessary to ensure compliance.
- Detailed information on product laws in foreign countries and customer requirements in various foreign markets.

- Translations of foreign standards, laws and Codes of Practice. THE also provides a (low cost) translation service for specific foreign language technical documents.
- A research service for gathering detailed information about foreign technical requirements for particular products.
- Assistance in seeking foreign approval for your company's products.

Some enquiries can be dealt with free of charge by THE over the telephone. If a charge is to be incurred the enquirer will be advised of this in advance. THE is subsidised by the government and thus able to provide cheap consultancy services. Also, government grants to client companies are available in certain circumstances. Small firms with less than 200 employees are eligible for a 50 per cent discount (up to a maximum of £100) on any charges they incur when contacting THE for the first time.

Robotics and flexible manufacturing systems

A flexible manufacturing system (FMS) consists of a collection of computer-controlled machine tools and transport and handling systems, all integrated through a larger master computer. The great advantage of a flexible manufacturing system is the speed and ease with which relatively small production runs can be set up and modified from one batch of output to the next. A wide range of versions of the same product may be economically produced. Hence the features of products can be adapted to meet the needs of several different markets. Accordingly, economies of scale and the benefits of standardisation and rationalisation of product ranges are less important in flexible manufacturing systems.

Most FMS arrangements rely heavily on robots for routine production. Robots have several advantages over manual labour: they do not complain, and they incur no training or staff development costs. The present generation of robots incorporate easily reprogramable computers which enable the nature of the robots' activities to be altered quickly. Hence, the same robot can be used for several different purposes: assembly line work (grasping, machining, etc, done from a fixed position), materials handling (shunting items from one location to another), clearing up, spray-painting, stamping, and many other diverse activities.

You might see the term 'manufacturing automation protocol' (MAP) used in these respects. It means the linking up of offices, assembly lines and processes in different locations in order to increase the efficiency of closed-loop manufacturing operations. (A closed-loop system is one whereby information on current performance automatically adjusts operations in order to adjust divergences between planned and actual activity, eg, the speed of a production line might automatically and instantly adjust itself according to the proportion of defective output that it creates.)

Optimised production technology (OPT)

This is as much an *approach* to production management as it is a specific procedure. It seeks to minimise work in progress by isolating and where possible, removing bottlenecks in material flows. Importantly, it does not assume that peak efficiency is attained by keeping every machine, worker and process fully employed all the time. The steps involved in installing an OPT system are as follows.

- Identify bottlenecks, eg, the time taken to set up machines or to adjust tolerances, delivery holdups, stockouts, etc.
- Devise work schedules to guarantee that equipment or processes associated with bottlenecks are fully supplied at all times – even if this means plant, equipment and labour standing idle further back in the chain of production.
- Integrate the entire system under a single coherent production plan.

To appraise the calibre of an OPT system, ask yourself the following questions.

- Can the company quote shorter periods for delivery of final products than before the system was installed?
- Has product quality diminished? Have customer complaints increased?
- Did the consultant suggest possible uses for the idle time and spare capacity generated by the new system?
- What is the true cost of the idle capacity that may have been created?

Just-in-time stock control procedures

With a Just-in-time (JIT) system, work is planned so that each production unit delivers to the next unit precisely the input it requires in order to proceed with the next stage of manufacture (or processing) and delivers the input just in time for the work to begin. No stocks of inputs are carried, there is no bunching of production lines or queues anywhere in the system. Successful operation of a JIT scheme requires precise scheduling of raw materials procurement, production, processing and despatch. There has to be a uniform daily demand throughout the entire sequence of manufacture, with minimal change-over time and reliable equipment. Production workers themselves are expected to operate the system – there is little defective production and inventory levels are sometimes as much as four times lower than before. This is made possible by requiring each worker to assume personal responsibility for quality and production control. Workers are organised into *cells* which organise their own work and are put in charge of the repair and maintenance of the equipment they use, quality control, and the timing of movements of work from one cell to another.

Evaluating a manufacturing management consultant

The range of assignments that manufacturing consultants might undertake is so diverse that it is difficult to identify common criteria for evaluating their services. In general, however, you need to ask the following sorts of question.

- How comprehensive were the consultant's recommendations? Did they encompass all relevant aspects of the work of the firm including its transport, packaging and goods handling procedures?
- Do you receive less complaints from customers about product reliability than before?
- Are customer requirements now fully integrated into product design and new product development procedures?
- Has the consultant's initial fee plus the administrative costs of implementing his or her recommendations been recouped by higher output and/or less defective production?
- Are the documents and manuals drafted by the consultant easy to follow and readily revised and updated?
- Has the consultant included free telephone advice (albeit for a limited period) following installation of the new system as part of his or her overall service?
- Are performance standards more clearly defined than previously?
- Are the records attached to the new system clear and comprehensive? In particular do they reveal sources of problems, identify inefficiencies in specific operations and individual workers, leadtimes, cost differences between various processes, etc? And do they measure idle time, overtime working and the extent of sub-contracting in sufficient detail?

Sources of information

British Standards Institute
(Technical Help for
Exporters)
Linford Wood
Milton Keynes MK14 6LE
0908 220022

Exports to Europe (DTI)
1 Victoria Street
London SW1H OET
01-215 4782/5336

**Institution of Mechanical
Engineers**
1 Birdcage Walk
London SW1H 9JJ
01-222 7899

**Institution of Production
Engineers**
66 Little Ealing Lane
London W5 4XX
01-579 9411

**Production Engineering
Research Association**
Nottingham Road
Melton Mowbray
Leics LE13 0PB
0664 501501

Chapter 6

Financial Management Consultants

Introduction — Accountants — Auditors — General financial management consultancy — Credit management — Raising finance — Management accountants — Sources of information

After reading this chapter you should:

- understand the range of financial management consultancy services available;
- appreciate the differences between financial accountancy consulting services and management accounting consultancy;
- know the advantages and disadvantages of using large and small accountancy firms;
- understand how accountants and auditors fix their fees and how to negotiate with an accountant in order to minimise your payment;
- know how to choose a credit factor or debt collecting service; and
- know where to look for help with venture financing, investment appraisal, cost reduction, etc.

Introduction

Financial management consultancy covers an extremely broad field, including accounting and financial management information systems, investment appraisal, fund raising, mergers and acquisitions, company turnaround and insolvency, taxation, debt collecting and credit control. Assistance towards the cost of certain types of financial management consultancy project is available through the DTI Enterprise Initiative (see Chapter 1) in the category 'Financial and Information Systems', which explicitly mentions the provision of advice on overall financial accounting systems, especially those involving information technology. However, EI assistance is not available for physical systems implementation, software programming, or the input of data to a system.

To most people, financial management means accountancy, and managers instinctively think first about approaching an accountant when considering taking financial management advice.

Accountants

There are two types of accountant – 'financial' and 'management' – and several recognised professional bodies that operate in the accounting field. While it is true that anyone can call themselves an 'accountant' and give financial advice, an accountant who has qualified through a series of proper professional examinations will belong to one (or more) of a small number of bodies; notably the Institute of Chartered Accountants (of which there are three regional variations), the Chartered Association of Certified Accountants (still referred to as the ACCA, which were the initials of its old title) the Chartered Institute of Management Accountants (CIMA), and the Chartered Institute of Public Finance and Accountancy (CIFPA). (You will not normally encounter members of the latter body outside the public sector.)

Only members of the Institute of Chartered Accountants and the ACCA (plus a couple of specialist bodies approved by the Secretary of State of Trade and Industry) are legally entitled to audit company accounts.

Accountants work as sole practitioners, in partnerships, as members of large national accountancy firms, or in industry and commerce as employees. From now on, when I use the word 'accountant', I mean a member of one of the bodies mentioned above.

Financial accountants

Financial accountants will prepare your final accounts, determine your maximum liability for tax, negotiate with the tax authorities on your behalf and audit your books. Tax is a difficult, technically complicated subject, involving many procedures and rules for appeal. A good accountant will not only understand the issues and procedures involved but will also be a competent advocate, fully capable of persuasively arguing your case before the tax authorities.

Among the numerous matters about which financial accountants offer advice and assistance are VAT, payroll procedures, design and installation of bookkeeping systems, preparation of cash flow forecasts and the maintenance of accounting records. Other important topics for which a company might require the services of a financial management consultant include:

- timing of share issues and deciding on share issue prices;
- seeking access to the stock exchange and/or the unlisted securities market;
- management of working capital;
- export finance (see Chapter 14);

- international borrowing; and
- management of the firm's portfolio of financial investments.

Choosing an accountant
The accounting bodies have allowed their members to advertise since 1984 and you now see advertisements for accountants in newspapers, trade presses and elsewhere. An obvious source of information on the whereabouts of suitable accountants is the published accounts of competing companies, which by law must state the names and addresses of their accountants. Also the professional accounting bodies will provide lists of qualified accountants in your area. Accountants are listed under that title in *Yellow Pages*.

Large accountancy practices provide a wide range of services, and will guarantee that work is carried out. Small local firms offer personalised service, instant attention (usually), a one to one relationship, and lower fees. However, a small practice will of necessity be 'generalist' in nature, the partners personally undertaking all aspects of accountancy work. Hence they may lack the highly specific functional skills (integrated and advanced computer accounting skills for instance) frequently available in larger accountancy firms. An advantage of dealing with a small practice is that the same people will do the work year after year. Big firms sometimes have high staff turnovers, so that the individuals who turn up at your premises may be different on each visit.

In selecting an accountant ask yourself the following questions.

- What is the accountant's experience of the problems attached to your particular type of business?
- How extensive are his or her ancillary services?
- Has the firm handled the accounts of major companies?
- Does the accountant possess the administrative resources to handle the assignment? If so, will these resources still be sufficient in a couple of years' time if your company grows?
- Will the firm guarantee a maximum leadtime for dealing with your requests for help and advice?
- Will the work the accountant does for your company be untypical of the work it normally undertakes? If so, what are the implications?
- How long will the firm spend on the project?
- Is the accountant prepared to justify fully all the component parts of his or her estimate of fees?

The problem with using an accountant for general management consultancy is the lack of knowledge of general management theory and practice typical of most accountants. Of course, accountants are expert in matters relating to financial management; but their knowledge of marketing, personnel, organisational design and development, and so on, is (to say the least) rather poor. At the time of writing only one of the major accounting bodies (CIMA) has management as a compulsory subject in its training curriculum. ACCA offers management as an option, while the curriculum of the Institute of Chartered Accountants of England and Wales does not provide for instruction in (non-financial) management *at all*.

Fees

Most accountants charge on an hourly or daily basis, but note (importantly) that the accounting bodies do *not* prohibit their members working on a payments by results basis (eg, investment advice may be rewarded according to the performance of a recommended portfolio). Fees vary accordingly to the type of work done, the time spent with the business, and the complexity of your company's accounts. The national average for combined auditing and general accounting service charges lies between 0.5 and 1.5 per cent of annual company turnover.

When asking for estimates specify the nature and extent of the work you require, giving plenty of background information on your present accounting system. Candidates will need to know the size of the firm, number of employees, its products, and details of any computer accounting packages (See Chapter 8) currently operating.

Dismissing your accountant

It is easier to dispense with an accountant who does not audit your books than with one who does because in the former situation this is a management rather than a shareholder's decision (see below). Note however that the dismissed accountant will hang on to your accounting records until all outstanding fees have been settled. If you believe payment is not appropriate you may have to sue, eg, for losses incurred through the accountant's incompetence or professional negligence.

To their credit, the major accounting bodies insist that all of their members in public practice have proper insurance to cover such actions, so you need not fear the accountant's insolvency if you win your case.

Auditing

Auditing has been described (with some justification) as a statutory nuisance. Limited companies are legally obliged to have their books audited once a year. And only chartered accountants (CA or ACCA) may perform this task. Yet auditors do not (normally) assume liability for falsified or misleading accounts. All they do is state that (i) the accounts give a true and fair view of the company's position – given the information supplied and available at a particular moment in time, and (ii) that the layout of the accounts meets statutory requirements. Auditors do not prepare or maintain the company's accounting records and statements (balance sheets and profit and loss accounts for example); and they are not responsible for the detection of fraud (directors bear this obligation).

However, auditors can be held liable for professional negligence (see Chapter 16) to third parties who rely on an audit report which was negligently prepared and who suffer losses in consequence – provided that the auditor could have reasonably foreseen at the time of the audit that the third party might use and rely on the report. This means that the third party should not be too distant from the affairs of the company. Also, outsiders are expected to be prudently cautious when reading audit statements and, where large investments are concerned, to conduct their own independent investigations.

Dismissing an incompetent auditor
Here you run into all the problems attached to dealing with a legally protected profession. Only shareholders are allowed to dismiss an auditor, *not* the directors of the company. If directors do attempt to remove an auditor then he or she is legally entitled to circularise shareholders with his or her version of events – *at the company's expense.* Moreover, if shareholders do dismiss an auditor, then under the internal rules of the accountancy bodies authorised by law to conduct audits the next accountant you approach to replace the dismissed auditor is obliged to write to the latter and ask for details of the dismissal. The dismissed accountant must then ask your permission to reveal these details (to protect confidentiality) and if you refuse (eg, because sensitive or personal relationships matters are involved) the accountant whose services you are seeking will *automatically refuse the assignment.*

Reducing your auditor's fees
Your auditor will claim that he or she is professionally obliged to comply with certain operational standards laid down by the accountancy bodies. Accordingly, your task is to reduce the amount of routine work the auditor needs to do (and hence be paid for) in order to achieve these standards.

- Arrange the company's accounting information system in such a way as to minimise the amount of time the auditor can claim to be necessary for collecting data.
- At the conclusion of an audit ask the auditor to specify any measures that you might implement in order to reduce the time he or she will need to spend on next year's audit.
- During an audit, ask the accountant to provide interim reports on any problems with your accounting system that are holding up his or her work.
- Provide all the auditor's support services from in-house resources – clerks, secretaries, programmers, etc.
- Have all relevant information available for immediate inspection on request, including systems files and flowcharts, up-to-date procedures manuals and so on.
- At the outset of the audit point out any problems with figures, any deviations from past trends, and major differences between this year's figures and those for last year. Provide fully documented justifications for these.
- Arrange and pay for all travelling and overnight hotel bookings yourself rather than leaving these to the auditor, who will add their cost to your final bill – with perhaps a 15 or 20 per cent mark-up.
- Avoid discussing minor matters with the auditor. This merely increases the time he or she spends with the firm and raises the final cost.

It is important to note that auditors provide a wide range of general accounting services in addition to their audit role. If you use some of the auditor's ancillary services (the contracts for which might be worth more than the total audit fee) you can threaten to withdraw your custom – without any of the legal and other hassles previously described – in order to pressurise the auditor into reducing his or her audit fee.

Evaluating an accountant's contribution
First and foremost the accounts your accountant prepares and/or audits must satisfy all legal requirements and not attract complaints from shareholders, debtors or the authorities (particularly the Registrar of Companies). Then ask yourself the following questions.

- How quickly was the work completed?
- Were all the items on the accountant's bill fully explained and justified?
- Has the accountant responded instantly to your requests for help?

- Has extra work been undertaken which you did not directly commission, and if so why?
- How responsive was the accountant to your suggestions and criticisms?
- Has the accountant offered useful comments about the general management of your firm?

General financial management consultancy

Financial management consultants are listed in the TFPL publication *Directory of Management Consultants in the UK* (see Chapter 1) and may be found in *Yellow Pages* under the heading 'Financial consultants'. A good source of information is *The City Directory*, published annually by Director Books. This gives lists of over 5500 City organisations: credit information services, financial market research organisations, financial advertising and public relations consultants, factors, stockbrokers, venture capital firms, currency brokers and so on. Some of the major specialisms are outlined below.

Credit management

Most firms experience difficulties in obtaining payment from some credit customers from time to time. Non-settlement of outstanding balances is a major problem in certain businesses; indeed, slack credit control is a common cause of business collapse.

Factoring

One solution is for a company to factor its debts, ie, turn over its invoices to an outside credit factoring business in exchange for immediate cash payment. The factor then assumes responsibility for collecting the money owed on the invoices. Factoring provides ready cash, but is expensive – only a percentage of the face value of a debt is paid, depending on the factor's assessment on how easily the debt can be collected. Since credit factors devote all their efforts to debt collecting they acquire special skills and achieve economies of scale (employment of legal advisors, access to credit rating information, standardised documents and so on) not usually available to individual firms. Sometimes, letters from credit factors will elicit positive responses from slow payers even though previous letters from supplying firms were ignored. Debtors will realise that a credit factor has the resources and determination to prosecute settlement of the debts. Some of the high street banks have credit factoring subsidiaries. Otherwise look in *Yellow Pages* under 'Factoring'.

Choosing a factor
Look carefully at how a factor operates – does the firm guarantee to take all your invoices or just some of them, and how quickly will you receive the cash? Note that some factors (who may refer to themselves as 'invoice discounters' rather than as factors *per se*) in effect 'lend' you money against the security of invoices – as opposed to buying them outright. You are still expected to attempt to collect the debt and they only step in when accounts become excessively overdue. Some factors, moreover, expect client firms to meet part of the cost of bad debts.

How exactly will you be paid by the factor? Usually you receive some proportion of the face value of the invoice immediately (eg, 75 per cent) plus, say, a further 15 per cent following the customer's settlement (leaving the factor with a ten per cent commission on the transaction). The factor might also levy service charges based either on the volume of invoices handled or on the value of lost interest on the initial payment to the client firm.

You need to compare the terms of various factors, and indeed to compare the costs of factoring with the benefits of not having to collect your own debts. Depending on circumstances, the following questions might be relevant to your choice of factor.

- How will customers react to having to pay their debts to a factor rather than yourself (especially if your debt collecting procedures have been somewhat free and easy in the past)?
- If the factor 'lends' you money against the security of invoices, will this affect your relationships with other lenders (particularly your bank) who might regard outstanding debtors as an important constituent part of the security you offer against loans?
- Is the factor willing to disclose the names and addresses of other clients whom you can approach for a reference?

Debt collection
Debt collecting firms will either be factors who purchase debts outright, or agents acting on commission. They are experts in the (complex) law of collection and in the methods and techniques of (legally) obtaining settlement. Debt collecting in Britain is governed by section 40 of the Administration of Justice Act (1970), plus the precedents established by a number of test cases brought under the Act. Of course, it is (rightly) illegal to use or threaten violence or even to harass unduly those who owe you money. Courts have rules

that, for example, calling on someone's home late at night is unlawful, as is sending several men or a man with a large dog to collect a debt. Other unlawful practices include:

- approaching a member of a debtor's family and making abusive or threatening suggestions;
- pretending to be a police officer or court official, or threatening criminal (rather than civil) proceedings;
- discussing a person's debts with his or her neighbours or posting notices about a debt in shop windows near to where the customer lives; and
- parking a vehicle conspicuously marked 'Debt Collector' outside the customer's home or business premises.

Clearly, serious debt collection is best left to the people who know what they are doing, and there is no shortage of consultants/agencies available to help you in these respects. Lists of debt collectors can be obtained from the Collection Agencies Association, and from Yellow Pages under the heading 'Debt collectors'.

Raising finance

Consultants are available to prepare fund raising proposals and business plans (see Chapter 15) and to argue your case to external financiers. The large accounting firms in particular have extensive contacts in the City, and will liaise with City institutions (underwriters, merchant banks, the Stock Exchange, etc.) on your behalf.

It is as important for a consultant to advise on the *type* of finance required (share issue, debentures, bank loans, etc) as on where to raise the money (eg, a full stock exchange quotation versus use of the unlisted securities market, or the use of overdrafts rather than long term financing). These issues typically resolve to the choice of capital structure and the extent of gearing within the client firm.

Choice of capital structure
A public limited company (one that sells shares to the general public) can finance expansion in several ways: shares, debentures or other loans, or through retained profits. Shares have the advantage that dividends need not be paid in loss making periods. However, outsiders gain votes as shares are issued – existing majority shareholders may lose control. Debenture financing involves no loss of control since debenture holders have no votes. But the risk of liquidation is higher because debenture interest must be paid in full, on time, regardless of current financial circumstances. Overdrafts and similar loans may be recalled.

Against this background, companies have been tempted to finance themselves entirely by ploughing back their own profits. There are no interest payments on retained earnings and there is no possibility of takeovers from outside. The danger is that while the value of a business goes up as profits are ploughed back, market prices of the company's shares may fall, since high retentions of profits necessarily reduce dividends. Shareholders are not interested in buying shares in companies that do not pay good dividends. Demand for such shares will be weak. Thus, paradoxically, increases in a firm's physical assets: land and buildings, plant and equipment, vehicles, work in progress; might be accompanied in the short term by declining share prices.

Of course, in the longer run, shareholders (who own these physical assets) are entitled to extra shares to cover increases in company asset values. These are known as bonus shares and are issued, periodically, in proportion to shareholders' existing holdings. In the short term however dangers exist that outsiders might be able to buy a controlling interest in the firm for less than the monetary value of the company's physical assets.

Public companies must consider carefully, therefore, the relative proportions of debentures, shares, and retained earnings they should include in their capital structures. Debenture financing is appropriate for steady, low risk industries (usually offering comparatively poor returns) whereas shares are better for riskier, less stable, high return environments where profits fluctuate and money for interest payments may not be available in some years. Retained profits are a free source of business finance (no interest or dividends are payable) but must be administered judiciously bearing in mind the consequences of lower dividends on share price. Companies whose shares are highly valued in relation to capital employed and which are earning high returns are likely to retain substantial parts of their profits.

Mergers and takeovers
Certain aspects of consultancy work relating to mergers and takeovers are described in Chapter 3, since many strategic management issues are involved. An accountant might be employed during a takeover/merger project solely to investigate the accuracy of figures quoted in published accounts of a company targetted for merger or takeover.

Assistance to small companies
Small companies which have been set up purely and simply to

restrict their owners' liability for business debts must still have their books audited annually, and go through all the formalities of reappointing auditors at an Annual General Meeting, of minuting the AGM, keeping share registers and other documents required by the 1985 Companies Act, etc. All this despite the fact that the 'AGM' might consist of nothing more than a conversation between (say) a husband and wife who are the only shareholders in the company (the share capital of which is perhaps as little as £100, of which only £2 might actually be called up).

Often the administrative details of this type of company are handled entirely by its accountant; who keeps the books, looks after the company's tax, prepares accounts, audits the accounts and manages all the financial affairs of the company. Indeed the accountant might have been instrumental in registering the company in the first place.

Venture capital
Venture financing means that an outside body (e.g., a merchant bank) buys shares in your business in order to inject capital, takes a big share of its profits in return and then sells the shares back to the company for an agreed price at a predetermined future date. Venture capital companies are looking for high-risk high-return investments offering at least a 30 per cent return. The venture capital market has grown rapidly in recent years, and many organisations now exist to link venture capital investors with likely propositions. You can find details in the following publications, *The City Directory, Venture Capital Report, Money for Business,* and *Investor's Chronicle* (which publishes a guide to venture capital facilities once a year).

Specialist and complex negotiations are necessary for raising venture capital, for which outside assistance (eg, from an accountant or solicitor) is usually required. The issues that will appear on the agenda of such negotiations include repayment amounts and schedules, the extent to which the venture capitalist will become involved in the management of the firm, accountability and reporting procedures, the formula for computing the investor's return, and whether personal guarantees are to be offered by the directors of the firm.

Normally, a venture capitalist will insist on a thorough examination of the target firm prior to advancing funds. This will involve legal and valuation fees the costs of which must be apportioned between the investor and the company in some agreed manner.

Management accountants

Management accountants are usually employed in-house to deal with such matters as cost accounting, internal financial management information systems, investment appraisal and budgetary control. However, some management accountants do act as consultants, particularly in the investment appraisal and costing and cost reduction fields.

Investment appraisal

This concerns the assessment of the profitabilities of capital projects and the determination of the criteria to be used in selecting investments. It uses conventional methods for computing discounted cash flow and a variety of *ad hoc* methods. Despite the mathematical sophistication of the (sometimes bewildering) techniques that consultants often apply to investment appraisal, appraisal still involves many subjective elements: the consultant has to look into the future and predict long-term interest rate movements and expected returns. When considering a consultant's investment appraisal report ask the following questions.

- What assumptions have been made when forecasting future interest rates and commercial environments, and how are these justified?
- If past observations have been used to predict future values, why does the consultant assume that past trends will continue?
- What is the difference between the consultant's most optimistic and most pessimistic estimates of expected revenues? If this is more than (say) twenty per cent is it really worth applying sophisticated forecasting methods to the problem?
- What is the maximum time in which the project will pay back the initial investment?
- How sensitive are the consultant's estimates to environmental changes?

Cost control

The precise measurement of manufacturing and selling costs can be extremely difficult, and a separate branch of management control, 'costing', has arisen to deal with these problems. Costing concerns the prediction and categorisation of costs, their allocation to individual products or activities, and the assessment of profitability.

Consultancies specialising in cost reduction will put your

business under the microscope to determine where expenditures may be cut.

Two things are needed for effective cost cutting: accurate information and an adventurous frame of mind. The consultant will identify the true cost structure of your firm (which prior to the consultant's work you may not have understood properly) and specify appropriate cost centres. He or she will critically appraise your existing methods for allocating overheads, and might suggest alternative schemes. Internal budgetary control systems will be examined, and new mechanisms recommended if they are not up to scratch.

Target cuts should relate to specific cost centres rather than apply overall: a general but vague commitment to reduce total costs is unlikely to succeed. Thus, the campaign needs careful planning, and detailed records of its subsequent success must be maintained. If a particular target reduction is not achieved, detailed explanations of the reasons for failure are needed. The consultant will look for cuts in each of the following areas.

Administration.

Here the consultant will examine such things as stationery and photocopying costs, utilisation of office space and equipment, information retention (filing) systems and other clerical procedures, and so on. Do not expect your consultant to work miracles in this area. In most private companies administration accounts for less than 10 per cent of total costs, so saving a few photocopies or making the secretaries use their typewriter ribbons for a little longer will not contribute all that much to total profitability in the long run.

Production.

Reductions in production costs might be possible through:

- trimming the range of support services offered to customers (acceptance of non-defective returns, repair and maintenance services, free advice on how to use goods after purchase, etc);
- value analysis (see Chapter 11);
- better utilisation of production staff (eg, de-skilling jobs to enable work to be done by cheaper unskilled workers);
- identifying the sources of machine breakdowns and implementing measures to prevent these interruptions (planned maintenance for instance);
- low stockholding (see Chapter 5); and
- installing a system for continuously monitoring the lowest cost sources of materials supply.

Marketing costs

Special problems apply here because certain aspects of marketing (especially advertising) generate income. A reduction in advertising is likely to reduce sales. Nevertheless, the effectiveness of current advertising should be regularly assessed,and distribution and transport costs cut to the bone. The consultant will look for possible cost reductions in the following areas:

- packaging materials and equipment;
- costs of discounts and special offers;
- salespeoples' expenses;
- mail order sales costs (postage, order processing, release from stores, invoicing and other documentation, etc).

The consultant will also examine your transport costs (see Chapter 12) and (importantly) possible losses arising from fraud, customer theft or employee cheating.

Sources of information

The Chartered Association of Certified Accountants
29 Lincoln's Inn Fields
London WC2A 3EE
01-242 6855

The Chartered Institute of Management Accountants
63 Portland Place
London W1N 4AB
01-637 2311

The Chartered Institute of Public Finance and Accountancy
5 Robert Street
London WC2N 6BH
01-930 3456

The City Directory (published annually)
Director Books
Fitzwilliam House
32 Trumpington Street
Cambridge CB2 1QY
0223 66733

Collection Agencies Association
5 Mill Street
Bedford MK40 3EU
0234 4566

The Institute of Chartered Accountants in England and Wales
Moorgate Place
London EC2P 2BJ
01-628 7060

The Institute of Chartered Accountants in Ireland
Chartered Accountants House
87/89 Pembroke Road
Dublin 4
0001 680400

The Institute of Chartered Accountants of Scotland
27 Queen Street
Edinburgh EH2 1LA
031-225 5673

The Institute of Internal Auditors
82z Portland Place
London W1N 3DH
01-580 0101/323 2826/7

Money for Business Magazine
Bank of England
London EC2R 8AH

Venture Capital Report
The Refuge Building
20 Baldwin Street
Bristol BS1 1SE

Chapter 7

Project Management Consultants

Introduction — What a project manager will do — The skills of project management — Where to find a project manager — Executive leasing and locum management — Briefing the consultant — Sources of information

After reading this chapter you should:

- understand the distinguishing characteristics of a 'project';
- know the advantages of using outside consultants for project management;
- appreciate the scope of a project manager's duties, especially as they relate to the management of professionally qualified staff; and
- know about locum management and executive leasing.

Introduction

It is increasingly common for smaller companies to engage external consultants to oversee major *ad hoc* projects such as the installation of a new production line, property development (see Chapter 13), computerisation of a firm's accounting system (see Chapters 6 and 8), setting up a distribution network, etc, rather than using their own staff. Consultants are especially likely when projects are exceptionally large, urgent, complex, or require expertise and/or resources not currently possessed by the commissioning firm. The practice has several advantages.

- A consultant will have previous experience of several similar projects, whereas internal staff would normally be tackling the work for the very first time.
- Existing staff will develop their own competencies just through observing an expert project manager in operation.
- Outsiders bring fresh perspectives to the company's project management problems, and have extensive contacts with other specialists in their particular field.
- It is usually far easier to dispense with the services of an outside consultant who mismanages a project than to dismiss an incompetent employee. The latter might claim unfair dismissal

(see Chapter 9) on the grounds of not having been properly trained for the job, or not being given sufficient authority, or complaining that he or she had a contract of employment which excluded the management of major projects, etc. Your legal relationship with a consultant is defined purely by the short term contract you have with that person. A consultant is a contractor and *not* an employee. Also you can include a penalty clause in the consultant's contract to cover (proven) incompetence or late completion of commissioned work.

What a project manager will do

There are two types of project: self-contained projects (construction projects for instance); and those which are themselves elements of another project or an on-going programme. In either case the duties of the consultant project manager are essentially the same (assessing the feasibility of the project, negotiating supply contracts with third parties, commencing and completing operations, and arranging support services) although for ongoing programmes the company's own staff will probably be more closely involved both with the consultant and with day-to-day operations because these internal employees might have to implement the next stage in the programme.

A project manager is at once a co-ordinator, a motivator and a planner of tasks. He or she must unify effort, forecast workloads, determine priorities and schedule jobs. The project will be broken down into logically ordered components, and targets for each element then precisely defined. Priorities are established, critical activities identified, and potential difficulties exposed. Resources may then be allocated and reallocated to hasten completion of the work.

The consultant must know about tendering, purchasing and other procurement procedures (leasing, hire purchase, etc) and, importantly, about the legal aspects of the supply contracts the project will involve. Specific responsibilities of the consultant project manager might include:

- conducting a feasibility study (see chapter 8) for the intended project;
- estimating costs and activity start and completion times (see below);
- work scheduling;
- deriving a critical path for the project (ie, determining which activities cannot be held up without lengthening the total completion time of the project as a whole and predicting how long these activities, added together, will take);

- negotiating the best possible supply prices with sub-contractors and suppliers of materials;
- quality management (see chapter 5) with regard to material inputs and project operations;
- 'progress chasing', ie, ensuring that inputs are delivered on schedule and that project activities are completed on time;
- monitoring and appraising the performances of members of the project team and reporting on these;
- negotiating penalty clauses with suppliers *vis-à-vis* late delivery of supplies;
- advising on insurance, licencing requirements, planning permission (see Chapter 13), etc, wherever required; and
- detailed costing of the project.

Usually the commissioning company finances the project and sets expenditure and other constraints, leaving the consultant free to determine cost entries and implement day-to-day budgetary and other controls.

The skills of project management

Although the fundamental characteristic of a 'project' is that it is unique, many of the skills necessary for effective project management are common to all types of project. The following are particularly important.

Project planning and control.
Projects can be bewildering in their complexity. There are, of course, certain well-established techniques for dealing with complicated projects (critical path analysis for instance); but the naive application of sophisticated quantitative project control methods – without considering the human factors involved – is unlikely to succeed. Professional project managers appreciate this and are normally competent to motivate and get the very best out of the project team. Also, consultants know all about the innumerable difficulties that cause projects to exceed their budgets or schedules: accidents, incompetence, withdrawal of financial support, supply problems, sudden changes in input prices, strikes, resignations of key workers, and so on. The experienced project administrator should be capable of predicting the likelihood of these occurrences and incorporate allowances for them into expected completion dates and project costs. 'Contingency budgeting' is a crucial aspect of the consultant's task.

The management of sub-contract labour and professionally qualified staff.
Project management typically utilises several functional disciplines

that need to be united into a common framework for attaining project goals. Functional specialists (accountants, researchers, lawyers and so on) often wish to pursue only those activities which are immediately relevant to their own professional fields; and conflicts and tensions between professionals and project managers (indeed between professionals themselves) may occur.

The consultant has two tasks in this regard. First, he or she must persuade professional specialists to alter their perspectives and working methods to fit in with the requirements of the project as a whole; second, the consultant should try to create management structures appropriate for the administration of specialist professionally qualified staff, eg, by having a separate project secretariat completely independent of other administrative arrangements within the firm. This issue is considered more fully in chapter 4.

Where to find a project manager

You can locate project management consultants through three sources.

- Specialist contacts within a trade, obtained perhaps through your trade association.
- A list provided by a professional body (see Chapter 1). Construction project consultants, for example, are listed in the Chartered Institute of Building's *Handbook and List of Members,* which has separate section on consultancy services.
- An executive leasing agency (see below) specialising in project management.

Engineering project management consultants are listed in *Yellow Pages* under 'Engineers – project'. Otherwise look in *Yellow Pages* under particular functional specialisations. For instance, numerous telecommunications consultants are listed under that title. Installing a major new telephone system (with perhaps a thousand extensions) is a substantial project in its own right. It involves a feasibility study, choice of equipment, installation of a call management scheme (automatic call distribution for example), and devising a system for monitoring telephone costs – metering, call logging, abbreviated dialling, call barring and so on.

To select a project manager you need to look for clear evidence of *substantial* experience of other projects of a similar type. In particular ask whether the potential consultant has concrete evidence of leadership, organisational, and human resource management skills. How extensive are the consultant's contacts with third party contractors? How do the discounts the consultant can negotiate with sub-contractors compare with those you could negotiate yourself?

Executive leasing and locum management

Acute shortages of skilled and competent senior managers in particular fields have caused some senior company executives to be prepared to hire themselves out to other businesses for short periods. A 'locum manager' will normally be a specialist in a certain area (electronics, computing and information technology are the subjects in greatest demand) and will be highly qualified and experienced in his or her line of work. The locum will be one or other of the following.

A senior employee of a company which – due partly to this person's ability and effort – has reached a level of efficiency where it possesses 'spare capacity' at the top management level, yet wishes to retain all its senior staff. Accordingly, the firm will lease out under-employed top managers to other businesses for specific tasks, eg, setting up a subsidiary company on the client's behalf, implementing a business turnaround strategy, reorganising a department, training the client's own managers in particular techniques, providing senior management cover during the temporary absence of one of the client's key personnel, and so on. The locum's fee will be payable either to his or her main employing company, or directly to the locum under schedule D.

A member of a consultancy firm specialising in locum management. Such an individual will contribute to the day-to-day running of his or her consultancy business (usually a partnership) as well as handling clients' projects. Often, the consultant will handle the work of several clients at the same time.

An executive who subscribes to a locum placement employment agency. Such agencies have hundreds (sometimes thousands) of former senior managers on their books and place them with client companies for short term assignments on a daily fee basis (currently between £200 and £500 per day). Note that unlike ordinary employment agencies, executive lease agencies charge large fees (up to £10,000) to the individual managers who wish to use their services. Thereafter the agency undertakes to provide the manager with a flow of assignments. The agency then charges further fees to client companies that take executives from the agency's books. The advantages of the system are that:

- executives possessing specialist management skills (especially those in which there is a severe shortage) can be located immediately;
- the cost is not expensive compared to hiring a permanent senior manager on a high annual salary while not fully using his or her particular expertise throughout the year; and
- executives from the agency will not come to the job with preset ideas about the client organisation and thus may apply fresh perspectives to the problems the client faces.

To find an executive leasing agency you can contact the Confederation of British Industry (which actually markets the services of one of the major locum management companies) or the Management Consultancies' Association (see Chapter 1). Some of the large general consultancies offer locum placement facilities and occasionally advertise these – usually in the trade presses of particular industries. Problems with locum management include:

- the possibility of becoming totally reliant on the locum's services – leaving too much to that person and not making the effort to observe and acquire his or her skills;
- the danger that a locum recruited from another company might suddenly be recalled to deal with a crisis in his or her main employing firm;
- possible neglect by the locum of your firm's needs, caused by his or her simultaneous involvement with several clients; and
- agency locums being of the wrong type or disposition (especially if they were supplied mainly because of the agency's obligation to provide assignments to managers who pay to be on its register).

A serious problem that can arise when temporarily leasing a senior executive from another company is that the lessor firm may in fact be trying to earn money from a member of its management team who is not contributing as much to the company as he or she might, eg, following a physical illness, a psychological breakdown, or other personal problems. Also it is not unknown for companies to offer for secondment their older and less efficient managers who otherwise would be prematurely retired. Such employees have great experience, but could lack the vigour, creativity, enthusiasm and enterprise that your project requires.

Briefing the consultant

First you must clearly identify the goals of the project. This requires an assessment of all the risks the project involves, because in rapidly changing environments it is often uncertain exactly *how* objectives can be achieved. State how much discretion the project manager is to be allowed in modifying objectives (deadlines, cost limitations, specific achievements, etc) as circumstances change.

Then you should discuss with the consultant your resource constraints and agree on the size of the overall project budget. Decide which of your internal staff will be involved in the project and (importantly) to whom they will report. Can the project manager give orders to your staff directly, or is the intervention of one or more company line managers required? You need to specify appropriate quality assurance procedures (see Chapter 5), and to state the minimum criteria that must be satisfied for the project to be regarded as a success. For certain major projects it may be necessary to decide who will be responsible for publicity and public relations: the company or the consultant.

Appraising a consultant project manager's work

A good project manager will devise a scheme for answering, 'what if' questions relating to various scenarios and alterations in presuppositions regarding resources, activity times and so on. He or she should have been able accurately to predict earliest and latest start times for various activities, given a particular set of resource constraints. Also the consultant should have listed activities to be undertaken by particular departments (everything involving electrical works for example), and all the jobs relating to each phase of the exercise. Peak-activity periods and potential bottlenecks should then have been identified and measures implemented to deal with the problems they create.

Three particularly relevant questions to ask when evaluating the quality of a project management consultant are as follows.

- Did the consultant devise a means for effective communication between the various members of the project team?
- Were the inter-relationships between all the activities needed for project completion identified and clearly explained?
- Was progress towards project completion systematically monitored; with regular reports on labour and equipment utilisation, resource requirements and cash flows?

Sources of information

Chartered Institute of Building
Handbook and List of Members
Highwood Publishers Limited
Premier House
150 Southampton Row
London WC1B 5AL
01-833 2124

Confederation of British Industry
Centre Point
New Oxford Street
London WC1A 4DD
01-379 7400

Chapter 8

Computer and Information Technology Consultants

Introduction — Who are computer consultants? — Information technology (IT) consultants — Selecting an IT consultant — Financial management support services — Management information systems — Facilities management — Systems analysis and the installation of new systems — Feasibility studies — Systems analysis — Commercial software — Systems design — CADCAM — Expert systems — Evaluating the consultant's contribution — Sources of information.

After reading this chapter you should:

- appreciate the problems and pitfalls attached to computerising a business system;
- understand the improvements in management information made possible by information technology;
- know where to locate various types of computer consultants and the extent of their services;
- appreciate the desirability of obtaining truly independent advice, entirely unconnected with equipment suppliers' agents;
- possess an outline knowledge of facilities management, systems analysis and design and the role of the financial management services consultant;
- be able to brief and evaluate a computer consultant; and
- understand how a computer consultant will conduct a feasibility study.

Introduction

Computer consultants assist clients to introduce information technology* (IT) to their firms; with computer assisted manufacture, computer aided design (see Chapters 5 and 11), robotics, and with computer assisted management control.

Computerisation has revolutionised management practice:

---

*Information technology is the acquisition, processing, storage, analysis and dissemination of information using computers.

indeed it has changed the way managers *think* about their work. Effective managerial control requires the collection, summary, and evaluation of data prior to taking decisions. Not only can computers handle enormous amounts of data, but also they enable the application of sophisticated control techniques which previously were not feasible because of difficulty and cost. Conventional stereotypes of managers behind desks, sifting through information propagated by reports, memoranda, and production and other statistics have been superseded by the reality of managers who sit before computer visual display units requisitioning and summarising instantly huge quantities of data, formulating models for analysing likely consequences of various courses of action and selecting criteria on which final decisions will be based. Decisions can be fed into computerised systems and implemented instantly.

Computerisation and its effects
The need for computerisation can be recognised in several ways: excessive amounts of management time spent in collecting and interpreting information, inaccurate or out-of-date records, non-availability of essential information needed for important decisions, high clerical costs for particular functions, and so on. Yet the consequences of computerisation may not be so clear. Installation of a new system can itself create the need for major organisational change, requiring new accountability and appraisal procedures, new departments, documentation, staffing levels, etc.

Improved quality of information
Information systems collect, store and retrieve data. In the past, the volume of data handled within a system has been constrained by limitations on available clerical labour and the inability of many people to comprehend and assimilate large quantities of information. Hence, various summary statistics were developed to ease the burdens of data collection and interpretation. Standard costing is a good example of attempted budgetary control through the preparation of a small number of concise variances to summarise expenditures and compare them with predetermined norms. Likewise, many financial accounting procedures were designed to enable easy checking of the accuracy of bookkeeping entries and to facilitate periodic extraction of summary data on sales, creditors, discounts received and given, and so on. Aggregate figures only were available, however, because of the difficulties and expense of cross-tabulation. Comprehensive detailed analyses with respect to various categories and subheadings were not generally possible.

Computerisation has cut the cost of data collection, and has made the reduction of large amounts of data into summary numbers easy. Cross-tabulation has become effortless, and the precise form in which data is presented can be chosen at will.

Integration of data

A great benefit of computerised data processing is the integration at source of each piece of information into the management control system of the entire organisation. Data is recorded once but then used for many different purposes in different departments. Thus, information on production costs will be diffused simultaneously to the accounts department, production planning and control, costing department, the purchasing manager, stores and stock controllers, and any other interested party. The data itself will be presented to each of these recipients in a form which is precisely relevant to their particular needs. It is not necessary for several departments to collect and prepare what is essentially the same information. This has implications for the structure of departmentalisation within the firm, since many functions which previously were independent may, with the assistance of an integrated data presentation network, be combined.

Problems with the computerisation of systems

Intelligent use of a computerised system will reduce costs, inventory holdings, manufacture and delivery times, and will improve product quality and reliability. Computerised procedures do however present special problems to those responsible for their control. Invariably, computerisation is accompanied by standardisation of methods and processes. Deviations from standards may be impossible even if such deviations are desired. Note that a hardware malfunction can disrupt totally the work of a firm. Destruction of files through accident or negligence can lead to major financial losses and enormous difficulties in trying to make good the damage caused. Software can also be a source of problems, errors might continue to exist even after programmes have been officially debugged. Large programs often contain subroutines which are hardly ever used so that mistakes might be discovered several years after a system has been implemented.

Who are computer consultants?

Computer consultants may be categorised as follows.

- Equipment and/or software producers who provide consultancy services regarding choice of model, installation of the system, training of the customer's staff in equipment/package use, and post-installation troubleshooting, maintenance and advice.

- Specialists in particular areas, eg, CADCAM, optimised production technology (see Chapter 5), management information systems, etc. Ideally the specialist will be mainly concerned with the technical aspects of his or her subject and not committed to installing any specific make of equipment. Often, however, these firms take commissions from equipment manufacturers in exchange for recommending their clients to purchase certain models and equipment types.
- General management consultancies and accounting firms with IT divisions.

IT consultants

Several of the large national chartered accountancy practices have diversified into IT consultancy. Indeed, such firms are today extending their services to include software development and equipment supply. A recent development is their practice of arranging what are in effect trade exhibitions whereby 30 or 40 hardware and related equipment suppliers demonstrate their systems to potential customers. The consultant then follows up leads from interested visitors: offering consultancy services, liaising with appropriate suppliers and acting as a systems integrator for the resulting deals.

The role of the IT consultant is to investigate inadequacies in existing information flows and to design new systems to overcome them. He or she will take a broad view of the situation, from data input through distribution channels right up to the final recipients of the processed information. The consultant will ask why information is needed, how best it might be used, and will devise and implement new methods for its analysis and presentation. An IT consultant will:

- explain the new technology and (importantly) how jobs will change in consequence of its introduction to a firm;
- demystify computer functions and create within the client company feelings of self-confidence about computer use;
- develop a *common* understanding of the purpose of the new system among all its users.

Some assistance towards the cost of IT consultancy is available through the DTI Enterprise Initiative (see Chapter 1) the computer aspect of which focusses largely on the provision of management information systems. The DTI scheme covers strategic computer

D B I ASSOCIATES LTD
CONSULTANTS IN THE MANAGEMENT OF INFORMATION

We were formed in 1984 to provide top quality, cost effective consultancy services throughout the UK. We have grown substantially and developed a strong base of major clients in both the private and public sectors.

Why choose DBI?

Specialisation. We are objective, independent IT consultants – not auditors, software developers or hardware salesmen. Our consultants are experienced professionals who understand user needs, usually from first hand experience as senior line managers.

Quality. A DBI director takes responsibility for each assignment. He arranges for quality assurance of our proposal and its presentation and then of the assignment itself. He makes sure the project plan is valid and monitors performance against it. He remains involved throughout.

Expertise. We have expertise and experience in most areas of IT from strategy and organisation studies to supplier selection and technical support, from project management to risk analysis. We can use leading methodologies appropriately, effectively and efficiently (for example, SSADM, PROMPT/PRINCE, CRAMM).

Our proposals always tell you what we will deliver, when, and who will carry out the work. We win business on the quality of our services and the ability of our people. Remember: any consultancy assignment is only as good as the individuals who carry it out.

We are

CONSULTANTS IN THE MANAGEMENT OF INFORMATION

It is all we do and we do it well.

We operate throughout the UK. If you would like to learn more about us, contact Richard Johnstone on 0926-312481 or write to: DBI Associates Ltd., Portland House, Portland Street, Leamington Spa, Warwickshire, CV32 5HE. (Fax 0926-882129)

system studies for larger companies, advice on computer systems for smaller businesses, and general consultancy on the integration of business information. However, the scheme does *not* cover the implementation of physical systems, software programing, or the input of data to a computer.

Desirability of independent advice

Companies cannot afford to make bad decisions in the IT field: a bad choice of system can ruin a firm. However, few senior managers possess the experience needed to make informed decisions about computers, so external guidance is useful and frequently sought. The choice of available equipment and software is bewildering, and truly objective and *independent* advice is obviously required.

Unfortunately, from the customer's point of view, many computer consultants have financial arrangements with a single hardware supplier whereby they always recommend clients to purchase one particular make of equipment. Indeed, the 'consultant' might actually be an agent working exclusively on the supplier's behalf. This can lead to the installation of unsuitable systems and hence to operating difficulties.

Arguments between clients and IT consultants who install systems are not uncommon. The latter might claim that the client's staff are abusing the equipment or are not intellectually capable of being trained in its proper use. The client firm, conversely, may insist that it was misled about the capacities and characteristics of the recommended system and that inadequate training was provided in the first place!

The Association of Independent Computer Specialists exists to put potential buyers in touch with consultants who have no links whatsoever with any equipment or software supplier. An excellent source of information about the locations and specialities of computer consultants is the *Computer Users Year Book,* volume 2 of which contains extensive lists of consultants – including facilities management firms (see below). Otherwise you should contact some of the larger general management consultancies (see Chapter 1 for advice on where to look for these), or the Computer Services Association. Look in the *Yellow Pages* under 'Computer consultants', 'Computer services' and 'Computer software'.

What IT consultants do

Nowadays the IT consultant is a management consultant first and a computer technician second. He or she must know about management objectives, business strategies, management information and management control. A consultant may help you choose a system (which normally means conducting a feasibility study), install financial management support services, do a complete systems analysis, or provide a comprehensive facilities management service.

Selecting an IT consultant

From initial enquiries list six or seven consultancies which appear experienced in your line of work. Outline your requirements to them and establish the extent of their services (eg, preparation of feasibility studies, systems analysis, choice of system, negotiating equipment purchase prices and maintenance contracts on your behalf, installing a new system, etc). The more services included in the package the more you have to pay, so take care that you are comparing like with like when evaluating different consultants' quotations. Now ask the following questions in respect of each consultant.

- Is the consultant genuinely independent of equipment suppliers and thus able to provide truly impartial advice? If the consultant receives commission from a supplier how much of this is he or she willing to pass back to your firm?
- Is low cost telephone advice available following installation? What redress do you have if this turns out unsatisfactory?
- Has the consultant experience of installing systems in your *size* as well as *type* of business? (Different sorts of problem may attach to setting up extremely large rather than small or medium sized configurations).
- Can the consultant guarantee immediate repair or replacement of equipment that breaks down?

Then, having removed unsuitable firms, ask each consultancy remaining on your shortlist to name half a dozen businesses similar to your own for which he or she has already installed a system. Telephone a couple of these and ask whether the consultant did a good job. (Previous clients might even invite you to visit their premises and have a look at the consultant's work).

Most consultants offer free (or at least low cost) initial evaluations, so request outline proposals and consider the following matters in relation to each proposal.

- Does the proposal take into account the present computer literacy and intellectual calibre of your existing staff?
- Is the proposed system well documented, with understandable operating manuals, user-friendly menu-driven instructions, etc?

- Has the consultant told you how long certain jobs will take to complete using alternative computing systems?
- Can various parts of the intended system be used for several different purposes?

Briefing the consultant

The consultant will want to examine your existing information gathering and processing procedures. If these are haphazard they must be corrected before the exercise begins. Categorise all the data you currently collect under appropriate functional headings (accounts data, stock control, cost data, etc) and specify the objectives of the exercise.

Be clear about what you require. Do you want a fully integrated system wherein one event triggers others (a stock issue causing an invoice to be printed, for example) or a simpler self-contained component part of a larger administrative whole (computerised accounts for instance). Remember that the more powerful and sophisticated the system the more highly trained (and paid) the operatives required to do the work.

Controlling costs

Firms frequently underestimate computer installation costs. Ask your consultant for *detailed* estimates covering,

- expected labour costs (of your own staff as well as the consultant);
- equipment prices or rental charges (plus a list of the advantages and disadvantages of renting as opposed to buying outright);
- the costs of consumables: stationery, printer ribbons, etc;
- training costs;
- other costs which might include:
  — modems and extra telecommunications charges; including the installation of extra lines;
  — working disks, backup disks and (importantly) disk security systems as required by the Data Protection Act;
  — increased electricity consumption;
  — maintenance contracts for hardware and for on-going software support services; and
  — new workstations.

A major cost in the early stages is that of running the existing system alongside the new scheme – indeed, extra (temporary) staff might initially be required. The firm cannot risk the failure of untested procedures unless a backup system is available and thus has to operate the old and new systems at the same time. As the new system develops, moreover, its deficiencies will be revealed so that even more money has to be spent on remedying freshly discovered problems in the new configuration. The establishment of links between old and new regimes is itself a costly activity requiring careful planning and control, and numerous phasing-in difficulties can be expected.

Financial management support services

The large IT consultancies (especially the IT divisions of the big general consulting firms) offer help with accounting and computer audit support services, with risk analysis, data security, and with the installations of management information systems. Some also provide a complete facilities management service.

Computerised accounts

One of the commonest uses of IT consultants is by small to medium sized businesses to install computerised accounts. The advantage of computerised accounts include faster invoicing, tighter credit control (information on outstanding debts is immediately available), lower inventories and better use of working capital. And of course, profit and loss accounts and balance sheets are prepared automatically, using inputs from files for various classes of transaction. Differences between packages (and their cost) relate not only to the volume of transactions they can handle but also to their adaptability to accounting periods, credit periods, payment terms and other variable factors. The range and quality of outputs from accounts packages may also differ; cheaper versions provide simple summary statistics, more expensive programs offer bar charts, pie diagrams, trend graphs etc.

As businesses differ, so too should their accounting systems. Thus, flexible packages that can be customised to meet the particular requirements of each firm are seemingly advantageous. Typically, however, the more versatile the package the greater its complexity. And there is no point in spending a lot of money on a sophisticated package which the existing staff are not technically competent to operate. The key elements of an accounts package are:

- separate files for the various ledgers (expenses, sales, creditors, etc);
- cost centres, usually defined as departments; and
- a means for combining the summary output of the several files into final accounts.

More complex systems can be fully integrated, so that as (for instance) a sale is recorded the system issues an instruction for the item in question to be released from stock, an order for replenishment of the stock is automatically printed if the stock issue causes the inventory of that item to fall below a predetermined level, an addressed invoice is generated, and news of the sale is instantly transmitted to other files such as a sales forecasting file that analyses sales by region. At the time of writing, this type of integrated system is not available 'off the peg' and must be custom built by consultant programmers. It is likely however that cheap, standard, integrated packages will soon be available.

In a limited sense, an accounts package provides its own (restricted) data base system. Sales ledgers for example offer information on customers' names and locations, on the value of the sales, discounts given, cash receipts and credit balances, plus other data. Reports can be commissioned on the basis of any one (or perhaps more) of these criteria, and similar exercises may be performed on any of the other ledgers.

Data security and the audit trail

Computerisation creates the need to alter internal self-checking and external audit procedures. Fewer people are involved in clerical activities, and little arithmetic work is undertaken outside the computer. Accordingly, the consultant installing an accounting system must devise measures for:

- forcing fraud into a state of collusion, ie, arranging company work so that no one person is able to enter certain files in order to substitute numbers, change bank account details, place extra people on the firm's payroll, etc, without colleagues being aware of this;
- establishing a system for independent random checking of the accuracy of input operatives' work;
- making sure that wherever possible, related data is submitted through independent channels unknown to other parties;
- randomly checking software packages against master copies to ensure they have not been altered;
- comparing running times for various activities, eg, if a payroll of 100 employees takes thirty minutes to process for one month and just over thirty minutes for the next (suggesting that an unauthorised extra name and address might have been put on the payroll).

On balance, it is likely that fraud is less rather than more likely in a computerised system. Fraudsters need technical knowledge about computers, and much co-ordination of accomplices (input operatives, personnel dealing with output documents, programers, etc) is required. Also, management can alter master files and key programs periodically.

Risk analysis

This involves computing the probable accuracy of forecasts at various future times. It is used in project management (see Chapter 7) for working out possible rates of return, likelihoods of completion dates being met, potential cost variations, etc.

Management information systems

An efficient management information system (MIS) will enable management to plan, co-ordinate, organise and control its activities. It will provide the information needed both for strategic planning and for day-to-day operational management. Strategic informational requirements include data on key business ratios (return on capital employed, ratios of debt to equity capital, interest payable on borrowed money, etc), on current trends in external capital markets, the firm's liquidity position, aggregate cash flow forecasts, market research data, and so on. Information needed for tactical control might include ratios of profits to working capital, of stock to current assets, sales to output, etc. The system should monitor rates of return achieved on specific investment projects and compare these with the returns initially forecast. Production bottlenecks and capacity constraints should be identified.

An important MIS function is to highlight potential difficulties with debtors and suppliers. What, for example, is the average delay between delivery of goods and the issue of invoices? How quickly do customers settle their accounts, and what are the effects of offering discounts for prompt payment? What is the ratio of creditors to purchases? How long, on average, do suppliers take to deliver goods, and to what extent can payments to suppliers be delayed? Other categories of information that an effective MIS should supply include the following.

- Marketing information:
    - effectiveness of sales personel;
    - responsiveness of sales to price changes;
    - market trends;
    - behaviour of competitors; and
    - adequacy of distribution channels.

- Financial information:
  — whether budgets are being adhered to;
  — lengths of trading cycles;
  — adequacy of cash inflows; and
  — needs for external financing.
- Work in progress information:
  — ratios of work in progress to production, stock to sales, etc;
  — identification of slow moving stock;
  — frequency and causes of stockouts;
  — stockholding costs; and
  — causes of machine breakdown and other interruptions in production.

Using a consultant to install an MIS

The installation of an MIS might, at first sight, appear a relatively straightforward task. There are only a few factors to consider – when, how and to whom information should be transmitted, and how best to summarise data in a form that enables its fast and accurate evaluation prior to taking decisions. In practice, however, unforeseen difficulties frequently emerge for which consultancy help might be required. The following sorts of problem are common.

Relevant information does not reach the right people. Managers commonly assume that colleagues and subordinates have been informed of particular facts when, actually, they have not. Transmission of every piece of information that might be relevant to an individual is not feasible; otherwise the firm would devote all its time, energy and resources to transmitting messages, most of which were of little practical use. Thus, choices have to be made, and dangers exist that the wrong people will receive information.

Breaks in the chain of command. Information should flow vertically through the enterprise from top to bottom through channels illustrated in its organisation chart. Often, information bottlenecks occur at supervisory and middle management levels since supervisors and middle managers not only receive information from above (and have to decide whether to act on it) but also collect feedback from lower levels. If a manager fails to act on relevant information received, the chain of command is broken – policies are not implemented; feedback on the success or failure of policies is not transmitted to high authority.

Horizontal flows of information among colleagues of equal rank may be interrupted if certain individuals deliberately conceal information or – through incompetence – do not pass it on.

Evaluating the consultant's contribution
The effectiveness of an MIS must be evaluated against its ability to assist in taking decisions: operational decisions, long and short term planning, budgeting, investment decisions, and so on. Ask yourself whether:

- the additional information generated by the system enables you to compare things (eg, costs and benefits of intended projects, returns on alternative investments, environmental circumstances, etc) in new and meaningful ways;
- the substance of the extra information created by the system is *already* known; and whether
- the consultant has fully explored the organisational implications of the proposed scheme. Perhaps the most likely of these is the need to rearrange the departmental structure of the firm. Computerisation tends to encourage centralisation of administrative procedures. Data is summarised and distributed automatically, circulating around a central control unit which can receive and monitor management information continuously. Less delegation from senior to junior managers is likely in a computerised system because higher management obtains better, faster and more comprehensive information. Consequently senior managers can exercise much tighter personal control.

The aim is to create cheaper and faster means for transmitting, summarising and presenting information. Note, however that responsibility for selecting the precise forms in which information is to be summarised and presented lies ultimately with the client firm. Bar charts, pie diagrams, Lorenz curves, etc, may be called up using the simplest of systems; yet there is no point whatsoever in confronting, (for example) a sales manager with a complex array of graphs and figures on promotional costs or market trends if he or she cannot understand what they mean! Thus *you* rather than the consultant must specify the formats in which information is required.

A problem that novice business computer users might not anticipate is the proliferation of information that sometimes occurs in new systems. Department heads (and other employees) frequently overstate their information requirements. Hence they are sent information they never use, possibly at the expense of others who do actually need the data. Periodically, therefore, the organisation should audit its internal (and perhaps external) communications to remove duplication, delete unnecessary transmissions and generally reduce the volume of data flows and messages.

Facilities management

This is analogous to the work of an export management company (see Chapter 14) or vehicle fleet maintenance management consultancy (see Chapter 12) in that the consultant will take over the client firm's entire computing function and become, in effect, the data processing department of the company. The client may or may not own the system and/or employ its own computing personnel. Hardware, software and computer operatives could be provided – possibly *via* third parties – by the consultant's firm. A client will (usually) pay:

- an annual lump sum fee;
- rental charges on equipment (when the client does not directly own the system);
- equipment maintenance costs; and
- an hourly charge while the system is in use, covering the wages of computing staff plus general support services.

Invariably, responsibility for providing data in a form acceptable for input to the system lies with the client company – the facilities manager simply processes the information and presents the results.

The client obtains a complete electronic data processing facility at low overhead cost and is relieved of all the burdens of training, organising and controlling computing staff. And the cost need not be prohibitive because the consultant might use the system for processing other clients' work thus enabling the consultant to reduce his or her total fee. Equally, a consultant could arrange for a part of your own computing work to be done on another firm's system.

Problems with using a facilities manager are that (i) your firm becomes entirely dependent on the consultant's advice and services for all its computing activities, and (ii) you lose control over computing costs. Also the facility manager might use your system for other jobs without letting you know.

Systems analysis and the installation of new systems

Perhaps the commonest of all uses of computer consultants is to advise on which computing equipment a company should obtain and then to install the new system. This involves feasibility studies, choice of system, and systems analysis and design.

Large versus small systems

Some consultants advise their clients to buy relatively powerful machines at the outset to ensure the availability of lots of space, flexibility, and the capacity to handle larger and more complex programs as the business expands. A system that is perfectly adequate for (say) a payroll program may be hopelessly inadequate for other more substantial tasks.

The alternative approach is to recommend the client company first to master a small and simple system – gaining skill and experience as it goes along – and only then progress to more sophisticated applications. This latter approach has many advantages: familiarity with an uncomplicated system means you know what you are talking about when you come to upgrade, and existing hardware can usually be traded-in or used for other purposes. Also, your staff has experience of computer methods and thus will not be intimidated by a larger and more powerful configuration.

Too often, businesses (especially small businesses) purchase as their first computer a machine that is far too complicated for their needs. Then specialist programming is necessary to install the system and untangle the numerous problems that occur. There are mismatches between printers and keyboards; staff become hopelessly confused, and consciously avoid using the computer. Old manual systems continue and all the potential benefits of computerisation: speed, cost savings, accuracy and reliability, huge data storage and so on, are lost.

Feasibility studies

Often, the consultant's first task is to study the feasibility of an intended new system. This study will examine critically all the costs and benefits involved and the longer term implications of the proposed installation. Specifically, the study should cover:

- which aspects of a certain function can and cannot be computerised;
- how computerisation will affect existing staff, including needs for training and redeployment;
- the form in which output information will be required, and how data flows can be arranged to meet output requirements most efficiently;
- costs involved: equipment, software, retraining, extra recruitment; and
- implications of the new system for management control.

Independent consultants not tied to particular equipment

manufacturers are best for conducting feasibility studies, since only rarely will a manufacturer's agent conclude that installation of the manufacturer's equipment is not feasible. Internal staff could conduct the feasibility study, but will not have the outside consultant's computer expertise and knowledge of available alternatives.

Senior staff who are to operate the new system must obviously be involved in its choice and installation, possibly by the establishment of a steering committee comprising representatives of affected departments but under the external consultant's overall control. Salespeople from various equipment/software suppliers might be invited to make presentations to the steering committee.

The consultant's initial report

This should contain a 'system specification' precisely defining the new system's operation from document input to final presentation of processed information. Usually, system specifications are shown as flowcharts, with detailed appendices describing sub-routines. The report should also state the extent of the training of existing staff necessary to introduce the system. Those concerned with software packages will normally require more training than the rest. Training, apart from instruction on equipment use and documentation procedures, should cover the new administrative structure, interdepartmental relations, and the responsibility and authority systems that the new regime will create. Basically, four steps are involved. First and foremost is the need to specify precisely what the system needs to do in order to solve the client's problems (which presuppose of course that the client firm knows what its problems are). This will require a 'systems analysis' of existing procedures (see below). Then the consultant will identify a suitable system, analyse and predict its costs and benefits, and may – for an extra fee – plan and install the scheme. Systems maintenance and development support may or may not be provided.

Systems analysis

A system consists of computer 'hardware' (the machine, disk drive, keyboard and printer) and 'software' (ie, the packages you use) plus a set of procedures for completing jobs. A payroll system, for example, has procedures which convert pay rates, overtime records, PAYE and national insurance contributions into pay slips and direct debits into employees' bank accounts. The task of systems analysis is to organise the interactions of these elements to produce desired outcomes.

Analysing needs
The first task in designing a system is to analyse the information requirements of each of the firm's functional activities (marketing, production, personnel, etc) in order to identify interrelations between them and hence to devise efficient input procedures and output designs. A 'master' file is needed for each key activity, fed by various subsidiary files. Master files are constantly updated and process raw data to provide useful information. The stock control master, for instance, is fed with facts on stock issues, receipts of supplies, requisitions, etc, and generates information on stock shortages, holding and acquisition costs, and replenishment data for various inventories. This output constitutes input to the purchasing master, which contains suppliers' names and addresses, delivery periods, prices and so on.

Those who are to use the output of the system should be involved in the system's design. This 'back-end' approach is known as 'logical systems design', since the process begins from the specification of an agreed format for output and then 'works back' through the various stages of the system, specifying the inputs and procedures needed to produce the predetermined format. In other words, the consultant asks the questions:

- What input data is required?
- How should it be stored and manipulated?
- How many files are needed and of what type, in order to generate the information?

And then he or she develops a system configuration to meet these needs. Hopefully, standard programs can be found that satisfy stated output requirements. If not, the output format chosen should be re-examined in case compromise outputs exist that enable most user demands to be satisfied.

The systems plan
To implement a systems plan (as opposed to *ad hoc* procedures) the firm must first identify priority areas for computerisation and then order and organise procedures for meeting these priorities efficiently and as part of a *total* business system. Management should ask itself what jobs need computerising, in what order, and with what sorts of linkages between the various activities? Procedures cannot be improved unless they are fully understood, and much effort is needed in analysing comprehensively the failings of the existing system. Indeed, consultants frequently report that client managements are shocked to discover how much they did not know about present arrangements.

Systems analysis should begin with a statement of the purpose of the organisation and its overall objectives, since only then does the compartmentalisation of the intended system into various functional parts possess a logical structure. Next, output requirements should be specified, including the formats of fundamental business documents (invoices, credit notes, stock requisitions, etc). Then, the reporting procedures that will govern the new system (ie, what information is needed by which manager, where, and when) must be determined.

In asking a department the question, 'What information do you need in order to perform your duties satisfactorily?' management invites an exaggerated response. It follows that consultants have an advantage over internal staff here because they will not be impressed by a department's overestimation of its own importance.

The next step is to redraft the business' organisation structure and to conduct detailed investigations into specific procedures. These enquiries will cover documents, data retention requirements, people-machine interfaces and interpersonal communications structures. The consultant can now design a new system.

Commercial software

Increasingly, hardware is less crucial to the choice of system than the availability of ready made or easily converted business software packages. In choosing a package for a certain application your consultant should examine the following factors.

- The program's ability to handle the volume of data entries required by the system eg, the number of customers' names and addresses that need to be held on file).
- Speed of operation. How long the program takes to load and operate.
- Quality of output: especially if the output is in the form of written documents that will be seen by outsiders.
- Ease of use. Ideally, a program should be capable of operation by an inexperienced person. Increasingly, standard programs are menu driven: instructions appear on the users VDU immediately the program is loaded and the user merely selects various options from menus of alternatives that periodically show on the screen. Note, however, that some of the instruction books that accompany packages are so badly drafted that even the loading of a program can be difficult for the untrained user.
- Flexibility. Good packages allow the user to modify, *via* menus, the basic structures of their operations and output. Note, however

that a package purchased to run on one system (IBM compatible for example) will not normally run on another – a different version of the same package will be required.

- Availability of support services from the program manufacturer. Many software suppliers offer free advice (over the telephone) on how to use their programs – including the correction of errors found in the program itself. The facility is normally available for three or six months from the date of purchase on payment of a supplementary fee.
- Whether the program is user-friendly, how much training (if any) is required prior to its use, and any problems or drawbacks associated with its operation.

Another relevant variable might be whether the package is new or well-established. A new program may be technically superior to its antecedents, yet contain numerous minor errors and logical inconsistencies that will only be ironed-out over time. Experienced computer users can usually identify and handle such problems, but novices might be completely bamboozled by these mistakes.

If greater specialisation is needed, 'custom-built' software may be commissioned from professional software designers. However, the extremely high cost of the straight purchase of existing programs encourages firms to alter their internal routines to make them compatible with available software rather than *vice versa*. Changing an existing administrative system is often cheaper than commissioning 'designer' software and has the added advantage that well established commercial programs are usually error free. Custom built software, conversely, may contain many errors (requiring the personal attention of the individual who wrote the program) which might not be revealed for several months (or even years) after installation.

Systems design

The aim is to create an integrated information and control system that is easily implemented and co-ordinated and which can be adapted and expanded to meet future needs. Thus, not only must the consultant evaluate your current working methods prior to computerisation, but must also devise a procedure for periodically (perhaps even continuously) reviewing and appraising the performance of the intended system. In other words, a 'development plan' needs to be drafted at the time of implementation.

Sub-systems
To do this the consultant will identify the *sub-systems* of functions

to be computerised (payroll, stock control, etc), and decide which should be tackled first. The easiest is probably the best, and usually the easiest of all is that for which a great deal of tried and tested software exists. Note immediately that choice of one project for initial priority necessarily precludes the completion of others, and a delay in implementing the first project (caused perhaps by program errors, inappropriate choice of software or inability to understand the instructions accompanying the first package purchased) will hold up the entire venture (at great financial cost because the existing system then has to be continued for a longer period after the purchase of new equipment). This fact reinforces the proposition that only easy projects should be undertaken in the early stages.

For each sub-system the consultant will prepare a statement of:

- its purpose and longer term objectives;
- anticipated costs and benefits;
- expected technical problems and possible causes of difficulty;
- staff training requirements;
- form of new documents required;
- how the sub-system relates to the wider system and how, specifically, it meets certain aspects of the overall system's needs;
- how the sub-system will be monitored when operating; and
- the extent to which it can be modified and adapted to satisfy anticipated future requirements.

Once the sub-system statements are ready the crucial projects may be identified. A project is 'crucial' if it affects several other sub-systems; computerised accounts are perhaps the best example since the accounting system affects so many others – planning, costing, stock, credit control, working capital management, tax and VAT, and so on. Great care is needed in ensuring that the sub-system first implemented will be fully compatible with the crucially important elements.

Next, named individuals should be put in charge of the implementation of particular applications. These people must become expert in the use of packages relating to their function; and must liaise with others where applications overlap (payroll and accounts for example). Eventually they should be able to suggest improvements in the sub-systems for which they are responsible. Resources will be allocated to these individuals through normal budgetary procedures: with project targets, schedules etc.

Timing of the installation
As the system plan develops, changes in the firm's organisation

structure may become necessary. Departments may need to merge, and some activities (inevitably) will become redundant. Inter-personal rivalries could develop at this point, so it is essential to try and identify possible causes of friction at the start of the project. The next stage is to detail (precisely) the final output documents that are to be produced and the summary control information (eg, monthly or semi-annual figures, quarterly profit and loss accounts, or weekly inventory levels) expected of the system. Raw data requirements, file structures, and processing methods can then be determined.

The advantages of a phased introduction, rather than a 'big bang' are that:

- staff gradually become fully familiar with particular packages and are not overwhelmed by errors and difficulties simultaneously arising in several programs;
- the capital cost of the additional hardware and software needed for a complete system can be spread over time;
- staff will transfer the knowledge they acquire from using the first packages to the use of others; and
- familiarity with the currently installed parts of the system enables staff to define precisely what they expect and require from the next application – they come to appreciate the characteristics of various types of standard program and they develop preferences for the packages of particular software manufacturers.

After the new system has been tested and proved fully operational, a scheme for monitoring its performance and for constantly updating its procedures is required. The system specification should by now be embodied in a written manual containing operating instructions, rules of procedure, copies of all standard documents, and lists of things to do if various malfunctions occur. This manual is necessary for ensuring continuity following staff changes, absences due to holidays or sickness, and for training purposes.

CADCAM

Another field in which computer consultants are active is the installation of systems for Computer Aided Design and Computer Assisted Manufacture (CADCAM, see also Chapters 5 and 11). These techniques involve not only design and manufacture but also testing, inspection, assembly, packaging, and despatch. All processes are fully integrated; raw materials, inputs, machining specifications, workshop instructions, tolerances, etc, are generated from initial design input data. CADCAM originated with the automation of production lines and associated measurement and analysis of machine tool movements. As firms with automated production acquired computing facilities they began to create data files recording all known machine tool movements and their effects. Special programs were then written to quantify and control production line work. Inevitably there was an explosion of innovative software linking design and production; and the advent of small, cheap, powerful computers has accelerated this trend.

Benefits of CADCAM

Often, firms acquire computers initially for data processing; especially for financial accounts. Accordingly, CADCAM software that can be quickly and easily fitted into existing data processing systems using equipment and personnel already employed by the firm has been developed and is now available commercially.

CADCAM systems require new attitudes towards questions of management control. Information is transmitted instantly between design, machining and asembly stages of production. Since there are no time delays or intervening agents there are few possibilities for breakdowns in communication, misunderstanding, or misinter-pretation between departments. Integrated computerised systems require fewer staff and are faster, more reliable and more accurate than those based on manual labour. Duplication of effort is avoided and costs are reduced.

Control of a CADCAM system does not rely on periodical data collection. Information on activity at any given moment in time is available and the implications of particular events can be immediately assessed. In this context, an effective manager is one who can take decisions quickly and is capable of utilising all the information resources available from the integrated system. The manager's primary concern will be to ensure that a failure in one part of the organisation does not cause the entire system to collapse.

CADCAM enables production controllers to interact with produc-tion control data intimately and continuously. Linkages with visual display units have allowed designers to alter scales of measurement on drawings, to rotate axes, alter specifications, simulate results and even animate their constructions. Partial CADCAM systems are available to which additions such as an inventory control system or cost data from computerised accounts can eventually be made, so that in due course all the firm's activities become computer controlled. Design, machining, assembly, packaging and despatch become as one.

Installation of a CADCAM system

In considering a consultant's proposals for installing a CADCAM system, ask yourself the following questions.

- Have the human resources implications of the intended system been fully considered? Redundancies might be avoided through human resource planning (see Chapter 9), retraining, voluntary severance, etc.
- If the company is beginning with a partial system, can additions be slotted-in quickly and easily? Modular as opposed to complete self-contained systems offer flexibility. Changes in manufacturing technique, materials inputs or environmental constraints may then be quickly accommodated since individual modular elements can be removed from or added to the complete system as circumstances change.
- How vulnerable is the intended system to technical change? Will your firm become locked into a particular design/manufacturing technology and if so what will happen if a leading competitor introduces a newer and better system in a couple of years' time?

Expert systems

Expert systems attempt to mimic the human expert, applying the same knowledge and procedures to problem solving as would a highly skilled professional person (eg, a medical doctor examining a patient). The facts and diagnostic processes contained in the package enable it to answer questions in a seemingly intelligent fashion. Packages themselves are divided into two parts: a shell which is a program to process information in a logical way, and a data base containing the information and rules about how it must be interpreted. The shell manipulates the data base according to a pre-set pattern, and various combinations of questions may be asked of the data. You ask questions in the form, 'What if. . . , and. . . , and if something else happens?' The answers should correspond to those of an expert instructor. Hence you use the package to *diagnose* simulated problems and in so doing develop your personal knowledge of the subject and how best to investigate logically the problems that it involves.

Expert systems have been applied to the training of telecommunications engineers (for fault diagnosis on printed circuit boards), to training operatives how to adjust complex electronic equipment and to training betting shop managers how to settle complicated bets (such as 'What are the odds if the number of runners in a horse race exceeds 12 and the race is a handicap and the chosen horse is placed third and. . . '). New applications of expert systems to business are constantly being discovered. For example, cheap packages are now available to prepare short lists for job applicants for interview following the receipt of numerous completed applications. Users simply type-in key information taken directly from each candidate's application form and then specify various criteria (typing/shorthand speeds, possession of certain educational qualifications, number of years' experience of a particular kind of work, etc) deemed by users as crucial for successful performance in the job. Criteria can be altered at will and hence different sets of shortlisted applicants generated according to the various sets of candidate characteristics.

Evaluating the consultant's contribution

To appraise the calibre of a computer consultant's contribution ask yourself the following questions.

- How well has the system satisfied the objectives originally set?
- Has the system operated within its budget, and if not why not?
- Have environmental circumstances altered so as to require changes in the system (new accounting standards or procedures for example) and should these changes have been predicted?
- Can specific examples of improved efficiency be identified?
- Have users expressed dissatisfaction with either the system's procedures or with the adequacy of its outputs?

Before becoming overly critical of your consultant's work remember that as staff become familiar with computerised procedures their expectations and demands of the system will naturally increase. Efficiency improvements that seemed spectacular at first will now be taken for granted, so it is only reasonable to expect staff to become dissatisfied, even frustrated, with the limitations of the current scheme and to want change.

Further questions to ask include the following, depending on the particular system and application.

- Has the consultant 'overstandardised' your administrative procedures to make them compatible with available software? Overstandardisation may create inefficiencies through forcing the firm's working methods into formats not really suitable for its needs.
- Did the consultant clearly explain at the outset what the system is *not* capable of achieving?
- Have you incurred any extra costs (special printers, disk drives, etc) not predicted by the consultant?

- Did the consultant analyse your business's needs and examine software alternatives *before* recommending particular equipment?
- How quickly do you get back up support following equipment failure or discovery of a fresh error in the software?
- How easily could you expand the system? Has it been modularised to allow for the addition and troublefree integration of additional units?
- Did the consultant overestimate, underestimate or accurately predict the system's capacity to handle your current volume of computer work?

Sources of information

Association of Independent Computer Specialists
c/o BEMA
Leicester House
8, Leicester Street
London WC2H 7BN
01-437 0678

Computing Services Association
Hanover House
73-74 High Holborn
London WC1V 6LE
01-405 3161

Computer Users Year Book
VNU Business Publications
VNU House
32-34 Broadwick Street
London W1A 2HG
01-439 4242

Chapter 9

Personnel Management Consultants

Introduction — Who are human resources management consultants? — Services provided by ACAS — Recruitment consultants/agents — Recruitment algorithms — Headhunters — Selection tests — Training consultants — Possible assignments: Installing grievance, appraisal and job design procedures; Drafting trade union recognition agreements — Evaluating a personnel consultant's contribution — Legal aspects of personnel — Dismissals — Legal complexities: Job evaluation — Redundancy planning — Sources of information.

After reading this chapter you should:

- know what is meant by human resource management (HRM) and how personnel management relates to it;
- be aware of the range of HRM consultancy services available;
- understand recruitment consultancy and the role of the headhunter;
- know why recruitment consultants frequently use selection tests, and the drawbacks and limitations of these;
- understand and be able to evaluate the work of an outside training consultant; and
- appreciate the legal problems that can arise in personnel management (laws on dismissal, equal opportunities, redundancy, grievance procedures, etc) and how a consultant might help overcome these difficulties.

Introduction

Personnel management is the major element of *Human Resources Management* (HRM), which is a wide-ranging subject covering industrial psychology, theories of learning and motivation, management/worker communications (including industrial relations) and the physical and psychological conditions of work. Whereas HRM is largely theoretical, personnel management concerns practical and mundane employee related duties: recruitment and selection, training and staff appraisal, maintenance of personnel records, health and safety, redundancy and dismissal procedures and so on.

Who are human resources management consultants?

There are four major types of consultant in the human resources field: recruitment consultants (who often act as agents as well), training and staff development consultants, specialists in motivation and staff appraisal, and consultants who deal with the legal side of personnel work (dismissals, redundancy planning, equal opportunities, and so on). Many of the large general consultancies have personnel divisions, primarily for the recruitment of senior managerial staff although other personnel assignments (assessing the human relations effects of the introduction of new technology for example) are also undertaken. There are in addition numerous small or single person consultancies offering personnel services, usually operating as trainers, headhunters (see below), or as occupational test administrators.

Personnel consultants have diverse backgrounds, reflecting the wide scope of human resources work. A few have law degrees; most will possess general management experience and/or qualifications. Some (but not many) will have the diploma of the Institute of Personnel Management (IPM). Note, however that one does not have to pass any examinations to join this institute.

Where to find HRM consultants

The IPM will supply lists of human resources consultants, including those prepared to work with very small firms. Also, the Institute's monthly magazine, *Personnel Management* is a useful source of consultants' names and addresses. In addition, there is the *Human Resource Management Yearbook*, edited by Michael Armstrong and published annually by Kogan Page. The second half of this comprises a substantial directory of names and addresses of HRM consultants, categorised according to major activity.

Consultants specialising in selection testing (see below) sometimes advertise in *Training and Development* magazine (published by the Institute of Training and Development) as indeed do other types of personnel management consultancy. If you want to undertake psychological testing on a large scale you should contact the British Psychological Society for further information.

Other useful sources are the BACIE journal, *Transition*, and the magazine of the Industrial Society which appears under the same title. Training and management development consultants advertise in all the above and in the *Training Officer* magazine. Look for personnel consultants in *Yellow Pages* under the headings 'Personnel Consultants' and 'Employment Agencies and Consultants'.

DBM
Drake Beam Morin Ltd

Locally and Globally
Drake Beam Morin is helping business
manage its most important resource:
People

Managing people in the 1990's will be a constant challenge, especially in four key areas:

- Separation – career transition counselling for employees separating from a company
- Performance – assessing, coaching and counselling employees
- Selection – interviewing and hiring the right person for the right job
- Corporate Revitalisation – consulting designed to support changing organisations

Drake Beam Morin is the world's leading provider of Outplacement and career management services. For more than 20 years DBM has been helping companies maximise profitability and productivity through appropriate human resource management.

For more information on DBM's many products and services, telephone or write:

Peter R Trigg DRAKE BEAM MORIN, LTD,
3 Arlington Street, St James's London SW1A 1RA, England 01 493 8444

Services provided by ACAS

For technical advice on dismissal and related matters and best initial contact is the enquiries desk of ACAS (which stands for Advisory, Conciliation and Arbitration Service). ACAS is a government agency that exists to promote good industrial relations in the UK by seeking to arbitrate in industrial disputes and to obtain out of court settlements in claims for unfair dismissal. You simply telephone your local ACAS office (the number is in the telephone book) and ask for general enquiries, your call will eventually be taken by an ACAS officer who is an expert in employment matters. ACAS officers are highly competent people and can often answer queries on the spot. If the issue is too extensive or complicated to be dealt with over the telephone you will be told where you need to go for further advice. Moreover, ACAS itself provides a low cost human resources management consultancy service, offering help in the following areas:

- negotiating machinery, bargaining arrangements, procedures for settling disputes and grievances;
- consultative and participation agreements, trade union recognition;
- communications and the disclosure of information to trade unions;

- labour turnover, absenteeism, human resource planning, productivity bargaining, hours of work and other conditions of employment, payments systems and job evaluation;
- industrial relations and employment legislation, including the law on unfair dismissal, sex and race discrimination, equal pay, recruitment, selection and induction;
- disciplinary, dismissal and redundancy procedures; and
- training in industrial relations.

Additionally, a subsidiary of ACAS, the 'Work Research Unit' will give information, advice and assistance on such matters as job design, ergonomics, motivation, job satisfaction, and the causes and consequences of stress at work.

Recruitment consultants/agents

The usefulness of recruitment consultants is perhaps summarised by the following true story. A certain organisation employed staff in four grades, A, B, C and D. A senior employee retired, creating an 'A' grade vacancy. Good internal candidates were available for the post, but the organisation's equal opportunities recruitment policy required that all posts be externally advertised in several diverse media. Nearly £3,000 was spent on advertising the vacancy in magazines and newspapers, plus additional sums on paying short listed candidates' travelling expenses. Then there were the costs of correspondence with applicants, clerical costs, and the cost of the management time absorbed by interviewing candidates (eight of the organisation's staff each spent a full day conducting interviews). Of course, one of the (excellent) internal candidates was appointed, thus creating a vacancy in grade B so that the entire process had to be repeated. Again, an internal candidate was appointed. The process was repeated once more in respect of the newly vacant grade C position, resulting finally in a genuine vacancy in the lowest grade D, which was filled from outside. Almost a full year was absorbed by this work during which temporary assistance had to be employed, adding still further to the total cost.

Managers within that organisation were oblivious to the inefficiency of their recruitment procedures. It cost more than £15,000 on advertising, administration, etc, to secure a single junior employee: considerably more than the annual salary of the person finally appointed. And this ignores the cost of temporary cover.

A consultant would have identified the huge cost of current procedures, recommended the implementation of fair and efficient (equal opportunity) internal promotion procedures (pointing out the motivational advantages of promotion from within), and would have attended to the recruitment of the junior employee at a fraction of the previous cost.

Recruitment consultancy really began during the labour shortage of the 1950s when the unemployment rate averaged less than one and a half per cent and the average period of unemployment was just over a fortnight. National newspapers began to carry special displays of job advertisements, giving excellent low-cost publicity to the recruiting firm as well as attracting high calibre labour. (Then as now many newspapers and magazines offered cheaper rates for job advertisements than for advertisements of a more general nature.)

Recruiters may be *ad hoc* consultants (headhunters for example – see below) or employment agencies. There are two main types of the latter.

Those which deal mainly with office staff: typists, clerks, machine operators, etc. Here the employer informs the agency when a vacancy arises and the agency then submits any suitable candidates it happens to have on its books. If an agency candidate is engaged the employer pays a fee to the agency, part of which is usually refunded if the employee leaves within a specified period. There is no charge to the candidate, who may register with several agencies. Problems occur if the agency submits unsuitable candidates for the vacancy because of the time and expense then involved in interviewing, testing, and processing applications.

Agencies which specialise in the recruitment of senior staff. These will analyse the job, prepare job and personnel specifications, advertise, send out application forms, interview and possibly test selected applicants. The employer is then presented with a short list of candidates.

The vacancy may be advertised, individually or as a component for a block of vacancies for different firms. Recruitment agents and consultants provide much advertising revenue to newspapers and magazines (indeed, some specialist publications, depend for their existence on job advertisements) and thus command discounts for bulk space purchases which they can pass back to clients.

In drawing up a suitable shortlist the consultant will:

- use his or her expert knowledge of job advertising media to select the media most likely to be seen by suitable candidates;
- relate job requirements to applicants' CVs; and
- screen out candidates he or she considers unsuitable using intuition, a recruitment algorithm, or by giving applicants a selection test.

There are perhaps two major disadvantages attached to using an agency: the difficulties experienced by the agency in understanding in a short time the kind of person that is compatible with existing staff; and the fact that agencies rarely follow up and validate their recommendations.

Briefing a recruitment consultant

Give the consultant comprehensive details of the duties attached to the vacant post and state the characteristics of previous occupants who performed exceptionally well in the position. Tell the consultant something about the *culture* of your company: whether it is authoritarian or democratic, the degree of formality of interpersonal relations, attitudes towards authority and responsibility, and whether initiative is seen as a desirable attribute for subordinate staff. Clarify the formulae for calculating the consultant's fee and (importantly) for payment of rebates if the appointee is unsatisfactory.

Fees vary, from as little as eight per cent of annual salary for a routine appointment to as much as 50 per cent of annual salary when complicated and highly specialised headhunting is involved. Think in terms of 15 to 20 per cent for most situations.

Beware of the possibility of early resignations. Most recruitment consultants offer a big refund if you have to sack an employee within a month of starting work, and a small amount if the person proves unsatisfactory and has to be dismissed after a month but before the expiry of (usually) one year. Check the contract to ensure similar provisions apply to workers who quit. Otherwise you could pay a hefty fee to the consultant and then lose both this and the employee if he or she resigns shortly after the appointment.

Recruitment algorithms

These began in the 1950s but are still widely used, albeit in updated and modified versions. And each consultant will have devised his or her own particular variation. The aim is to match the requirements of jobs with the attributes of candidates. Accordingly, the consultant will need from you a detailed job specification from which the personal characteristics of suitable candidates may be derived. If the job description provided is inadequate the consultant will ask questions to establish precisely all the tasks and competencies the job requires. This might not be easy because managements sometimes prescribe impossibly high standards for new entrants to their firms; resulting in a restricted choice of candidates and meaning that the person finally appointed is almost certain to fail!

Next the consultant will draft a 'person specification' formally defining the background, education, personality and other relevant characteristics of the ideal appointee. The person described might not exist, but the qualities laid down will provide criteria for preparing a short list and for deciding which questions to ask during interviews. While putting together the person specification the consultant will probably refer to a standard algorithm to guide his or her thoughts about the competencies needed for the job. Among the earliest of these was the 'Fraser Plan' (named after its author, J M Fraser), and first published in 1954.* This has five headings, each of which can be used to analyse both the characteristics of the job and the personal qualities desired in the successful candidate. It is worth going through the Fraser Plan because it illustrates the idea and because it forms the basis of many other variations. The headings are as follows.

Impact on other people
Does the work involve much contact with others, and if so what specific communications skills are involved? To what extent does the job require someone who makes a strong impression on other people? Is the ability to lead crucial to the post, and if so what type of leadership (tight or flexible, autocratic or democratic, directive or participative) is necessary? Does the job demand someone who mixes easily, or are such matters unimportant for this work?

Qualifications and experience
What educational certificates should the successful candidate possess, and why? Should candidates have attended certain training courses? What work experiences are relevant to the post? Companies often specify entry qualifications not really justified by the objective requirements of the job. A consultant will point this out, if only because insistence on unnecessarily high entry standards will significantly reduce the number of candidates available for the position.

Innate abilities
Does the work require someone who, for example, can quickly assimilate large quantities of information, interpret complicated issues, think quickly, take decisions on the spot, and so on?

Motivation
Is the job appropriate for an extremely ambitious person, or is it more

---

*Latest edition is Fraser, J.M., *Employment Interviewing*, Macdonald and Evans, London, 1970.

suitable for an individual not concerned with developing a career? Certain jobs are necessarily repetitive and lack intellectual stimulation. It is usually a mistake to appoint individuals who possess great drive, creativity and enthusiasm to such positions.

Emotional adjustment

Employees who cannot easily withstand stress should not attempt harrowing or emotionally arduous work. Some jobs can be very distressing. Dealing with irate customers, coping with belligerent operatives or unsympathetic colleagues is necessarily stressful. To what extent do you require a person who can withstand stress or similar emotional difficulties?

Having drafted a person specification the consultant will next suggest the sorts of question you need to ask during interviews. Advice might also be offered on the general conduct of interviews: reception of candidates, putting people at ease, avoidance of interruptions, seating arrangements, not asking irrelevant questions, assessment of candidates, interview performances, etc.

Problems with recruitment algorithms

These matching exercises could result in the appointment of stereotypical candidates who lack the flair and creativity needed for important work. Truly creative people do not always follow conventional career patterns and hence might not possess the experiences and characteristics listed in a carefully drafted person specification. And much subjectivity still applies: what seems a pleasant disposition to one person may appear as surly and aggressive to someone else!

It is usual in these circumstances to look for common factors among candidates. For instance, has the applicant a good record of passing examinations first time, or were several attempts required? Does the applicant's CV show significant gaps in particular subject areas (mathematics or english, for example)? Did the candidate drop out of particular courses? How much responsibility did the candidate carry in his or her previous post? Is there any evidence of the candidate's willingness to attend courses and update skills? Did the applicant remain long with any one employer without being promoted?

The fact that any of these are true does not necessarily mean the candidate is unsuitable, only that the issue should be further explored during the interview.

Headhunters

In expanding industries it is likely that the best people will *already* have good jobs and thus will not be seeking a fresh appointment. Accordingly, 'headhunters' (or 'executive search consultants' to give them their proper title) will locate suitable candidates and approach them directly in order to establish whether they are interested in a vacant post. Headhunters work in strict confidence, possibly without revealing the name of the recruiting firm in the first place. They have specialist knowledge of particular industries and of the most successful managers within them. And they can advise on the terms and conditions of employment necessary to attract this level of staff. Using a headhunter offers several advantages.

- It can be cheap because no advertising or administrative costs are involved.
- It can result in extremely rapid appointments since even if the individual first targetted is not interested in the job, that person might know of an equally high calibre candidate elsewhere and pass on news of the vacancy on the headhunter's behalf.
- Only candidates discovered by the headhunter need be considered.
- Although a firm can do its own headhunting, an executive search specialist will know the locations of suitable candidates and be able to approach them at once. Also the consultant will know how to present the vacancy attractively in order to induce the target to quit his or her current job.
- You are guaranteed a supply of eminently well-qualified candidates (headhunters commonly work on the basis of no appointment no fee).

It is important to note that executive search and selection firms are not human resources management consultants *per se*, although many selection consultants do in fact possess personnel management qualifications. Usually, search consultants are either members of an executive selection division of a large consultancy which provides a full range of human resource (and other) services – job evaluation, redundancy planning, appraisal, etc – or members of a firm that specialises exclusively in executive selection.

The MCA Code on Executive Search

Consultancies that belong to the Management Consultancies Association (see chapter 1) must adhere to a special code of practice when undertaking headhunting assignments. This code includes the requirements that the consultancy will:

- take steps to ensure that the client firm actually has a genuine vacancy (ie, that it is not using the exercise merely as a device for

obtaining information on competing firms by giving bogus job interviews to people already employed by competing businesses);
- not place an individual with one client and then subsequently approach that person with a view to placing him or her with another company;
- only charge fees to recruiting firms and not to candidates;
- provide candidates with comprehensive and accurate information about vacancies; and
- regard all personal information obtained on candidates and clients as totally confidential.

Selection tests

Some consultants administer tests to job candidates as part of their overall service. Indeed, certain consultancies do little else. Beware. There is much pseudo-psychological humbug circulating in this area, and it is easy to spend large sums of money on useless tests. Consultants who use tests do so for a number of reasons:

- giving tests impresses both clients and candidates (influencing the latter is especially important in 'sellers' markets' where the recruiter needs to persuade applicants that the client firm is better to work for than competing companies);
- sometimes all the candidates are so alike it is impossible to distinguish between them using other criteria;
- arguably, tests inject an element of true objectivity into selection procedures;
- it may be necessary to hire a large number of employees in a short period; and
- testing can be a cheap method of recruiting staff – 30 or 40 candidates can be tested at a single sitting using only one person to administer the test.

Selection tests may relate to intelligence, personality, or attainment. The latter type of test (typing speed or driving ability for instance) is relatively straightforward, while intelligence testing is so specialised and difficult that nowadays it is rarely used for employment purposes.

More controversial are the tests of personality that consultants sometimes advise be given to candidates for managerial positions. They are supposed to show whether an individual has a personality compatible with the needs of a job.

Personality tests
The tests are used either to assess management potential or as self-

awareness exercises for existing managerial staff. Unfortunately there are many serious problems attached to personality testing, as is obvious even from the manner in which they are compiled.

How personality tests are devised

A psychologist prepares a list of questions the answers to which he or she believes reveal various aspects of an individual's personality. The aim is to identify dimensions of personality such as introversion/extroversion, intuition, whether someone is judgemental, empathetic, submissive, dominant, etc. Note immediately that there are various schools of thought in psychology, which differ over such (crucial) questions as:

- what personality is and how (indeed whether) it can be measured;
- whether individuals possess a 'core' personality (as most of the tests assume) that is constant over time, or whether personality changes with age, experience, education or following traumatic events (getting the sack or the death of a close relative for example); and
- how observed behaviour and responses to questions should be interpreted.

Next the test is given to several (usually small) samples of people whose personality types are already known with a view to seeing how accurately the test predicts the personalities of these individuals. Then the test is administered to a larger group of respondents considered truly representative of the sort of people the test is intended to evaluate. Average values of the responses of this group are then computed. For instance, a test that aims to identify individuals who possess management potential will be given to a group of *existing* senior managers and their average patterns of response recorded. It is now assumed that anyone who subsequently takes the test and responds in the same manner as the average of the senior managers initially tested probably possesses senior management potential!

Inevitably, these tests have been accused of being naive, simplistic, misleading, and downright dishonest; for many reasons. The managers used to define 'normal' or desired test responses typically represent a distinct and unique socio-economic and cultural group, not necessarily representative of other societies and cultures. Why not use, for example, agricultural workers in mainland China to establish 'normal' responses?

These tests are alleged to discriminate against ethnic minority and female candidates. Indeed, in the United States several tests which previously were widely used have now been withdrawn following successful civil law suits against the people administering them brought by women and ethnic minority job applicants who were rejected on account of their poor performance.

Critics suggest, moreover, that there is little genuine proof that these tests select the best candidates. To be useful a test must be *reliable,* ie, give consistent results when repeated, and *valid* ie, measure what it claims to measure and not something else (booklearning is easily mistaken for intelligence for example). Without doubt, people get better at tests the more they practice. Certain candidates may have received instruction about how to respond to personality test questions in order to create the most favourable impression.

The use of personality tests

The copyright of a test lies with its creator, who normally will sell licences to use it to other people. Licences may cost several thousands of pounds per annum, so licence holders charge their client companies a capitation fee according to the number of candidates tested on the client's behalf.

Publishers of tests usually restrict their sale to people who have been trained in their use. Each test must be given in precisely the manner described in the test manual, and the results interpreted by a qualified person. Critics of this practice allege, however, that in so doing publishers and psychologists conceal the foundations upon which tests are constructed, prevent discussion of the validity or otherwise of their assumptions, and thus exclude all possibilities for external scrutiny, criticism and academic debate. And people who take such tests but are then not happy with the scores they are awarded cannot challenge the marking criteria and propriety of the test.

If your consultant suggests applying a test to the candidates short-listed for the vacancy, ask the following questions.

- Will it be possible to relate test results to subsequent performance?
- How does the test suggested relate to your *particular* vacancy?
- Is the test of American origin and if so how does the consultant justify its applicability to the UK? Who *actually* devised the test and how was its accuracy determined (how big a sample was used, were women and ethnic minorities properly represented in the sample, have follow-up studies confirmed the initial results, etc)?
- Where can you read about the origin and development of the test and details of its methodology?

- Can the consultant refer you to previous satisfied users of the test?
- Does the test seek to isolate a specific personality characteristic and what does possession of that characteristic really mean?
- Will the test provide more information about the candidate than is already known?
- If a candidate obtains an extremely high test score and then turns out to be so incompetent in the job that he or she must be dismissed, will the consultant give a refund on the consultancy fee?

Never evaluate a test by taking it yourself, because you are not necessarily typical of the type of person likely to succeed in the vacant position. Also, you will probably take the test in private, knowing the results will not be revealed to third parties, and you might cheat a little by giving yourself extra time. Candidates, conversely, will be extremely nervous and self-conscious while taking the test and this is bound to diminish the quality of their performance.

Training consultants

Training consultants normally deliver training courses and/or instructional materials as well as advising on client companies' employee training needs and the suitability of various training methods. The aim is to improve the employees' performance in the shortest training time and at the lowest cost. Few trainers (especially management trainers), are academics – although most will have some sort of academic background. This is because the areas in which industrial training needs are greatest are usually those in which state provision through colleges and government training schemes is least satisfactory. The majority of trainers operate in the following fields.

- Sales training, particular aspects of marketing and legal aspects of personnel.
- Analytical skills, organisation, delegation and control, time management.
- Interpersonal skills, communication, leadership and co-ordination, motivation of subordinates.
- Creative abilities, problem solving, capacity to initiate new activities.

What a trainer will do
Trainers have a wide range of training methods at their disposal:

lectures, group discussions, interactive video, coaching, business games, role-playing, computer-based training, etc. The trainer will study course participants' aspirations and abilities, and hence devise a programme specifically relevant to their particular needs. The following matters must be determined:

- the speed at which material is to be presented;
- targets for each trainee;
- how progress is to be assessed (ie, the grading and assessment system) and excellent performance rewarded; and
- relationships between the intended course and participants' job requirements, especially whether the competencies learned on the course are easily transferred to other fields.

Briefing a training consultant

State *exactly* how you want employees' performance to improve following the course, and how improvements are to be measured. You need to identify knowledge and skill deficiencies among the existing staff and to outline your employees' backgrounds and levels of motivation. Training needs might be identified from:

- underperformance by subordinates, evidenced by low quality output, lack of initiative, bad decisions or general incompetence;
- the acquisition of new and unfamiliar equipment or the introduction of new working methods; and
- perusal of subordinates' job specifications to identify gaps between what they are doing and what they should be doing.

Together with your consultant you need to define the knowledge (what the employee needs to know), skills (what he or she must be able to do), and attitudes (how the worker should perceive the job) necessary for satisfactory performance. Then detail all the training inputs needed to remedy current deficiencies. This will enable your consultant to draft a 'training specification' from which a training plan may be devised.

Evaluating a trainer's contributions

Improved performance should result from all training activities. For manual workers the success of a training programme might be quantified in terms of better productivity, higher quality of output, less absenteeism, lower staff turnover, greater adaptability, fewer accidents and less need for close supervision. Unfortunately, improved performance in many jobs is difficult to express quantitatively and some skills acquired on courses undertaken today might not be used until the future.

Training can improve workers' morale, create better interpersonal relationships, instil in employees a sense of loyalty to the organisation and provide other intangible benefits. Note however that it is not sufficient merely to ask workers whether they *feel* more efficient in consequence of attending a course; hard objective evidence is also required. Courses which participants have particularly enjoyed (especially residential courses) may be popular not because of their intrinsic educational value but because of their holiday camp atmosphere, recreational facilities, friendships established among course members, and so on. Always ask the question 'What difference would it make if this training did not take place?' If the answer is 'not much', then you must critically reasess the value of your training activities.

Employee remuneration consultants

Remuneration policies have two objectives: to attract and retain good quality staff, and to provide incentives for increased effort. Consultants specialising in this area will:

- devise schemes for encouraging long-term employee loyalty to the business;
- identify key relationships between staff incomes and the firm's successes and failures;
- ensure that employees' remuneration packages are tax efficient;
- establish logical and practicable salary structures; and
- predict the cash flow implications of differing employee remuneration schemes.

Salary structures

Ultimately, salary levels are determined by the forces of supply and demand. In the shorter term, however, management needs to make certain that differentials between salary grades are consistent and rationally determined. The ideal salary structure will (i) allow for progression through a scale that coincides with the level of attainment of the salary earner at any given point, (ii) have a rationale that is understood by all the staff, and (iii) be cheap and simple to operate. Unfortunately, modern systems tend to be complicated and in consequence may fail to achieve any of these objectives.

The major reason for the intricacy of so many contemporary remuneration schemes in the UK is of course the tax system, which frequently encourages businesses to pay their staff through fringe benefits rather than 'salary' as such. Accordingly, a person's total remuneration package might include a salary, a pension, a performance bonus, a lump sum on termination, a car, housing assistance, medical benefits, low interest loans, expense accounts, and many other items.

Fringe benefits are generally taxable but may be taxed at a lower marginal rate than the recipient normally pays. Accordingly, employees normally welcome a significant part of their remunerations being paid in this way. Remuneration consultants are expert in guiding clients through the tax aspects of the fringe benefits maze.

Employee share schemes

Constructing and implementing employee share schemes is an increasingly important part of the typical employee remuneration consultant's work. Such schemes can involve general payouts to workers in the form of shares, or (more commonly) provision for the exercise of share options. Employee share option schemes became available via the 1984 Finance Act, which enabled workers to agree to monthly (say) deductions from wages that would then entitle them to exercise the option of buying shares in their own companies at a (low) predetermined price a certain number of years in the future.

The harmonisation of marginal rates of income tax and capital gains tax that occurred in 1988 seemingly removed the (significant) tax advantages given to share option schemes under the 1984 Act because straight cash bonuses are today taxed at exactly the same rate as Inland Revenue approved share options. Also, share options cannot be exercised by workers until at least three years after they have been agreed.

On the other hand, capital gains tax resulting from a share option scheme is not payable until the employee *actually* sells his or her shares (whereas income tax on a cash bonus is immediately payable under PAYE), and there is currently no tax liability whatsoever in respect of the first £5,000 of capital bonus. Moreover, profit sharing systems which automatically invest recipients' incomes in company shares are free of all income tax provided the shares are held for five years.

Companies too can benefit from remunerating their workers via shares and share options, for a number of reasons:

- The net cost to the company of employees exercising their share options at any particular moment will be small relative to other ways of remunerating workers. Note also that through accepting remuneration in shares rather than cash, employees are in effect helping to finance the business.

- No employer's national insurance contributions are involved.
- Money paid into trust funds established to 'purchase' the company's shares on employees' behalf may be set against corporation tax. This money immediately returns to the company in the form of subscriptions for shares.

Employee share schemes, therefore, still have a great deal to offer, although their details are necessarily complicated and expert consultancy assistance is normally required.

Further possible personnel consultancy assignments

Other matters for which you might seek the help of a personnel consultant are as follows.

Installation of a grievance procedure

The Employment Protection (Consolidation) Act of 1978 requires that all contracts of employment, which by law must be issued to employees within 13 weeks of starting work, contain details of the employer's grievance procedure (EPCA, s 1(4)(b)). This does not mean that an employer *must* have a grievance procedure; only that if one exists then its particulars must be communicated to employees in the contract of employment. No organisation is so well managed that its employees never need to complain and even if the firm is objectively a good employer, staff may still *feel* that complaints are justified. Well constructed grievance procedures enable firms to resolve complaints quickly, fairly, and without risk of inconsistent decisions. The employer is seen to be trying to be fair and, of course, the absence of formal procedures will severely prejudice an employer's case if the grievance eventually results in legal proceedings.

Job design

This is the process of deciding which tasks and responsibilities shall be undertaken by particular employees and the methods, systems and procedures for completing work. It concerns patterns of accountability and authority, spans of control and interpersonal relations between colleagues. The purpose of job design is to stimulate the interest and involvement of the worker, thus motivating the worker to greater efforts. Jobs may be *enlarged* or *enriched*.

Job enlargement means increasing the scope of a job through

extending the range of its duties and responsibilities. This contradicts the principle of specialisation and division of labour whereby work is divided into small units, each of which is performed repetitively by an individual worker. The boredom and alienation caused by the division of labour can actually cause efficiency to fall, thus, job enlargement seeks to motivate workers through reversing the process of specialisation.

Job enrichment involves the allocation of more interesting, challenging and perhaps difficult duties to workers in order to stimulate their sense of participation and concern for the achievement of objectives. Extra decision-making authority may be assigned to workers, or they might be given duties requiring higher skill levels, or be required to have greater contact with customers and/or suppliers. Equally, existing single tasks might be combined into a composite whole, or workers might be made responsible for controlling the quality of their output or allowed greater discretion over how they achieve objectives. Your consultant will analyse existing job descriptions, interview staff and devise questionnaires intended to isolate the factors that make your employees' jobs boring or interesting. Then, he or she will specify the changes necessary to make boring jobs more interesting, eg, by regrouping activities (taking some interesting work away from certain individuals for reallocation to others), allowing workers to alter the pace or methods of their work or allocating broad rather than specific targets. Participation in the setting of objectives can also enrich employees' work, especially if workers are encouraged to contribute completely new ideas.

Devising a system for effective employee appraisal
Often this involves organisational design (see Chapter 4) in order to create departments or sections that are easy to appraise (ie, where output is measurable and can be sensibly compared with the outputs of other units).

Performance appraisal is the analysis of employees' past successes and failures, and the assessment of their suitability for promotion or further training. It generates useful information about employees and the nature of their work. And it monitors the feasibilities of targets set in management by objectives programmes. Employees know they are being evaluated and are told the criteria that will be used in the course of the appraisal. Indeed, knowledge that an appraisal is soon to occur could motivate an employee into increased effort aimed at enhancing the outcome of the assessment.

The commonest method of performance appraisal involves having line managers report on each of several characteristics mentioned on a predetermined checklist in respect of each subordinate. Headings for assessment could include: punctuality, reliability, enthusiasm, productivity, speed of work, accuracy of work and so on. Also, the form might ask the assessing manager to consider the appraisee's:

- knowledge, skills and/or formal educational qualifications acquired and/or utilised during the review period;
- abilities to delegate, plan, supervise, establish priorities, assume responsibility, cope with stress, exercise leadership;
- personal qualities: appearance, personality, disposition, enthusiasm, compatibility with colleagues;
- critical faculties: creativity; judgemental, problem solving and decision taking abilities; and
- interpersonal skills: verbal and written communication, willingness to accept new ideas, relationships with superiors/subordinates/clients.

Evaluating an appraisal scheme
To evaluate the usefulness of an appraisal system ask yourself the following questions.

- Do appraisal forms absorb excessively long periods of time to complete and administer?
- Is the scheme appropriate for the intellectual level of the departmental managers who must undertake the appraisals?
- Did the consultant offer training in appraisal techniques (performance review interviewing for example) as part of the deal?
- Has the scheme created resentment among employees, and if so why? (The purpose of PA is to improve performance, not to discipline staff.)
- What measures has the consultant introduced to prevent all employees being classified as 'fair' or 'average' by those conducting the appraisals? Note how this can prevent assessors becoming involved in arguments both with subordinates and with their own bosses. But it means the appraisal scheme becomes effectively useless.
- Is there any evidence of better motivation among the staff as a direct result of the scheme?
- Can information derived from the appraisal system be conveniently applied to the firm's promotion, training, management succession, and general staff development programmes?

- Have interpersonal communications between managers and their subordinates improved in consequence of the system?

Drafting a recognition agreement regarding trade unions that seek to enter your firm

Suppose your company is approached by a union which demands recognition. You will want to assess (i) the extent of support for the union among employees, and (ii) the wider implications of unionisation for the well being of the firm. Estimating the level of support might not be easy, since not only should the *present* number of union members be counted, but also the number of employees likely to join the union if it is recognised. Also, management must determine the threshold membership at which recognition will be granted. Is this to be a third of all workers, or 51 per cent, or two-thirds, or whatever?

Often, unions are only partially recognised at first, say to represent workers in grievance or disciplinary interviews, but not for collective bargaining over pay and conditions. Then, further issues are gradually incorporated into negotiating procedures – pension schemes, working conditions, holiday arrangements, shift work systems – until eventually all aspects of employment, including pay and working conditions, are covered. The aims of recognition policy are to dovetail negotiating procedures into the administrative structure of the firm, to establish mechanisms for defusing potentially dangerous conflict situations and to ensure that appropriate unions represent the workers.

Evaluating a personnel consultant's contributions

Appraising a personnel consultant is normally straightforward because he or she either will or will not have completed some prespecified task – recruiting a certain employee, implementing redundancies, installing an appraisal system, etc. To evaluate training courses many firms simply ask trainees what they thought of the programme. Unfortunately, however, trainees sometimes enjoy a course even though it was not objectively worthwhile. Conversely, trainees do not always realise the true value of certain courses, particularly if they find them difficult.

You should, of course, expect a consultant to possess expert knowledge of Codes of Practice and particular statues relevant to his or her specialist field. And you need always to compare the consultant's fee with the cost of providing equivalent services 'in-house'. How long, for example, would it take the company's own staff to devise a job advertisment, prepare information on the vacancy, draft an application form, sift through applications and conduct interviews rather than use a recruitment agency?

Legal aspects of personnel

Many issues arising in the personnel field (dismissal, job evaluation, maternity leave, employment protection) have legal implications. Initial (free) advice on employment legislation is available *via* ACAS and then, for a fee, through a personnel and/or general management consultant. If complications arise, however, you will be told to consult a solicitor.

Using a solicitor

Lists of solicitors specialising in employment matters are available from the Law Society or (more easily) from your local Citizens' Advice Bureau (which hold such lists for the benefit of aggrieved workers). Unfortunately, solicitors vary enormously in their knowledge, calibre, general efficiency and enthusiasm. And the legal profession is so closed and internally regulated (solicitors do not really compete with each other) that it is extremely difficult to find out who the good ones are. Other serious problems with using a solicitor for personnel work are as follows.

- Solicitors can be extremely expensive compared to other consultancy services. By law, solicitors' fees have to be 'fair and reasonable', taking into account (i) the complexity of the problem, (ii) its urgency and (iii) the time spent on the case. But if you are unhappy with the final bill all you can do is have it assessed by the Law Society (itself consisting of solicitors and representing their interests) or by an officer of the court, who will also be a lawyer!
- If your solicitor's performance is unsatisfactory and causes you financial loss you will want to sue for compensation. But then you need to engage *another solicitor* to handle the case, and solicitors are usually extremely reluctant to accept such work.
- Much of the work on the problem might in fact be done by junior unqualified staff, even though you are being charged the full rate for a qualified solicitor.

Shop around before engaging a solicitor. Ask for estimates of costs, and ask business and other contacts (including personnel and management consultants) for recommendations. Make sure, of course, that the solicitor you choose is experienced and expert on employment legislation.

When briefing a solicitor remember always the need to minimise the amount of work he or she can claim to have completed when preparing your bill. Provide the solicitor with *all* the information relevant to the case, and outline the circumstances surrounding the issue as fully and clearly as possible. This reduces the time spent on queries.

Specify exactly what you want the solicitor to do, and how much money is available. Insist that any possible additional expenditures be cleared with you *before* they are incurred.

Dismissal

You need not necessarily approach a solicitor for advice on the legal aspects of dismissal – consultants, ACAS, Chambers of Commerce and trade associations can often provide satisfactory advice on these matters – but you *must* be aware of the possible complications that could arise and hence know the circumstances in which a lawyer's assistance is required. In general dismissal is the termination of employment by:

- the employer, with or without notice; or
- the employee's resignation, with or without notice, when the employer behaves in a manner that demonstrates refusal to be bound by the contract of employment. This is termed 'constructive dismissal'. It means the employer is behaving so unreasonably that the worker has no alternative but to quit, or
- the failure of the employer to renew a fixed term contract.

Dismissal without notice is known as 'summary' dismissal. This might occur when a worker's behaviour makes impossible the fulfilment of a contract of employment. Examples are theft, persistent drunkenness, violence, abusiveness to colleagues or customers, wilful disobedience, or incompetence that immediately causes damage to the employer's business.

There is an important difference between 'unfair' dismissal and 'wrongful' dismissal. The former can only happen when the person dismissed is an 'employee' of an organisation in the sense defined by the Employment Protection (Consolidation) Act (1978). At the time of writing, a worker is able to claim unfair dismissal only if he or she has worked continuously for an employer for at least two years full time, or two years part time doing at least 16 hours a week or five years part time doing at least eight hours a week. Continuity means the absence of gaps in the worker's service of more than a week, although holidays, time off for sickness (up to six months at a stretch), and 'normal' layoffs (teachers' long summer vacations for example) do not break continuity. A series of short term contracts, issued one after another, will build up worker's continuity to exactly the same extent as a single contract for a longer period. Thus, a worker employed on (say) renewable one year contracts is regarded in law as equivalent to someone on a permanent contract after the appropriate number of years have elapsed.

'Wrongful' dismissal in contrast may be claimed by any dismissed worker, regardless of length of service – a worker who has been with the firm for only a few days may be 'wrongfully' sacked. This occurs when the worker is dismissed with insufficient notice, and results in civil proceedings in a county court. The aggrieved party sues for damages equivalent to the actual loss incurred. Note that unfair dismissal cases are heard by relatively informal three person 'industrial tribunals' and not the county court. There are major differences in procedure between county courts and industrial tribunals, and whereas costs in the latter are intended to be minimal (and in normal circumstances are never awarded to the other side) costs in the county court can be huge.

Reasons for dismissal

The Employment Protection (Consolidation) Act 1978 lists four major reasons for which staff may be fairly dismissed: genuine redundancy, gross misconduct, inadequate performance, or some other substantial reason. Dismissing people under any of these headings can be complicated and the help of a personnel consultant is essential if you are not familiar with the rules. The term 'misconduct' for example has no legal definition, each case must be considered on its individual merits. Gross misconduct (theft, violence, etc) justifies summary dismissal in certain circumstances but the law insists that you 'act reasonably' at all times, and it is up to you to prove that misconduct vindicating dismissal actually occurred. You must be able to specify where and when the misconduct took place and how it affected the worker's job and/or workmates. Then you have to demonstrate that the worker's past record was taken into account and how exactly the organisation suffered on account of the event. Also, you need to show that the dismissed person was not selected unfairly from others who were equally guilty, that dismissal rather than some lesser action was required, that formal warnings were issued, proper investigations carried out and that a fair dismissal procedure was followed, including right of appeal.

Similar complexities apply to 'inadequate performance'

(incapability) which means that the employee cannot satisfactorily complete his or her work. You are expected to warn people of their inadequacies and give them the chance to improve. If you promote somebody who turns out to be useless at the higher level of work, you should offer the opportunity to revert to a less arduous job before dismissing that employee. Always keep documentary evidence of an employee's incompetence and *do not* write glowing references for a worker immediately prior to dismissal, since such documents can subsequently be used as evidence against your allegations of inadequate performance.

Tribunals will hold that some dismissals are automatically unfair and the victims of these sackings do not always have to satisfy the same eligibility criteria for being able to claim unfair dismissal in a tribunal. Three circumstances give rise to unquestionably unfair dismissal: sacking a pregnant woman simply because she is pregnant, dismissal for union membership or activity or for refusing to join a union, or dismissal of workers when a business changes hands unless significant technical, economic or organisation changes warranting the dismissal of staff also occur at the same time.

The ACAS Code

Without doubt the most important guidelines on dismissal procedures are contained in the ACAS Code of Practice entitled *Disciplinary and other Procedures in Employment*, (HMSO, 1986). Failure to observe the Code does not render the firm liable to legal proceedings, nor does it make a dismissal automatically unfair, but the Code is admissible in evidence before courts and tribunals and if any of the Code's provisions appear to a court to be relevant for deciding any question arising from the proceedings then it will be 'taken into account in determining that question' (EPCA 1978, s 6(11)). A lawyer or personnel consultant should have a detailed knowledge of this Code and its proper interpretation. if he or she does not then something is very wrong.

The Code offers advice on how rules should be drafted, who should be authorised to dismiss employees, procedures for conducting disciplinary interviews, how to issue formal warnings, appeal procedures, and so on.

The law relating to industrial relations

There are laws on strike ballots, picketing, sympathy strikes, closed shops, secondary actions and 'going slow'. Note that it is legally 'fair' to dismiss employees who go on strike, provided *all* strikers are sacked and not just some of them. (Unless the workers picked out for dismissal have committed some special misdemeanour, eg, violence on picket lines.) Consult ACAS for advice on these matters. Otherwise you will need specialist legal help.

Further legal complexities

It is unlawful to discriminate unfairly with respect to race or sex in employment matters. Equal opportunities legislation covers job advertisments and recruitment, terms and conditions of employment, appraisal and the provision of access to training or promotion opportunities. However, discrimination is allowed where membership of a particular sex or ethnic group is a 'genuine occupational qualification' for the job (chinese waiters in chinese restaurants for example), and further exemptions exist – employment in religious organisations that operate a sex bar for instance. Responsibility for seeking to eliminate unfair discrimination in Britain lies with the Equal Opportunities Commission and the Commission for Racial Equality, both of which issue detailed Codes of Practice and offer substantial help and guidance to employers in these respects.

Another problematic issue is the entitlement of pregnant employees who have completed more than two years' continuous service to paid maternity leave and to full reinstatement after the child is born. All pregnant employees must be given paid time off to attend antenatal appointments, regardless of length of service. Details (which are complex) are available from job centres, Citizens' Advice Bureau and from ACAS.

Job evaluation

Job evaluation concerns the appraisal of the relative values of jobs compared to other jobs undertaken within the organisation, focusing on the *characteristics* of each job rather than on the personal attributes of the occupants of specific positions. Its purposes are firstly to establish a hierarchy of graded posts according to their objective worth to the business (so that individual occupants of these posts may be fairly rewarded), secondly to remove pay anomalies and petty differentials, and thirdly to reduce the number of separate grades of pay.

The law on job evaluation is extremely complicated at the present time. This is the result of the 1983 amendments to the Equal Pay Act whereby today any person can claim equal pay relative to a member of the opposite sex employed by the same firm who does work of 'equal value' as determined by a 'proper' job evaluation. The legislation was designed to enable women who perform jobs not usually done by men (typists, office cleaners, etc) to claim fair rewards for their contributions. Hence, a woman need not identify a man who is doing identical work for the firm on higher wages, she just has to demonstrate that her job is *worth* the same in terms of its demands. Such demands might relate to effort, skill, responsibility, working conditions or decision taking capacities required for effective performance. The comparability of these demands with those embodied in a job done by a member of the opposite sex will be established by a formal job evaluation study. The legislation insists that job evaluations be done using 'analytical' methods, ie, all relevant factors must be considered and weighted objectively according to their importance in a job, normally using a points system. Common criteria equally applicable to all employees should be applied and wages related directly to each job's contribution.*

Redundancy and human resource (manpower) planning

Implementing redundancies might require the assistance of a public relations consultant (see Chapter 10), and important legal problems may be involved. Note that management consultancies which advertise 'Management of Change' as one of their specialisations are usually expert in redundancy planning and procedures.

What redundancy is

A worker is 'redundant' when the firm no longer requires work of the type done by that employee. Thus it is the worker's *job* that becomes redundant and not the particular worker. To implement redundancies a statutory procedure must be followed and some financial compensation (details of current rates are available from job centres or ACAS) offered to workers with more than two years' continuous service with the company. Firms are obliged to warn relevant trade unions of impending redundancies and to consult with them before discarding staff. The company *must* seek alternative work for those involved, and workers under notice are legally entitled to paid time off to look for other jobs. Criteria used in selecting individuals for redundancy (eg, length of service, age, capability, past conduct, qualifications, etc) have to be 'objective' and fair. The firm must disclose its reasons for declaring workers redundant and is expected to stop recruitment, ban overtime and to seek volunteers for redundancy prior to laying people off.

---

*For a comprehensive discussion of these issues see chapter 7 of my book, *Managing People* (Kogan Page, 1989).

Human resource planning
This can help avoid redundancies. It concerns the comparison of existing labour resources with forecast demand and the scheduling of activities for training and redeploying employees. Large companies will prepare their own human resources plans. Smaller firms may seek the services of a consultant.

In the latter case, the consultant will first want to prepare a 'skills inventory' of all the client's employees, listing their qualifications, experiences, and *everything* they can do. This necessarily means asking staff for personal details not strictly relevant to their present jobs (why, for example, should an accounts clerk report whether he or she can speak a second language) and the exercise may thus be resented. However, resentments quickly disappear when employees realise that the purpose of the questions is to avoid their possible redundancy by making it possible to find them alternative work.

Next, the consultant will analyse the firm's labour turnover and examine the consequences of high turnover within certain grades or categories of staff. The labour force will be classified according to age, type of work, length of service, educational and skill levels and potential for promotion. Then, potential labour shortfalls and/or surpluses are predicted and measures suggested for how they might be overcome, eg, via natural wastage, early retirement, retraining, reallocation of duties, etc.

High labour turnover is undesirable for several reasons: recruitment and training costs increase, new entrants are relatively unproductive during the early stages of their service, and additional demands are placed on the remaining staff. Your consultant's report should indicate:

- whether high turnover is concentrated in particular groups (eg, younger people or workers doing certain kinds of job);
- the extent to which employees with long periods of service are leaving the firm;
- the percentages of the employees who started with your firm on a certain date who are still with the firm six months later, 12 months later, 18 months later, two years, etc.

High turnover can indicate serious deficiencies in personnel policies, and a major audit of these should follow a large increase in the turn-over rate. This audit should consider whether pay, holiday entitlement, working hours, and other conditions are comparable with those of competitors, whether the work is overspecialised and hence excessively monotonous, and whether promotion opportunities exist. Recruitment and induction methods might be faulty. The wrong people may have been selected for jobs and/or inadequate information conveyed during induction courses. Grievances arising from routine working practices might have remained unresolved for long periods for want of an efficient grievance procedure.

Note, however, that zero labour turnover rates can also indicate problems: *some* turnover is to be expected in any large organisation. Zero turnover could mean that wages are far too high in the firm in question or that not enough work is expected.

Sources of information

Advisory, Conciliation and Arbitration Service (ACAS)
11–12 St James' Square
London SW1Y 4LA
01-214 6000

British Psychological Society
48 Princess Road East
Leicester LE1 7DR
0533 549568

Commission for Racial Equality
Elliot House
10–12 Allington Street
London SW1E 5EH
01-828 7022

Equal Opportunities Commission
Overseas House
Quay Street
Manchester M3 3HN
061-833 9244

The Industrial Society
Peter Runge House
3 Carlton House Terrace
London SW1Y 5DG
01-839 4300

Institute of Personnel Management
IPM House
Camp Road
London SW19 4UW
01-946 9100

Institute of Training and Development
Marlow House
Institute Road
Marlow
Bucks SL7 1BN
0628 890123

Kogan Page Ltd
120 Pentonville Road
London N1 9JN
01-278 0433

The Law Society
113 Chancery Lane
London WC2A 1PL
01-242 1222

***Training Officer* magazine**
Marylebone Press Ltd
Lloyds House
18 Lloyd Street
Manchester M2 5WA
061-832 6541

***Transition* magazine**
British Association for Commercial and Industrial Education (BACIE)
Personnel Publications Ltd
1 Hills Place
London W1R 1AG
01-734 1773

Chapter 10

Marketing Consultants

Introduction — What a marketing consultant will do — The marketing audit — Briefing and evaluating a marketing consultant — Sales promotion consultants — Direct marketing consultants — Public relations consultants — PR methods — Marketing research consultants — Advertising agencies — Sources of information

After reading this chapter you should:

- appreciate the differences between various types of marketing consultancy and be aware of the services that each type of consultant can provide;
- understand how a marketing research consultant will analyse markets and the behaviour of customers;
- be able to specify objectives for a marketing consultancy exercise;
- have an outline knowledge of the roles and major activities of advertising and public relations agencies; and
- know what to expect in a marketing consultant's report and be able to appraise the work of a marketing consultant.

Introduction

Marketing is more than just 'selling', though increases in sales are obviously the ultimate aim. Rather, marketing is a collection of activities, including:

- choice of suitable selling prices for your products;
- merchandising (eg, arranging special displays and/or selecting the best shelf locations for various products in retail outlets);
- sales promotions (coupons, competitions, money-off offers, etc);
- advertising and public relations;
- marketing research; and
- making the best use of sales representatives.

Marketing people frequently refer to the *marketing concept* when discussing policies for producing and promoting goods. This is simply the idea (i) that firms should offer for sale the goods and services that consumers actually want to buy (and thus should conduct extensive research to establish customer requirements) and

(ii) that marketing staff should be fully integrated into all aspects of the work of the firm – including the choice of new products, their design, quality, and method of production.

Sometimes, firms manufacture goods that are easy to make rather than the products really wanted by customers. The resulting output might be technically excellent, but not necessarily the output that customers wish to buy!

Why engage a marketing consultant?

An external consultant can adopt a birds' eye view of your marketing strategy and suggest the very best combination of marketing activities (referred to as the *marketing mix*) for your company. Consultants are particularly useful for:

- convincing production staff of the need for product diversification and modification in order to satisfy consumer demand;
- steering research expenditures away from excessive research into manufacturing and process development and towards research into the feasibility of producing the goods that are necessary to serve lucrative new market segments;
- sidestepping pitfalls created by unexpected actions on the part of competitors;
- persuading accountants and other senior non-marketing managers of the long-term cost-effectiveness of expenditures on intangible marketing activities such as corporate identity projects, public relations, or the design of creative new advertising messages; and
- incorporating marketing issues into corporate plans.

Marketing qualifications

Few marketing consultants possess academic marketing qualifications since, alas, few UK public sector higher education establishments recognise marketing as a *bona fide* subject. However, most general business degrees and diplomas and all MBA programmes include introductory courses in marketing. Also the Communication, Advertising and Marketing (CAM) Foundation and the Chartered Institute of Marketing (CIM) offer examinations leading to diplomas in the marketing field. Consultants possessing these qualification will put the letters 'Dip. CAM' or MCIM (Dip.) after their names. The Institute of Marketing is the contractor for the marketing component of the DTI Enterprise Initiative and as such will provide you with lists of marketing consultants registered under the scheme.

Many top class creative marketing people possess an art college qualification, having learned about printing, design, graphics, etc. Unfortunately, few British art schools teach marketing or business administration.

What a marketing consultant will do

A general marketing consultant (specialists such as public relations or direct marketing consultants are discussed later in this chapter) will:

- objectively assess the competitive environment in which your firm operates;
- identify who your customers are, where they are located and what they really want from your output (see also the section on 'market research' below); and
- conduct a comprehensive audit of all the firm's marketing activities.

The marketing audit

This is a comprehensive review of the effectiveness of the firm's marketing methods. It has two parts: an analysis of the company's internal marketing situation, and an appraisal of the external environments within which the business exists. Deficiencies in current marketing methods should be revealed; the potentials of various markets identified, and the profitabilities of various products and market segments assessed. Internal analyses should cover the following.

Effectiveness of the sales force.
Sometimes a small percentage of the sales force is responsible for a large percentage of total sales. If this is the case, why does it occur? Are variations attributable to, say, transport problems in certain areas, or are they due to differences in sales technique. How can the methods of successful salespeople be passed on to others?

The product range.
Is rationalisation of products feasible or desirable? Are the sales staff knowledgeable about the firm's output? Should new products be introduced or current models modified for various market segments?

Communications.
Here the consultant will examine the efficiency of your advertising,

your corporate image, public relations, packaging, and sales promotion methods. He or she will (or should):

- define target audiences for your advertising messages and state the characteristics and whereabouts of these;
- specify the customer responses that the firm's advertisments and corporate image need to evoke; and
- compare advertising requirements to current advertising activities.

The external audit must analyse the competition: its strengths and weaknesses, expected behaviour, and its capacities to act. What is the firm's market share? (Measuring this might not be easy, and market share is large or small depending on how you define the market.) Have competitors recently taken any of your large customers and if so why? What can be learned from competitors' marketing methods?

Distribution systems must be examined, including the usefulness of intermediaries and all the costs and benefits that a change of outlets or distributors might involve.

Analysing markets

A major function of the external review is the systematic analysis of markets. Which market segments are expanding and which are in decline? Have consumer tastes altered? Are future changes in consumer tastes likely to occur?

The term 'market segmentation' describes the breaking down of a market into self-contained and relatively homogeneous sub-groups of consumers, each with its own special requirements and characteristics. Products and advertising messages can then be altered to make them appeal to particular segments.

Markets may be segmented with respect to consumers' locations, ages, incomes, social class, or other demographic variables; or according to consumer lifestyles, attitudes, interests and opinions as they effect purchasing behaviour. It does seem that many consumers buy goods that fit-in with a chosen lifestyle (healthy, sophisticated, rugged, etc) and with their perceptions of what they *ought* to purchase in order to pursue that lifestyle. Once the lifestyle to which potential consumers aspire is identified, advertising messages can be modified in appropriate ways. Make sure that the segments your consultant identifies are:

- cost effective in that they can be reached without enormous additional advertising expenditures;
- large enough to be worthwhile; and

Research Economics Marketing
Information Technology

Our **REMIT** *is to offer consultancy
and reports based on a combination
of original thought and established
analytical techniques.*

REMIT'S *consultancy staff offer
experience in pharmaceuticals,
healthcare, trade development,
defence, competition, information
technology, consumer durables,
food/beverages.*

————◁●▷————

For more information telephone
Janice Haigh on 01-837 5498
or by facsimile on 01-833 5716

R E M I T
C O N S U L T A N T S
L I M I T E D

4 2 2   S t   J o h n   S t r e e t
L o n d o n   E C 1 V   4 N J

- sufficiently homogeneous in terms of customer characteristics and tastes to justify modifications in products and/or advertising messages.

Briefing and evaluating a marketing consultant

Appraisal of a marketing consultant's contributions is perhaps easier than for other types of consultant because the final aim of his or her activities is obviously to increase market shares and/or profitable sales. Even intangible marketing activities such as public relations and corporate imaging have increases in sales revenues as their long-term objective.

Often, firms approach marketing consultants when something has gone wrong (loss of important customers, bad publicity, or a dramatic decline in market share for example), or if they simply *feel* that their marketing efforts are not as effective as they might be (eg, in comparison with leading competitors). Specify your objectives clearly and at length. State the sources of your problems as you perceive them (for example, a competitor's price cut, failure to develop new products, inadequate advertising) and explain *exactly* what you expect from the consultant. In particular, decide in advance whether you want:

- an entire marketing strategy, including advice on the goods to

produce and which markets to enter (see Chapter 3); or
- help with the application of a particular marketing technique; PR, research, sales training, direct marketing, new product testing and introduction and so on; or
- information about your markets and competitive position (eg, how consumers see your firm and its output, market opportunities, strength of competition).

Make the point that you are looking for *measurable* improvements in profitable sales following implementation of the consultant's recommendations, and that if the consultant believes these are not possible then he or she should say so (with reasons) at the beginning of the report. Payment by results is perhaps more appropriate for marketing consultants than for others (although few are willing to accept this). Performance related payment encourages consultants not to overstate the value of their possible contributions and to report honestly when a firm's market situation is hopeless.

Sales promotion consultants

Consultants are available to assist with all aspects of sales promotion: couponing, design of competitions, distribution of free samples, estimating response rates, etc. A list of SP consultants is available from the Institute of Sales Promotion, which has a Code of Practice and insists that its members satisfy certain standards and behave in certain ways. Also you can find sales promotions consultants listed in *Yellow Pages*, and through advertisements placed in 'direct marketing' magazines (see below).

Typically, SP consultants implement as well as suggest promotional strategies; so you can ask to see examples of previous work prior to making your choice. To brief an SP consultant you need to provide full details of the characteristics of your brands, package sizes, markets to be covered, product distribution system (including the whereabouts and calibre of retail outlets) and how much you are willing to spend. You also need to state your objectives, which might include:

- stimulation of impulse purchasing;
- encouraging customer loyalty;
- attracting customers to the firm's premises;
- penetration of new markets; or
- improving the rate at which customers repeat their purchases etc.

The consultant will devise a set of promotional techniques to achieve the specified aims (free samples to enter new markets, reduced price offers to encourage repeat purchase, money-off coupons to attract customers to the premises, etc). He or she will estimate redemption rates, suggest an appropriate number of customer proofs of purchase, look after the legal aspects of the promotion (competitions are especially complicated in this regard) and may arrange for the production of the coupons and/or other promotional literature necessary.

Direct marketing consultants

Direct marketing covers direct mail, telephone selling, catalogues, and 'off-the page' selling *via* cutouts in newspaper and magazine advertisements.

Who are direct marketeers?

Direct marketing (DM) consultancy is a fast growing and highly competitive line of work, offering fast returns to new entrants while carrying a high degree of risk. This is because direct marketing is *fully* accountable; clients immediately know whether a direct marketing campaign has succeeded or failed so that consultants' advice and activities can be immediately evaluated. The industry itself distinguishes between 'suppliers' and 'consultants'. The latter are concerned with:

- planning and testing direct marketing programmes;
- suggesting new administrative arrangements to deal with the increased volume of enquiries and/or orders that a campaign will generate;
- integrating DM into the client's total marketing strategy;
- estimating the costs of DM exercises;
- drafting profiles of possible DM customers (lifestyle, reading habits, propensity to purchase using mail order, etc);
- training the clients' staff in DM methods; and
- evaluating alternative approaches to direct marketing (maildrops versus off-the-page advertisments for example).

'Suppliers' conversely, consist of telemarketing agencies, fulfilment houses, computer bureaux, list brokers and mailing agencies. Note that suppliers will also provide advice and general DM consultancy services whenever required.

Fulfilment houses

These are businesses that handle the responses to maildrops and direct mail advertisments, receiving the orders from customers and despatching the goods. On the consultancy side, fulfilment houses will advise on probable response rates (and hence the amount of stock of the 'offered item' to hold) and the best way to organise the offer. The characteristics of a good fulfilment house are that it despatches goods accurately, quickly, and uses packaging that minimises breakages and misdirected mail. Make sure your chosen fulfilment house has insurance covering the items it handles on your behalf because, legally, you are still the owner of these goods. And determine who is to be responsible for losses incurred through pilfering at various stages in the distribution chain.

Most fulfilment houses charge a basic fee, plus warehousing costs computed at so much per cubic foot. The costs of refunds to customers, (eg, because of customer dissatisfaction with the offer item) and goods lost in transit are normally borne by the client firm. There may or may not be a further administration charge to cover secretarial and other clerical expenses – if there is it will be calculated on an hourly basis depending on the time and effort involved.

Computer Bureaux
A DM computer bureau will enter target customer names and addresses onto a database, constantly update and correct the entries, cross-tabulate names and addresses according to various characteristics and print the results. Bureaux are used to enable client firms to avoid filling up their own computer systems with the typically huge data files that are needed for effective DM campaigns.

Mailing agencies
Mailing agencies send out DM letters and other sales promotions literature. They should be evaluated against their price, speed of service, and capacity to handle the volume of literature involved.

Telemarketing
A telemarketing agency will prepare lists of telephone numbers of people likely to buy the product, and then make the calls. In selecting/appraising a telemarketing agency, ask yourself whether it:

- simply makes and receives calls to and from preselected target customers or whether it provides additional creative advice and assistance (ideas for entering new market segments, for example);
- carefully measures the percentage response to a campaign;
- has the capacity to handle the volume of calls anticipated; and
- will provide feedback on customers' comments about the campaign.

Preparation of mailing lists
Names and addresses of potential DM customers are available from telephone and business information directories, from the company's own customer records, or by purchase from list broking firms. Lists must be up-to-date, accurate and carefully targeted. The ACORN survey (see below) can be extremely useful in these respects. Otherwise, you can purchase lists of, for example:

- readers of certain subscription magazines;
- members of certain clubs and organisations (the Automobile Association or various animal welfare charities for instance);
- owners of particular domestic appliances, or heavy purchasers of expensive luxury consumer items; and
- rich and poor people in various age groups.

In selecting a list broker you must make sure that all names and addresses are genuine, and that it fully understands your specific DM needs. Examine the list broker's experience of your industry, its major clients (which you can ask for references) and any specialist lists it offers that cannot be obtained elsewhere.

Help with writing sales letters
DM consultants or advertising agents will draft DM sales letters on your behalf. This is a specialist field and specific copywriting skills are required. The letter must be short, convincing and attractively presented; condensing the maximum amount of information into a limited space. Consultancies that write sales literature might also print it, put it into envelopes, mail the letters and collect the replies. To evaluate the quality of a consultant's contributions in this respect ask yourself the following questions.

- Are recommended sales messages specifically related to the needs of target audiences?
- Has a mechanism for evaluating the effectiveness of a specific maildrop been suggested?
- Is the manner in which the customer is supposed to respond to the message (filling in an order form, making a telephone call, visiting a showroom, etc) entirely clear?

Where to find a direct marketing consultant
The DM trade association is the *British Direct Marketing Association* (BDMA), which issues lists of its members to prospective clients. You can also look under the headings 'Direct mail' and 'Circular and sample distributors' in your local *Yellow Pages*, where you will normally find very many businesses (including consultants)

engaged in this work. Numerous advertisments by DM consultants and agencies appear in the magazines *Direct Response* and *Direct Marketing World*.

Decide in advance what exactly you want your consultant/agent to do. Are you looking for creative advice on DM strategy, or for technical assistance such as the organisation of databases containing consumer names and addresses, or help with packing and mailing the product?

Public relations consultants

Help with public relations (PR) is available from three sources: specialist PR consultancies, the PR departments of the big advertising agencies, or from a 'marketing communications' consultancy firm.

What PR consultants do

PR concerns the creation and maintenance of goodwill. But goodwill from certain 'audiences' (consumers or governments for instance) is more important than from others eg, competing firms). Hence a PR consultant will help you (i) define the various 'publics' you need to influence, (ii) define the messages to which these publics will most favourably respond, and (iii) decide how best to reach target groups. This may involve research into how your firm, its operations and products, are perceived by outsiders and into the media seen most often by the firm's leading publics (eg, which newspapers are read by the people you most need to influence). Then you have to define your PR objectives, which might be to:

- establish a brand image;
- create awareness among the general public of the existence of the firm;
- overcome prejudice against use of the product (religious or cultural prejudices for example);
- increase the number of enquiries;
- improve the ratio of enquiries to sales;
- reduce selling costs, especially the costs of distribution and/or of using salespeople 'in the field'; or
- achieve a higher profile in the local press and on local television.

Who are PR consultants?

Many of today's successful PR consultancies began either through the defection of specialist PR staff from large advertising agencies or from firms established by practising journalists who used their writing and influencing skills and intimate knowledge of the media for PR purposes. All the major advertising agencies continue to maintain substantial PR departments.

The large PR firms are 'full-service' and undertake the complete range of PR functions: media relations; copywriting, events, political lobbying, news releases, etc. Increasingly, consultancies are involved with direct implementation of suggested programmes, including the physical printing of brochures, distribution of literature, research, providing staff on short term secondment to client firms, and so on. Note that you need not use the same consultancy for all your PR activities; you can shop around and use different firms for different aspects of your PR work.

PR people tend to have journalistic, art college or media studies certificates and diplomas rather than public relations qualifications *per se*, reflecting the origins of the function.

Most PR businesses are limited companies, but without extensive outside shareholdings: the directors will usually be the owners of the firm. Typically you will deal with an 'account director' with whom you agree a PR strategy and budget. This individual then buys-in appropriate production services and determines – subject to your approval – suitable publicity and events for achieving the agreed objectives.

Marketing communications consultants
These see PR as part of the wider marketing communications field (which includes package design, display of products, merchandising etc) and thus offer an integrated package of communications activities, including:

- *media relations* – press releases, seminars, briefing sessions for journalists;
- *preparation of in-house leaflets, pamphlets, and other copy*, and the illustration and printing of such literature;
- *obtaining publicity* through devising newsworthy publicity stunts, competitions, arranging a factory tour for Royalty etc.
- *communications audits*, including checking the adequacy of existing investor and employee relationships (see below) and suggesting improvements in these;
- *media training* – how to be interviewed on radio and television, how to answer journalists' questions;
- *speech writing* for company executives who have to make important presentations to external audiences.

Why use a PR consultant?

Typical problems requiring the assistance of a PR consultant include:

- product positioning (see Chapter 3);
- the need to implement extensive labour redundancies while avoiding the reputation of being a 'bad employer';
- threats of parliamentary legislation or the imposition of local authority rules that will damage the business, thus requiring intensive lobbying of politicians in order to have the proposed legislation scrapped (some PR consultants specialise in this work, employing practising politicians who are expert in parliamentary and other legislative processes and who know therefore how to prevent or delay laws being passed and how to prevent effective implementation of new laws even after their parliamentary or local authority approval); or
- convincing shareholders to accept the company board of directors' advice to resist a takeover attempt.

The latter is an example of 'investor relations', which involves the attractive presentation of company reports and annual accounts to shareholders in order to convince them the company is well managed and financially sound. The consultant will write the document and arrange for it to be printed using appealing typefaces, a glossy multi-coloured cover, photographs, line-drawings, diagrams and other illustrations. Large American companies are currently experimenting with similar approaches to 'employee relations' aimed at motivating workers in firms. This is sure to become a future PR growth area in the UK.

Exhibition planning and organisation

Exhibitions are an important aspect of PR and much thought and effort is necessary to choose which exhibitions to attend and in designing and managing exhibition stands. The problems are numerous. If you engage a consultancy to advise you about exhibitions ask how it will deal with the following matters.

- Most consumers visit exhibitions to browse rather than to buy. How do you obtain the names and addresses of those callers on your stand who, subject to a follow-up letter or telephone call, are actually likely to purchase your products? And how can you identify important people who influence major buying decisions within their companies?
- Gimmicks may be highly effective in attracting visitors to your

stand, but you could attract the wrong people. An audience may be greatly impressed by the music, dancing, demonstration or whatever it is that you provide; yet not be remotely interested in your products.

- What criteria will be used to determine how big a display to mount at any given exhibition?
- Having a large and attractive stand at an exhibition could induce your competitors to do the same, thereby wiping out the benefits of exhibiting.
- How can the employees who staff your stand at an exhibition be prevented from treating the exercise as a holiday – paying more attention to the social aspects of their involvement with the exhibition than to finding customers? What specific targets can the staff be given and how can the attainment of targets be measured?
- How is exhibiting to be dovetailed into the company's general marketing plans? What marketing objectives does exhibiting seek to achieve?
- What is known in advance about the numbers and characteristics of the people who will visit the exhibition, their lengths of stay, needs and buying habits?
- Is the proposed stand well located *vis-à-vis* the layout and illumination of the exhibition centre and the anticipated traffic flow?

Certain consultants specialise in exhibition stand planning and administration. An excellent source of names and addresses of exhibition stand organisers is *The White Book* (1988), published by Birdhurst Ltd., which has a large section entitled 'The Conference and Exhibition Industry' carrying dozens of listings. Otherwise, you can find them by contacting exhibition organisers, the British Institute of Management, the Design Council (see Chapter 11), the Institute of Marketing, the Institute of Sales Promotion or the Advertising Association. Such consultants occasionally advertise in the BIM journal *Management Today* and in Design magazine. Look also in *Yellow Pages* under the headings 'Conference/exhibition facilities and services', 'Exhibition stand contractors' and 'Exhibition and show organisers'. A consultant will advise you on such matters as:

- whether to undertake pre-exhibition promotions (eg, maildrops to people likely to visit the exhibition);
- visual presentation of the stand; colour scheme, headlines, staff uniforms etc;
- the best ratio of staff to stand space;
- style and quantity of leaflets, brochures and other literature required;

- how to evaluate the effectiveness of the firm's exhibiting efforts (eg, how to measure the sales resulting from stand enquiries); and
- budgetary control over exhibition activities: stand erection and removal (including electrics and water where appropriate), cleaning, insurance, printing of leaflets, hotel reservations for staff, hire of furniture, etc.

Choosing a PR consultant

The questions you should ask when selecting a PR consultant are as follows. See also the criteria suggested for choosing an advertising agent in a later section.

- Does the consultant have a formal procedure for controlling the quality of the PR work done for your firm? If not, why not, and if so, was this properly explained?
- How many of the consultancy's employees will be actively engaged on the account and what are their roles and status?
- How frequently will progress towards achieving agreed objectives be reviewed?
- What proportion of the consultant's fee is attributable to intellectual input rather than to operating costs? If the proportion exceeds 15 per cent, how does the consultant justify this?
- Does the consultancy have access to European PR consultancies capable of carrying your European work following 1992?
- Does the consultant offer a *forward media monitoring service* whereby it routinely provides its clients with details of forthcoming radio and television programmes and newspaper articles that will feature topics of interest to clients' customers?
- Has the consultant suggested means by which the cost-effectiveness of PR expenditures may be evaluated?

Briefing a PR consultant

First you need to be clear about your PR objectives, what *exactly* do you want to achieve through PR? Much money can be wasted on superficially attractive PR activities – sponsorship, exhibitions corporate identity programmes – which cannot be evaluated in concrete terms. Hence you should specify detailed targets; which might include:

- creating favourable awareness of the business among a certain group of opinion makers (evidenced by subsequent survey data confirming a change of opinion with this group);
- increasing shareholders' satisfaction with the management of the company;

- influencing suppliers;
- improving the firm's image in the local community;
- motivating employees by bonding them to the firm; or
- getting a local authority to change its mind about refusing planning permission for an extension to the company's premises.

PR methods

The consultant will suggest a variety of techniques for putting your message across; sponsorship, newsletters and press releases, badging (T-shirts, balloons, car stickers, etc), events (open days, publicity, stunts, visits by celebrities, etc), competitions, and so on. Essentially you are paying for creativity, though PR consultants are increasingly interested in arranging the implementation of suggested schemes; actually buying, producing and distributing promotional materials (such as balloons or car stickers).

Dealing with adverse publicity

Bad publicity can ruin a business. Suppose your firm is attacked in the local press. A PR consultant might attempt to:

- broaden the issue by pointing out that other organisations have done or are doing the same thing as your company so that it is unfair for any one firm to be singled out;
- widely publicise the company's attempts to overcome the problem;
- present convincing counter-arguments and/or discredit those launching the attack.

Corporate imaging

A firm's image, ie, the mental impression it projects to outsiders is created by the identity it establishes with its letterheads, logos, the architecture of its premises, the tone of receipt of telephone calls, etc. PR consultants are experts at devising congruent and favourable images (of quality, innovation, dynamism, reliability and other desirable attributes) for client firms.

Like it or not, your business has several 'audiences' – customers, bank managers, suppliers, local authority trading standards officers, community neighbours, employees – that you need to impress and which will respond (albeit unconsciously) to the aura of the firm. The outward disposition your business projects will create in outsiders thoughts about and feelings towards the firm that will encourage them to behave positively or negatively when dealing with the company, without their necessarily being aware of why this is so.

Great care is needed when selecting an image, because techniques for projecting one type of corporate personality might not be appropriate for projecting others, and once established an image may be extremely difficult to change. The first important decision is which of the firm's potential activities to emphasise and which to ignore when devising corporate identity messages, since the business name, letterheads and other promotional material cannot possibly refer to all the firm's possible operations and market opportunities. For example, a small building firm whose target customers (householders) wish to replace some guttering or have other relatively minor repairs completed will be put off approaching this firm if it has created for itself an image of being concerned mostly with large scale house extensions or major shopfitting.

A business that is technically excellent can fail through having the wrong image. *Impressions* of ability can be as important for winning orders as actual competence to produce and deliver goods.

Many PR firms operate press cutting services in order to monitor clients' images as they appear in the trade and other press. Note, however, that although retaining a consultancy just to inform you what your corporate image is may flatter your self-esteem, it is unlikely to be cost effective in the longer term. Rather you should aim constantly to *improve* your image in ways that will feed back to improved company performance.

Crisis (disaster) consultancy

During 1988 and 1989, a series of major transport and other disasters occurred in Britain involving heavy loss of life. Identifying a new market opportunity for their services, some PR firms have responded to these events by offering a complete and self-contained media relations package for use immediately following a disaster involving a client firm. The client pays an annual retainer (plus the consultancy's expenses in the unhappy event of a disaster actually taking place) and in return is able to 'turn over' to the PR firm all the public relations attached to the tragedy.

Thus, consultancy staff will race to the scene of the disaster the instant that news of it is released and it is they, and not the client firm's employees who brief journalists, conduct news conferences, give interviews to local and national television, issue press releases, etc, avoiding at all times any statement implying the client's negligence or responsibility for the accident and presenting the company's behaviour – especially its relief efforts and offers of compensation – in the most favourable light.

Marketing research consultants

Market research (MR) is the analysis of the sizes, structures and locations of markets: marketing research is research into any and all aspects of marketing (advertising recall, effectiveness of corporate imaging exercises, finding the best shelf location for a particular product, etc). Typical issues requiring the attention of a marketing research consultant are:

- deciding whether expenditures on a certain type of advertising have been worthwhile;
- discovering the characteristics of users of the product (average age, sex, income level, type of residence, newspaper reading habits, etc);
- assessing how much to spend on attractive (but functionally non-essential) packaging;
- determining whether sales would fall significantly following a big increase in selling prices;
- finding out the sorts of new product that consumers really want to buy and ascertaining whether the firm's existing products satisfy consumer requirements;
- measuring the distribution of sales with respect to various retail outlets and discovering why some outlets sell more than others;
- discovering the basic motivations that cause consumers to buy the firm's products.

Why use a marketing research consultant

Effective MR enables the firm to produce goods that consumers actually want to buy, rather than having to sell goods which circumstantially the firm happened to produce. The precise identification of consumer needs and wants (the two might not be coincidental) and the location of the most lucrative market segments are difficult activities requiring specialised competencies. Marketing researchers use a variety of statistical and survey techniques which you might not possess the time, knowledge or inclination to learn about and copy.

In deciding whether to engage an external consultant rather than doing research in-house ask yourself the following questions.

- How much data on the issue which is causing you concern is available within the company or from easily accessible published sources?
- How risky is the decision you will have to make?
- How serious will be the consequences of a bad decision?
- How urgently and in what detail is the information needed?

What a marketing research consultant will do
The consultant will determine (i) what data is required to achieve research objectives (ii) the nature of the data (quantitative or qualitative), and (iii) a strategy for obtaining the information: sample surveys, observations, analysis of published data, interviews and so on. Questionnaires will be drafted and mailing lists and lists of telephone numbers of potential telephone interviewees compiled. A panel of representative consumers of your product might be assembled for interrogation.

MR consultants often use the services of one or more of the national research organisations such as the Television Audience Research Bureau, various government agencies attached to the offices of the national census, the *Family Expenditure Survey Annual Reports* (Department of Employment) and the major opinion pollsters, eg, GALLUP or the MORI poll. An important source of information for market research firms is the government financed agency, CACI. This produces 'ACORN' (which is the acronym for an ongoing research project called 'A Classification of Residential Neighbourhoods'). ACORN is a precise and detailed categorisation of UK consumers according to the type of residential area in which they live. CACI itself is an offshoot of the government population census. It provides a range of consultancy services, notably in the fields of demographic market segmentation and the location of retail outlets. It is able to link consumer buying habits, lifestyles, income levels, housing and employment characteristics and geographical location.

Where to find marketing research consultants
The large advertising agencies (see below) have MR departments; while general marketing consultants usually have contacts who specialise in the marketing research field. You will find MR firms listed in *Yellow Pages* under the headings 'Market research and analysis', 'Information services' and 'Marketing and advertising consultants'.

Television companies conduct extensive marketing research on (i) consumer buying habits, (ii) the socio-economic composition of their respective regions and (iii) what type of people watch certain programmes and/or watch television at certain times of the day. Some of this information (which can be extremely detailed) is free, some is available only to firms paying an annual subscription. Major *ad hoc* research projects must, of course, be directly commissioned and paid for separately by a lump sum fee. Details are available from the Independent Broadcasting Authority.

Otherwise the Market Research Society is probably the best

contact in the first place. This is a professional body for those engaged in MR and publishes the *International Directory of Market Research Organisations*, which is a listing of all the major survey companies and other information gathering institutions.

Briefing a marketing research consultant
Define precisely all the extra things you want to know by the end of the exercise. This means pinpointing what you do *not* know about your markets. Ask yourself honestly whether you know:

- exactly *which* type of person buys your products;
- *when* and *where* customers buy the products;
- the mood of consumers at the moment of purchase;
- consumer buying habits and lifestyles;
- the images and messages your customers find most appealing;
- why consumers purchase your products ˙and not those of competing firms; and
- how customers learn about your goods.

A preliminary investigation might be necessary just to establish the extent of your ignorance about these matters.

Tell the consultant what *you* believe to be the data required to solve the problem under investigation, and the degree of accuracy that you expect in his or her report. Offer as much assistance in assembling in-house data as you are able to provide.

The research consultant's report
Expect to see plenty of charts, graphs and diagrams in the consultant's final report. These clarify issues and neatly summarise large amounts of complex information. The report should have an introduction stating the research methods adopted and explaining their relevance to the objectives of the exercise. Key characteristics of the samples used should be described and the sensitivity of the results quoted to changes in the composition of the samples must be mentioned. The report will have conclusions, but do not anticipate *recommendations* in a marketing research consultant's report: the purpose of MR is to discover and interpret facts rather than to suggest actions; if you want policy recommendations you must usually ask (and pay) for them separately.

Advertising agencies

When asked to define a marketing consultant many people

instinctively think of advertising agents, and it is indeed the case that advertising agencies undertake a wide variety of general marketing consultancy work.

Agencies may be 'full-service', meaning that they cover the full spectrum of advertising duties, or specialist (sometimes referred to as *à-la-carte*) dealing only with a certain aspect of the advertising business: media relations, creativity and production, industrial goods advertising, television commercials, etc.

Media relations
Often, the services of an agency that places your advertisments with newspapers, magazines or television companies are free, due to the fact that the agency is allowed to retain a commission (normally 15 per cent) taken from the money you pay to the media owner. If, for example, your bill for advertising in a certain newspaper is £100,000 you pay this amount to the agency which only passes on £85,000 to the newspaper. If you deal direct with the newspaper you have to pay the full £100,000 because the media only give the discount to agencies. To qualify as a 'recognised' agency with the various media owners' associations (the IBA or Newspaper Publishers' Association for example) the agency must demonstrate that it is creditworthy, well established, soundly managed and possesses a substantial capital base.

Any advertising that attracts a media commission is referred to as 'above the line' advertising. Other advertising – direct mail, public relations, sponsorship, etc – is said to be 'below the line'. All below the line work is paid for through fees (see Chapter 2), rather than commission.

Above the line commissions pay for general strategic advertising advice given by the agency to the client, campaign planning, and the initial rough drafts of advertisements. However, any further work – production of materials, research, actually making commercials, market analysis, etc, must be paid for separately over and above the agency commission.

A survey conducted by the *Keynote Reports* organisation in 1987 revealed that 15 to 20 per cent of client companies were able to persuade their advertising agencies to give them rebates on the 15 per cent (or so) commission the agencies received from the media, so try negotiating this possibility with the agency to which you are considering giving your work, especially if you:

- will not be using the agency's full range of services;
- promise to pay the agency's invoices the day they arrive;
- will be doing some of the administrative work yourself.

Choosing an advertising agency

Biggest is not always best where agencies are concerned (although the large agencies do undertake the greatest proportion of all UK advertising business). Rather, creativity and the ability to understand and help solve *specific* advertising problems (remember that agencies are churning out advertisements week after week for many hundreds – perhaps thousands – of clients, resulting sometimes in work that is stereotyped, dull and lifeless) should be the essential criteria. Nevertheless, large agencies do possess certain advantages, including:

- international connections (they can handle your advertising for any country in the world);
- wide-ranging *marketing* as well as advertising skills, and the ability to provide a fully comprehensive service;
- their employment of top class (and highly paid) creative staff; and
- avoidance of your having to pay for several profit margins through engaging a variety of freelance services (photographers, copywriters, etc).

Media independents

These are agencies which specialise exclusively in planning and buying media space (including television broadcast time) on behalf of clients. Their existence results from the explosion of media opportunities – new television channels, satellite and cable TV, new commercial radio stations, magazines, giveaway newspapers, etc, – and the rapid escalation in media costs that has occurred during recent years. A media independent will find its way through the enormously complex system of media rate cards, special discounts, bulk purchasing possibilities, etc, in order to obtain the best possible price (up to 20 per cent cheaper than is available through conventional agencies, according to some media specialists). Such savings can make it worthwhile to use separate agencies for the firm's creative, media placement, and general marketing work.

A major advantage of the media independent is its ability to aggregate the business of many small clients into a single large contract to be placed with a particular newspaper, magazine, television company or whatever. Substantial bulk quantity discounts can then be obtained.

To brief a media independent you need to define your target audience and what precisely you hope to achieve from your advertising. The agency will then draft a media placement plan to secure maximum coverage of the market and the highest level of impact on target consumers. This involves the critical analysis of:

- which media are best for projecting the creative aspects of your advertisements (colours, designs, logos and so on);
- the time periods needed to book media space; and
- cost per thousand target customers.

You can obtain a list of media independents from the Association of Media Independents.

Creative and production agencies

Such agencies exist to think up new ideas for advertisments and/or to produce finished copy or television commercials. In the case of television advertisments the agent will first produce a 'storyboard' for client approval. This comprises a few hand drawn sketches depicting key scenes in the intended commercial plus sample dialogue. You may or may not wish to be closely involved in the preparation of the storyboard, depending on how precisely you briefed the agency about your needs and how much you know about the relevant procedures.

Where to find advertising agencies

The best source of information about the whereabouts and specialities of advertising agents is perhaps the *Advertisers' Annual,* published by BMP. Volume 1 of this publication has data on over 2500 agencies, plus lists of sales promotion consultants, sponsorship consultants, recruitment advertising agents and PR firms. Moreover, lists of each agency's recent clients and contact telephone numbers are also provided. General marketing consultants and marketing research agencies are listed in volume 2. The same publisher produces *The Creative Handbook* which also provides a comprehensive list of advertising agencies.

Otherwise, lists of the various types of agents are available from the Advertising Association and the Institute of Practitioners in Advertising (though note that only a minority of agencies actually belong to the IPA). The CAM Foundation might also help. Look also in Yellow Pages under 'Advertising agencies'.

Do not be alarmed if your intended agency holds the accounts of competing firms. A good agency with a sound reputation for quality, price and service and possessing extensive contacts in your particular industry will *inevitably* attract clients offering similar products. And the agency's experience in dealing with competitors' accounts might improve the work the agency does for your company. The fact that an agency holds competing accounts can indicate the agency's strengths rather than representing a weakness.

The agency brief
Specify your reasons for advertising. Do you want to penetrate new markets, introduce a new product, retain existing buyers, or what? Different advertising techniques might be necessary for each purpose. The agency will want full details of your output; its selling points – quality, price, etc. – and of what you consider to be your target audience (although the agency itself should help you define this). You must also specify any constraints you wish to impose, eg, no humorous portrayal of the product, no use of sex, technical information requirements, etc.

Your main point of contact with your selected agency will be with an 'account manager' who in turn will liaise with the creative, media relations and production staff who work on your account. You tell the account manager your advertising objective, receive information from that person on how the project is progressing, and meet with him or her periodically to discuss any problems that arise.

Appraising the calibre of an advertising agency
To evaluate the quality of your agent's contributions, ask yourself the following questions.

- Has the agency fully justified its recommendations of specific media in terms of their coverage, market penetrations, memorability of the messages they carry, etc?
- How extensive are the agency's contacts with ancillary services such as photographers' studios, printers and typesetters, exhibition stand designers, direct mail agencies, etc?
- Have all the 'extra' costs for which the firm might be liable been properly explained?
- Has your account been handled by junior agency staff rather than by the senior managers who discussed your requirements with you in the first instance?
- Are the advertisements produced on your behalf truly original or have they been cannibalised from agency stock?
- Were you mislead about the leadtime the agency requires for producing and/or placing advertisements?
- Has the agency sub-contracted aspects of the work on your account (photography for instance) to outside freelancers and then imposed a service charge on the cost of the work? You are paying for two profit markups in this case, and you could be better off independently shopping around for third-party services.
- Is there a high turnover of agency staff employed on your account, resulting in a lower quality of service?
- Does the agency provide regular reports on how it believes the

campaign is proceeding?

- Has the agency applied a quality assurance programme to ensure that the creative quality of the advertisements produced for your firm is constantly maintained?
- Does the agency evaluate the effectiveness of the campaigns it devises as an integral part of its service? If so, how useful are these analyses?
- If a particular advertisement or campaign appears to have been unsuccessful, did the agency conduct an investigation to find out what went wrong – without your having to ask?
- Has the agency requested your permission to use the advertisements it has drafted for your firm as an example of its work to show to potential clients?

Sources of information

Advertisers Annual
British Media Publications
Windsor Court
East Grinstead House
East Grinstead
West Sussex RH19 1XA
0342 26972

Advertising Association
Abford House
15 Wilton Road
London SW1V 1NJ
01-828 2771

**Association of Media
Independents Limited**
123 Dartmouth Park
Avenue Road
London NW5 1JL
01-485 2569

**British Direct Marketing
Association**
1 New Oxford Street
London WC1A 1NQ
01-242 2254

**British Institute of
Management**
Management House

Cottingham Road
Corby
Northants 0536 204222

CACI
59–62 High Holborn
London WC1V 6DX
01-404 0834

CAM Foundation
Abford House
15 Wilton Road
London SW1V 1NJ
01-828 7506

Campaign magazine
Marketing Publications Ltd
22 Lancaster Gate
London W2 3LY
01-402 4200

The Creative Handbook
As for **Advertisers Annual**
above

Design Council
See Chapter 11

Direct Marketing World
magazine
Ferrary Publications
Boundary House
91-93 Charterhouse Street
London EC1M 6HR
01-250 0646

Direct Response magazine
4 Market Place
Hertford
Herts SG14 1EG
0992 501177
(The magazine also publishes the
Direct Marketing Guide, which is
a listing of consultancies and
agencies in the DM field)

**Independent Broadcasting
Authority**
70 Brompton Road
London SW3 1EY
01-584 7011

Institute of Marketing
Moor Hall
Cookham
Berkshire SL6 9QH
06285 24922

**Institute of Practitioners
in Advertising**
44 Belgrave Square
London SW1X 8QS
01-235 7020

**Institute of Sales
Promotion**
Panstar House
13-15 Swakeleys Road
Ickenham
Middlesex UB10 8DF
0895 74281/2

Keynote Reports
ICC Publications
28-42 Banner Street
London EC1Y 8QE
01-734 5059

Market Research Society
175 Oxford Street
London W1R 1TA
01-439 2585

Marketing Week
Centaur Week Communications
Ltd
St Giles House
50 Poland Street
London W1V 4AX
01-439 4222

**Public Relations Consultants
Association**
10 Belgrave Square
London SW1X 8PH
01-245 6444

The White Book
Birdhurst Ltd
PO Box 55
Staines
Middlesex
0784 464441

Chapter 11

Design and Creativity Consultants

Introduction — The design process — Design as a technical activity — Value analysis — Designing for visual appeal — Aesthetic versus technical design — Who are designers? — Why use a design consultant? — Where to find a design consultant — What a design consultant will do — Briefing a design consultant — Evaluating a design consultant's contributions — Sources of information

After reading this chapter you should:

- know the different categories of design consultant and how they specialise;
- understand the concept of a 'design strategy' and the problems attached to the practical implementation of a design strategy;
- appreciate the key elements of the design process; and
- know how to brief and evaluate a design consultant.

Introduction

Much ambiguity surrounds the word 'design' and, in consequence, the precise role of the design consultant. On the one hand, design is an aesthetic concept focussing on the creation of visually attractive and otherwise sensually pleasing items. Equally, however, design is a technical function, seeking to reduce production costs and generally improve technical efficiency.

The design process

The design process can be broken down into sections:

- specification of the function of a product;
- determination of consumer tastes and preferences;
- assessment of materials required; and
- evaluation of available alternatives and choice of design.

Essentially, the designer's role is to translate marketing or work study ideas into practical specifications. Designers are able to control many variables: quality of the finished product, machining tolerances, processing methods, and purely aesthetic characteristics.

At the same time, however, they face numerous constraints regarding costs, market acceptability and the availability of resources. A good design will:

- minimise materials and labour inputs;
- maximise the efficiency of production;
- reduce machining and processing expenses; and
- be functional, yet attractive to customers.

Design strategies

A company's *design strategy* is the totality of its policies for ensuring that designs are cost effective, technically feasible and visually appealing. The strategy should relate designs to material inputs, product reliability and customer demand.

The *composition* of products must be analysed, since new methods or materials for their manufacture may have become available since the products were first conceived. Note here the important relationship between design and the length of life of a product. Innovative designs may appeal to large numbers of consumers, but result in short product lives because competitors might react either by introducing their own new designs, or by copying yours while incorporating different and cheaper inputs into the product's construction.

It is not possible to understand the work of a design consultant or how he or she should be briefed or appraised without knowing a little more about the design function: technical, aesthetic, and in terms of 'value analysis'.

Design as a technical activity

A utilitarian interpretation of design is to see it simply as a link between production research (rather than marketing research) and actual manufacture. According to this view the designer is expected to convert new ideas for products into drawings and specifications sufficiently detailed for production to commence. Hence the designer will examine the equipment, labour and general facilities needed and available for manufacture, and then define dimensions, shapes and necessary product features.

While the designer takes into account the need for the product to be suitable for human use; he or she will at all times seek to economise on labour, materials and the utilisation of plant and equipment. Value analysis is an essential aspect of the designer's technical role.

Value analysis

This is a technique for reducing production costs by studying the *functions* of the item being produced. In this context, a function of a product is a characteristic that makes it operate properly (eg, lift a weight, transport an item, heat a room, or whatever). Functions are examined in detail, using predetermined procedures, and are then related to production costs. In other words, the designer first asks the question 'What is this item intended to do?', and then 'Is there a cheaper way of achieving this purpose?' The consequence of the analysis might be the abandonment of a particular input and its replacement with a cheaper substitute, or a change in the process of manufacture.

Products that consist of many component parts are more likely to benefit from value analysis than single units, since multi-component products offer greater scope for cost reduction through removal of unnecessary functions. Every aspect of a product should possess an identifiable purpose, fulfilled at minimum cost.

Standardisation

The purpose of standardisation is to remove unnecessary differences between produced items since longer production runs, lower unit manufacturing costs, easier movement of goods and more efficient stockholding are possible with standardised units. Component parts become interchangeable and can be used for several purposes. Producers gain many advantages from standardisation.

- Fuller use of existing machines and labour, easier work planning and scheduling.
- Quicker inspection, better quality control.
- Reduced average stockholdings.
- More specialisation and division of labour.
- Simplification of clerical records.

Designing for visual appeal

Aesthetic aspects of design have important marketing implications. Designers must consider the psychological significance of goods – why people want to buy them and the satisfactions they provide – as well as technical convenience. Good designs will create in products certain favourable yet intangible attributes (warmth, hygiene, purity, cleanliness, ease of use, etc) that enhance their public appeal.

This is increasingly important as more and more products become technically alike: frequently, the electrical or mechanical differences between competing brands are negligible (consider for instance domestic appliances such as electric kettles, or vacuum cleaners) so that the styling and the shape of an item becomes a highly significant factor in the purchasing decision.

Accordingly, extensive marketing research (see Chapter 10) may be needed prior to finalising a design, especially where packaging is concerned: some consumers are more influenced by a package's shape and colour than by the quality of the product it contains.

Aesthetic versus technical design

Should aesthetic or technical considerations dominate design? A good example of this dilemma was the design and production of the Austin (and later British Leyland) 'Mini'. Prior to the Mini, UK motor manufacturers had invariably created new motor cars around a technical engineering specification. Mechanical, electrical and production engineers were told to build a technically first-rate vehicle (economical to run, long-lasting, easy to service) and then – when the technical specification was complete – design staff were instructed to make the vehicle look as attractive as possible.

Austin reversed the process. It hired designers – including fashion goods designers, people with architectural experience, ergonomists and furniture designers – and gave them the brief to 'design a motor car that the consumer of the 1960's wishes to buy'. Then, and only then, technical engineering staff were ordered to manufacture the vehicle that the design staff had devised. Moreover, from the outset the aesthetic design specification was regarded as near sacrosanct; engineers were not allowed to make changes except in the direst of circumstances.

The result, of course, was an international best seller: the Mini was undoubtedly the car that motorists of the 1960s and 70s wanted to purchase. But relative to other small cars, the Mini was expensive to produce, due largely to Austin's insistence that technical engineering considerations be subordinate to the vehicle's aesthetic design. Indeed, it was said at the time that had the car been a foot longer then production and maintenance costs might have been cut by up to ten per cent! Against this, however, is the likelihood that the Mini would not have had the customer appeal that it clearly did possess if technical staff had been allowed to alter the dimensions and layout of the vehicle.

The ideal design

A company should aim to design *both* the product *and* its

production process simultaneously. Thus, design specialists need to be knowledgable about marketing as well as production management. Actually, simultaneous concern with product design and production methods implies that separate design personnel ought *not* to be required, since the company will either have worked backwards from the marketplace – identifying consumer needs and demands and consciously creating a product specifically designed to meet the requirements of the market, or will have deliberately created an entirely new design which it believes will capture the market.

In either case the design function should be integrated into the management system so intimately that no separate 'marginalised' design activities should occur independent of other functions.

Who are designers?

Design consultancies have mushroomed during the last five or six years (the market grew by 35 per cent over a five period according to a survey conducted in 1988).* Work related to marketing (notably corporate identity and retail design assignments) represents a particularly buoyant market, as does office design.

Today's trend is towards design consultancy firms becoming directly involved in the manufacture and/or supply of items (eg, merchandising materials, fixtures and fittings or packages) as well as merely providing designs. The slowest growth rates in design consultancy relate to the design of products. This is not surprising since the demand for industrial designers depends heavily on the state of manufacturing industry and as UK manufacturing has declined so too has the demand for industrial designers (although certain manufacturing sectors, notably electronics and high-technology products, have expanded sharply in recent years).

Currently, most product design assignments involve the initiation and development of entirely new products rather than the redesign and updating of existing items. However, this could change dramatically in the run up to 1992 (see Chapter 14) for the following reasons. The harmonisation of product standards across the entire community will generate much work for industrial designers (it will no longer be necessary to produce several versions of the same

---

*This survey, published under the title *The Design Consultancy Marketplace,* was conducted by the management consultancy James Capel. It reported that the average age of design consultancies is 11 years, and that 6.3 per cent of consultancies controlled 57.7 per cent of the total spend. A summary of the survey is contained in the September 1988 issue of *Design* magazine.

product in order to satisfy the technical standards required by the laws of different EC countries). Hence designers will be needed to standardise existing designs to meet newly established EC specifications. New designs will also be necessary in order to modify and adapt existing products to suit the needs of newly available European market segments.

Also, certain UK manufacturing activities are bound to expand following 1992. Moreover, the demand for corporate identity specialists will probably expand over the next decade as the number of European mergers and takeovers continues to increase.

Categories of designer

There are three basic types of designer. The first is the top-class free lance who designs specific items for clients on a custom order basis. He or she will normally be the owner (or certainly a very senior employee) of a small design consultancy firm that might work on a single assignment for several weeks – perhaps months – at a stretch. Such a designer might insist on retaining the copyright of the designs he or she creates as a formal requirement of the consultancy contract (although the client firm will use and market the consultant's design under its own name).

The second category consists of development designers who adapt and modify existing concepts and specifications to suit clients' particular needs. Again, the consultant might be engaged by one firm for long periods. Third there is the jobbing designer who earns a living by simultaneously feeding numerous design sketches, models and draft specifications to very many client companies. This work is fundamentally *ad hoc* and could consist either of original designs or interpretations of existing material. However, there are few relationships between jobbing designers and the companies to which they sell their work – rather like an artist selling paintings to customers.

Why use a design consultant?

Large firms may already employ design staff but be looking for fresh ideas; small businesses (except those in fashion goods and similar industries) can rarely afford a full time designer and thus must rely exclusively on externally created designs. In either case the consultant can bring a new perspective to the firm's design problem, drawing upon a wealth of experience and ideas gained through previous assignments. External consultants are particularly useful for:

- helping to evaluate the production feasibility of a new product;

- assessing the production costs and marketing implications of intended new products;
- translating vague product ideas into concrete specifications; and
- converting the results of manufacturing research and development into working plans and models.

A design consultant who specialises in your particular industry might know more about the alternative (or near alternative) materials available to produce your product than you know yourself. He or she should be an expert in materials characteristics, durabilities, causes of materials fatigue, and the effects on materials of wear, tear, shock and vibration.

Where to find design consultants

The Design Council is the principal design body in the United Kingdom and the potential source of much useful information. (Note that the Council acts as general co-ordinator for the design aspect of the DTI Enterprise Initiative). It publishes two magazines, *Design*, and *Engineering*, the former of which contains numerous advertisements by design consultants.

The design component of the DTI Enterprise Initiative (see chapter 1) offers help with feasibility studies for new products, materials selection, ergonomics (ie, designing workplace furniture and equipment to fit in with the needs of the human body), plus advice on general design management and strategy. Advertisments for the scheme state moreover, that it also applies to mechanical and electrical engineering design, industrial design and styling, and (importantly) to packaging and point of sale materials. However, grants are *not* available for, as the DTI puts it, 'isolated activities not part of an overall design strategy'. Routine production of sales literature and redesign of letterheads, etc, are specifically excluded.

Rather, the design initiative is concerned primarily with overall conceptual assistance: *how* to devise attractive packages and point of sale materials, *how* to improve the company's design management, *how* to develop products to make them more acceptable to the market, and so on.

What a design consultant will do

The consultant's role will vary depending on whether he or she is appointed for technical or aesthetic work. Technical designers seek to ensure that items can be manufactured easily and that externally purchased components may be conveniently dovetailed into products. Additionally, they are concerned to reduce packaging costs and the amount of space required to store products. Note, however, that designers neither choose the products the client firm will manufacture, nor how products are to be sold. They are *not* marketing consultants; they merely design goods according to the brief they are given. Do not expect from the consultant anything more than patterns, drawings, specifications of the intended product, plus advice on materials and where they may be acquired (perhaps from sources controlled by the consultant).

Computer aided design (CAD)

Often, a design begins with a rough sketch, transferred immediately to a computer using a mouse or some other line-drawer. Then the design can be spun around on the designer's VDU and he or she can rearrange elements, extend or reduce dimensions and add or subtract components.

Increasingly, computer aided design is linked to computer assisted manufacture, and many design consultants today specialise in CADCAM work (see Chapter 5 for details of manufacturing aspects). The consultant will possess his or her own software, though may wish to use clients' hardware facilities. CAD offers the designer vastly improved control over the design process, greater flexibility in investigating alternatives, and huge reductions in the time (and cost) needed to draft proposals.

Moreover, modern CAD programs incorporate numerous facilities for performing calculations on stored data. Thus weights, volumes, surface areas, centres of gravity and so on can be computed for each design possibility and the various values of these variables then automatically translated into final production costs and specifications.

Elements of design

Design is a creative process, yet it is not possible to define precisely what makes 'good' design. Consider the shapes of motor vehicles for instance; these have at various times been functional, ostentatious, elegant, garish, or puritanical depending on contemporary public taste. Why, for example, did the huge tail fins on early 1950s American cars suddenly go out of fashion? How do you account for the transition from the angular shaped vehicles of the 1970s to the smoother bodied vehicles of today? (This is hardly likely to have much to do with speed, given the speed limits in force and the enormous congestion of British traffic.)

Designers need inspiration prior to creating designs, and the pursuit of inspiration is an essential component of the designer's daily work.

Some designers are pragmatic in their approach, relying for inspiration on formal theories of line, contrast and proportioning, and on the precise measurement of prescribed materials and tasks. Others depend entirely on random brainwaves for their most creative designs.

To be acceptable, a design should be functional, producable, and attractive. An item's functionality relates to how well it works: how it serves the function for which it is intended (see previous section on 'value analysis'). Producability refers to the ease with which the design can be manufactured – its cost-effectiveness and the quality and reliability of the final output. A product's attraction might depend on its size, colour, on the description written on its package, on functionally non-essential decorative additions to the product, or on its layout and general visual appearance.

The creative process
Design involves originating new concepts or rearranging existing ideas. The process often begins with a brainstorming session. Here, appropriate senior managers from the client company meet with the design consultant and relevant members of his or her staff in order to churn out ideas about the client's design problem. The important point about brainstorming is that you do *not* consider the feasibility of suggestions during the session – a separate meeting is convened for precisely this purpose at a later date. Rather, you simply list every idea on any aspect of the issue that comes into a participant's head. Participants need consciously to try to be inventive and imaginative, looking at problems from different angles instead of head-on. It is a strict rule of brainstorming that committee members are *never* criticised for suggesting superficially absurd or trivial ideas.

Morphological analysis
This is an extension of brainstorming that seeks to discover fresh opportunities by cross-referencing ideas. Suppose, for example, that you are considering extending your range of products and considering that three new products, A, B and C might be produced. Three markets – the teenage market, middle-aged consumers, and older people – are available. You begin a morphological analysis by listing the products and stating how each one might be used by each of the three types of consumer thus creating $3 \times 3 = 9$ ideas for desirable features to be incorporated into the products. A third dimension (package design for example) is now added and further ideas generated, eg, how best to package product C for the teenage market. This will generate $3 \times 3 \times 3 = 27$ ideas, and so on. Each idea is then evaluated critically, leaving only the best for detailed investigation.

Morphological analysis adds form and structure to a brainstorming session, but it does have problems. Ideas are generated geometrically, leading to enormous numbers of suggestions and consequently the need for long periods of time to weed out those which are unsatisfactory. Also many of the ideas thrown up will not be feasible because of external constraints; so that a great number of suggestions – while extremely interesting – will have no hope of implementation.

A consultant's creativity is perhaps best judged by what he or she has done previously, although there is no guarantee that past successes will be repeated. Nor is it possible to recognise creative potential from a person's demeanour. There is no physical appearance or mode of behaviour that ensures that an individual will be creative. However, you should expect your consultant to be able to generate a large number of new ideas rapidly, and to give interpretations of issues that you had not thought of before.

Note that the fact that you are looking for help in the creative sphere might itself suggest a deficiency in the organisation structure and/or management style of your company. Does your firm actively encourage its staff to suggest innovations and alterations to products? Is your communication system overloaded with committees and complicated slow-moving decision taking procedures? Are creative individuals rewarded by promotions, pay rises, explicit recognition, etc. How willing are employees to come up with fresh ideas and if they are not at all willing, why is this the case? Do employees feel themselves too busy to spend time on creative activities? How much autonomy is given to departments and sections to think up and implement creative ideas?

Briefing a design consultant

Designers need information about product functions, consumer types, existing market moods and structures, and customer preferences. And they must know your expectations regarding:

- the quality, durability, cost and general standards of performance of the company's products;
- any priorities you wish to impose, eg, create the lowest cost item subject to the incorporation of certain minimum product features, or (alternately) design the product that consumers really want to buy and leave salespeople to worry about the resulting price;
- budgetary constraints on use of labour or materials; and
- the compatibility of intended new products with an existing corporate image.

Also, you should clarify whether your fundamental aim is to cut costs (by standardisation or value analysis) or to increase the variety and attractiveness of products. Then, list and briefly describe all you know about (i) customer requirements and the prices you believe customers are willing to pay, (ii) customer sensitivity to changes in fashion, and (iii) whether customers want reliability in the product, after-sales service, etc. Is yours a 'throwaway' product for which 'built-in obsolescence' is appropriate, or are durable and high quality products required? Justify the assertions you make when briefing the consultant.

Evaluating a design consultant's contributions

It is impossible to measure creative output accurately. One really good design can be worth more than a hundred that are mediocre. Nevertheless, you might ask yourself the following questions when considering whether it was worthwhile hiring the consultant.

- Were suggested designs technically feasible?
- Do you have any evidence – direct or circumstantial – of increased sales resulting from the designers work? And if not, why not?
- Has the consultant looked ahead and *anticipated* changes in consumer preferences rather than simply reacting to existing consumer demands?
- Did the consultant liaise properly with production and marketing staff?
- Has there been an increase in customer complaints since the new designs were introduced?
- Have machine and labour utilisation, materials wastage rates and production efficiency in general improved in consequence of new designs?
- Can the designs be manufactured using existing tools and equipment rather than having to purchase additional and/or different tools and equipment? If not, did the consultant explain that this would be the case at the very beginning of the exercise?
- Have the consultant's designs created the need for additional maintenance or after sales service?
- Is the consultant fully aware of the designs and design management policies of your leading competitors?

Source of information

Design Council
(Publishes ***Design*** and ***Engineering*** magazines)
28 Haymarket
London SW1Y 4SU
01-839 8000

Chapter 12

Transport Management Consultants

Introduction — Who are transport consultants? — What transport consultants do: Fleet maintenance management; Vehicle purchasing and leasing — Controlling vehicle operations — Briefing a transport consultant — Appraising the consultant's contributions — Sources of information

After reading this chapter you should:

- appreciate the management control problems that arise following the acquisition of a fleet of vehicles and how a consultant might assist in overcoming these problems;
- understand the factors to be considered when deciding whether to buy or lease vehicles;
- possess an outline knowledge of the work of a fleet maintenance management consultant; and
- be able to appraise the work of a transport consultant

Introduction

Transport is not a function that immediately springs to mind when considering management consultancy. Yet transport is a major business cost, so even a small percentage saving in transport expenditure can justify a consultant's fee.

Small firms cannot justify the capital costs of buying their own fleet of vehicles. Yet outside carriers can be extremely expensive and it is thus natural for companies to wish to purchase a fleet of delivery vehicles just as soon as their volume of business warrants the necessary capital expenditure. Having purchased their own vehicles, however, new management problems emerge. Vehicles must be serviced and maintained, journeys must be carefully routed, drivers have to be controlled, decisions made about the rates at which vehicles are depreciated, and so on.

Who are transport consultants

Consultants are available to help with most aspects of the transport function. If you rely on outside carriers then the Post Office and

British Rail are obviously among the first organisations to approach. Both offer comprehensive information services regarding journey planning, packaging, insurance and documentation (the latter being especially important for overseas trade, see Chapter 14). For road transport you have to telephone road hauliers and compare their prices, geographical coverage and speed of delivery. You will find road hauliers listed under 'Road Haulage Services' in *Yellow Pages*. Names and addresses of road hauliers belonging to the Road Haulage Association are available in a directory that can be obtained free of charge from the RHA.

The *Yellow Pages* entry for transport consultants appears under that title, though in fact the term 'transport consultant' covers several varieties of activity, including:

- agency commission work involving negotiating the best possible contracts with outside carriers on behalf of client firms;
- administration of the maintenance and repair of large fleets of clients' vehicles;
- estimating running costs per mile, the costs of idle time, efficiencies of various drivers, etc;
- integrating the transport function into a firm's line and staff system after it has decided to acquire its own fleet of vehicles;
- preparation of Europe wide transport action plans in preparation for 1992 (see Chapter 14); and
- freight forwarding (see Chapter 14).

Many of the large national garage chains offer transport consultancy services, notably for fleet vehicle maintenance (see below). The same applies to the national car hire companies. Also, some of the large general management consultancy firms have their own transport consultancy departments.

Further lists of consultants can be obtained from the professional bodies in the transport field. These are the Chartered Institute of Transport and, for foreign deliveries, the Institute of Freight Forwarders.

What transport consultants do

Although no accurate figures are available most transport consultancies are concerned with the maintenance and management of fleets of company vehicles.

Fleet maintenance management (FMM)
These consultancies in effect take over the entire maintenance

function in relation to clients' fleets of vehicles. Certain FMM consultants are only interested in very large fleets (certainly more than 50 vehicles) although others (including some of the car hire companies) will handle much smaller sizes of fleet – possibly as few as seven or eight vehicles. Clients pay the consultant a fixed fee per vehicle per month. In return the consultant contracts to ensure that all the client's vehicles are constantly in a roadworthy condition, at a cost far lower than would be possible if the client undertook vehicle maintenance in-house. Also the client is saved the administrative cost of processing numerous monthly invoices for maintenance and other vehicle running expenses.

Consultants are able to offer attractive rates because they are experts in the costs and techniques of vehicles maintenance, especially preventative maintenance. Thus they can predict the faults likely to develop on certain types of vehicle and hence will implement measures to stop these occurring. Moreover, they know the very best replacement components to use, the most reliable sources of component supply, and the lowest component (and other maintenance) prices available. For routine vehicle maintenance, they operate groupage systems whereby all their maintenance contracts with their own clients (some large, some small) are put together into a composite whole so that they can place very large contracts (involving hundreds, even thousands, of vehicles) with third party garages that will actually do the day-to-day maintenance work. Because the orders are so large, garages give big discounts (which consultants pass back to their clients) resulting in low maintenance costs per vehicle.

Spare parts and routine service material are purchased in bulk by the consultants' own firms for use on clients' vehicles (even though the actual servicing is done by outside garages). Again the orders placed are so large that big discounts are available. Thus, for example, replacement tyres will be fitted to your company's vehicles at a 50 per cent discount on the normal trade price.

Where major repairs are involved, consultants know *precisely* the extent of the work necessary and the proper rate for the job. Also they operate extensive and detailed computerised checking systems on the maintenance records of the vehicles for which they are responsible. Given a vehicles's mileage, they know *exactly* how much petrol its user should be claiming, whether oil or tyres are being changed suspiciously frequently, and so on. And they can identify vehicles with significantly expensive maintenance histories – indicating perhaps unauthorised use or a particularly bad driver.

The consultant might have negotiated a bulk purchase deal with a petrol supplier whereby your drivers receive company fuel cards (BP *Supercharge* for example) *as if* they were employees of a much larger organisation. Petrol is thus cheaper and there is tight control – through the consultant's computerised accounting system – over expense abuse. Similar arrangements apply to emergency breakdown services. For example, AA, RAC or other emergency services might be available through the consultant at major fleet discount rates even though your company only possesses a few vehicles.

If a newly purchased vehicle is defective the consultant will return it to the manufacturer on the client's behalf. Vehicle manufacturers are anxious not to upset fleet maintenance consultants and so might replace – without argument – marginally unsatisfactory vehicles they would not be prepared to replace had the demand come from an individual purchasing firm. Equally, the consultant will take care of insurance claims for major repairs once vehicles are out of guarantee. Indeed, consultants who purchase vehicles on clients' behalf can often negotiate longer guarantee periods with suppliers than would normally be the case.

The trade magazine for the fleet management industry is *Fleet News*, which is distributed to known fleet vehicle operators. It is not usually sold in newsagents so you may have to contact the publisher in order to obtain a copy.

Vehicle purchasing and leasing

If you need to acquire several vehicles at the same time it could be financially worthwhile seeking consultancy advice. At first sight, the question of how to obtain vehicles appears simple – you just telephone around and enquire about current new vehicle prices. In fact, the issue can be extremely complicated and, if it is not handled properly, may involve substantial yet unnecessary financial costs. The main options are as follows.

- Outright purchase financed either by cash or using borrowed money. Relevant factors affecting this choice include:
  - interest rates, the firm's cash flow situation, other demands on capital resources and the alternative investment opportunities that are available;
  - part-exchange and trade-in facilities attached to the deal;
  - phasing of payments to the vehicle supplier; and
  - timing of repayments of the capital of a loan.
- Having another company buy the fleet and then leasing the vehicles from this company for a specified period. The lessor

might be a specialist leasing operator, a vehicle supplier (eg, a large garage), a car hire firm, or a general fleet management consultancy acting on behalf of a finance company.

- Contract hire. Here the lessor assumes full responsibility for repairing, maintaining and eventually replacing the vehicles. The contract will normally include all the costs of taxing, insuring and running the vehicles (excluding petrol). Accordingly, the price quoted includes allowances for expected resale value, anticipated intensity of usage (which largely determines repair and maintenance costs), and for insurance and tax. With this method you (literally) contract to hire a vehicle – lock stock and barrel – whereas under a conventional lease you and not the leasing company are responsible for vehicle running costs.

- Contract purchase. An important aspect of the work of commercial fleet management consultants in recent years has been to find ways of dealing with the maximum limits (currently £2,000 per year per vehicle) imposed by the Inland Revenue on the rate at which vehicles may be written off for tax purposes, and with the fact that leased vehicles do not qualify for any writing down allowance whatsoever.

Vehicles which are 'purchased' may be written off at a maximum of 25 per cent per annum (up to a ceiling of £2,000 pa) so that only vehicles costing less than £8,000 qualify for full tax relief. Unfortunately, few executive vehicles or commercial trucks cost less than £8,000. Hence, various 'contract purchasing' schemes have been devised to overcome these difficulties. Contract purchase operates as follows.

A third party (a garage, finance company or fleet management firm) purchases the vehicle, which is delivered to your premises. Instead of 'leasing' the vehicle you have a contract purchase arrangement which exhibits all the features of a lease agreement – you pay a monthly lump sum in return for which all maintenance, servicing, repairs, etc, are taken care of by the firm from which you obtain the vehicle – but at the end of a prespecified period (four years for example) you purchase the vehicle at a predetermined price.

The fact you will eventually own the vehicle means you are entitled to claim the 25 per cent pa writing down allowance (up to £2,000 per year), and because the deal is effectively a 'finance lease' equivalent to hire purchase you are exempt from value added tax on the monthly lump sum payments.

Under the 'used vehicle agreement' which will accompany the deal you eventually buy the vehicle at either a guaranteed price or at a price determined through some prespecified formula regarding mileage, wear and tear, etc. If you now sell the vehicle at a loss (eg, to an employee who, nevertheless, continues to use it for company purposes) you become entitled to *further* tax relief on the loss you incur *via* the balancing allowance that arises on disposal of the vehicle.

Each fleet management consultant will have his or her own variation of this system, and careful analysis and planning are necessary to ensure both that the scheme attracts the maximum corporation tax and VAT relief and that it is entirely legal. Some fleet management specialists claim they are able to obtain 100 per cent relief on any vehicle, regardless of the price of the initial purchase.

Choice of an option
All these options have their advantages and drawbacks. A consultant will examine (i) the administrative costs attached to various alternatives, (ii) the ease of budgeting associated with the options, (iii) the value to the firm of being assured that a replacement vehicle is instantly available following a breakdown, (iv) the utility of not having resources tied up in the ownership of vehicles, and other relevant variables. Seemingly small matters such as who is to bear the cost of transporting broken down vehicles to garages for repair, or whether all vehicles are to be serviced at the same time regardless of their condition, can make a huge difference to total expenditure.

Replacing vehicles
The problem here is deciding whether anticipated repair costs on older vehicles are likely to outweigh the costs of trading them in and buying new ones. Most of the previously mentioned criteria are relevant to the decision, plus the following:

- relationships between age, mileage and maintenance costs for various types of vehicle (some are known to last longer than others);
- the costs of the inconveniencies caused to the firm by increasingly frequent breakdowns, eg, the possibility of losing important customers by not delivering on time; and
- whether new vehicles are likely to rise in price in the near future.

Consultants are useful here in that they know from experience the ages and mileages of different makes of vehicle beyond which, on average, it becomes uneconomic to continue their operation. Moreover, consultants can suggest optimum timings for major overhauls – up to and including engine changes – in order to maximise the cost-effective lives of various vehicle types.

Controlling vehicle operations

New costing and budgetary control procedures may be required following the acquisition of a fleet of vehicles. It becomes necessary to compare the costs of operating particular vehicles, to identify possibilities for curbing expenditures, and to establish how often vehicles need to be serviced.

Firms that do not use fleet maintenance management consultants must decide whether to repair and maintain vehicles themselves or have this done outside. The choice should depend on:

- whether the volume of work justifies the employment of staff to undertake continuous vehicle maintenance and repair;
- the price and quality of work done in local garages;
- the availability of space and vehicle repair facilities (a pit, a small workshop with appropriate tools and equipment) within the firm's premises; and
- whether outsiders can be relied upon to offer immediate attention (including overnight working) in extremely urgent cases.

Vehicle security can be another headache. Policies are needed to avoid pilfering from loads, prevent lorry hijacks, for the installation of security devices, etc. Security consultants as well as transport specialists provide advice, information and services in this field. You can find them in Yellow Pages under the heading 'Security services and equipment'.

Drivers' wages are a major part of the cost of a transport operation, and it is thus essential that drivers' time be used as efficiently as possible. General management consultancies, particularly those with separate transport management departments, are usually the best to use for this type of work because they have wide-ranging knowledge and experience of work study and organisation and methods techniques. The consultant will:

- find ways of reducing time spent at loading and unloading points;
- examine the efficiency of the equipment and methods used for loading and unloading;
- draft forms and records for drivers to complete describing their activities;
- identify sources of delay during journeys; including time spent in heavy traffic, laybys and cafeteria; interruptions due to breakdowns, and so on;

- analyse procedures for changing the driver of a vehicle as one driver starts and another finishes a shift in order to minimise the time the vehicle is standing idle;
- devise incentive schemes to induce drivers to reduce journey times legally and safely; and
- arrange for discount booking facilities with the hotels used by drivers who need to break a journey overnight.

A consultant might also devise a new routing system to save time and/or mileage and to carry the maximum sizes of loads to destinations. Efficient routing requires the evaluation of many factors, notably;

- traffic congestion and hence average vehicle speeds obtainable on alternative routes;
- suitability of vehicles for slow moving traffic in terms of petrol consumption, effect on maintenance costs, etc;
- customers' sensitivity to inaccurate estimates of arrival times;
- opportunities for return loads;
- the number of calls necessary and the mileages between them;
- sizes of deliveries;
- customer opening hours; and
- whether customers require separate items to be delivered simultaneously.

Briefing a transport consultant

Apart from considerations of cost; customer requirements should determine the form of your transport policy. Accordingly a transport consultant will need to know all about your existing distribution system; about customer demand patterns and locations; the frequency and size of customer orders; and about the causes and consequences of your current distribution problems. Advise your consultant about market trends, sales volume growth and your plans for introducing new products. Present a detailed summary of current transport costs and tonnage volumes, broken down into figures for particular products and markets and describe and state the locations of any warehouses or depots owned by the organisation. Note how it can sometimes be cheaper to despatch larger loads to warehouses and hence save on the number of journeys that have to be made.

Appraising the consultant's contribution

To evaluate the usefulness of your transport consultant, ask yourself the following questions.

- How diverse are the consultant's trade contracts? Is the consultant placing business with a variety of suppliers and sub-contractors in order to get the best possible prices?
- What proportion of the discounts obtained by the consultant is passed back to your company? (It is not uncommon for consultants to pass on 100 per cent of such discounts to their clients, relying entirely on the monthly fixed charge per vehicle for their income.)
- Does the consultant guarantee same-day or next-day replacement of broken down vehicles?
- Has the consultant sought to integrate your transport facility into the company's total physical distribution system?
- Have all the costs attached to your transport operations been fully explained and itemised?
- Has provision been made for future additional transport requirements if you need to expand the business?
- Did the consultant take into account the desires and delivery requirements of your customers when drafting his or her recommendations?
- Has the consultant given you any useful advice on how to package your products?
- Has the consultant pointed out possible changes in transport and distribution technology that might disrupt your current transport arrangements?
- Did the consultant examine the transport policies of competing firms within your industry prior to making recommendations?
- Has the consultant left you with a set of standards against which you can monitor the costs and performance of your transport activities? Standards might relate to driver performance/utilisation, maintenance costs, average intervals between breakdowns, vehicle utilisation rates, etc.

Sources of information

Chartered Institute of Transport
80 Portland Place
London W1N 4DP
01-636 9952

Fleet News magazine
Response Publishing
Wentworth House
Wentworth Street
Peterborough
0733 63100

Institute of Freight Forwarders
See Chapter 14

Road Haulage Association
104 New Kings Road
London SW6 4LN
01-736 1183

Chapter 13

Property Management Consultants

Introduction — Who are property management consultants? — What property management consultants do — Property services management — Commercial estate agents — Rent reviews and lease renewals — How property management consultants charge — Property development consultants — Evaluating a property consultant's work — Sources of information

After reading this chapter you should:

- know what property management involves;
- understand the roles of commercial estate agents, surveyors and developers in property management consultancy;
- possess an outline knowledge of the criteria that a property location consultant will apply when seeking premises for a client company;
- appreciate the main costs attached to property maintenance and how a consultant may be used to keep these to a minimum;
- understand how a consultant can assist with negotiating rent reviews, lease renewals, sale and leaseback arrangements, etc.

Introduction

A company's involvement in property management may arise from several sources: maintenance of existing buildings, acquisition of new premises, redesign and modernisation of retail outlets, expiry of a lease, property extensions, rationalisation of offices, and so on. Some large businesses own their premises as a matter of policy; others (especially manufacturing businesses that need custom designed buildings for specialist plant) have no choice but to purchase and develop their own property, because outside financiers are not prepared to develop purpose built factories which have no alternative uses. Firms that rent their premises are necessarily concerned with the interpretation of leases, rent review negotiations, sub-letting, etc.

All businesses, therefore, are responsible for property to some extent. And they require sound and effective property management policies in order to maximise their property returns. Indeed, it is not unusual for companies which own their premises to find that the appreciation in their capital values over certain periods substantially exceeds the business's profits during those years. Moreover, firms that rent premises can achieve considerable savings through close attention to maintenance arrangements, rent review formulae, possibilities for sub-letting, etc.

It is thus hardly surprising that an increasing number of individuals with knowledge of property matters are setting up as consultants specialising in property management affairs.

Who are property management consultants?

Property management consultants fall into one or more of the following categories.

* *Property location.* Selecting the best geographical area for premises and finding suitable buildings/offices for rent or purchase in that district.
* *Legal and procedural aspects of property administration.* Representing clients in rent review negotiations, renewing leases, arranging mortgages.
* *Property development and conversion.* Organising building work, sub-letting, advertising for tenants.
* *Estate management and general property management services.* Arranging insurance, rent collecting, property maintenance, surveying and valuation, etc.

All the major national chains of estate agents have commercial property divisions, and numerous property management consultants are listed (under that title) in *Yellow Pages*. Consultancies which specialise in locating premises can also be found under the *Yellow Pages* heading 'Estate consultants', and in the TFPL publication *Directory of Management Consultants in the UK* (see Chapter 1).

Surveyors

Chartered surveyors are today very active in the general property management field. You can locate them through the Royal Institute of Chartered Surveyors and through the consultancy services section of the Chartered Institute of Building's *Handbook and List of Members*. Surveyors who undertake property management consultancy will not only value and identify defects in property, but will also:

* administer repairs and buildings replacements;
* install planned maintenance programmes (see below) for clients' property;

- co-ordinate site work and the activities of other consultants;
- represent clients in negotiations regarding third party compensation claims and building insurance assessments; and
- advise on the *profitability* of investing in a certain property *vis-à-vis* rates of return on the investment and its potential for profitable long-term development.

Surveyors normally work on a percentage commission basis – usually between 2 and 10 per cent depending on the amount of work involved.

Architects

For substantial property developments the bulk of your consultancy services could be provided by an architect. Today, many architects offer comprehensive property management packages, including the negotiation of planning permission, supervision of contractors and the installation of building services as well as the traditional functions of buildings design and choice of construction materials. An architect is liable to cost between 6 and 12 per cent of the final value of the project. You can obtain lists of architects from the Royal Institute of British Architects.

What property consultants do

Depending on the consultant's speciality, he or she might advise on such matters as tenancy protection, local government restrictions on use of premises, and on whether in your circumstances it is better to lease property than to buy. The latter is an important consideration involving many factors, for example:

- expected appreciations in property prices in a certain area;
- the convenience of being able to offer owned premises as security for loans;
- lease restrictions on an occupier's capacity to make structural alterations and/or to sublet; and
- rent, maintenance and other costs.

Property search

Nearly all property management consultants offer their clients a property search service, usually (but not always) charging a time related fee for this. The consultant will examine the market growth potentials of various districts, population catchment areas of particular locations, the whereabouts and calibre of competition, income levels and other socio-economic characteristics of the local population, extent of passing trade, security of premises against burglars and vandals, and so on.

Briefing a property search consultant

In general, the more detail you include in the consultant's brief the less you will have to pay, because less time is then needed to provide the service. Accordingly, you should always draft the brief with great precision and provide the maximum amount of relevant information. If the consultant insists on a lump sum or fixed percentage commission regardless of the quality of the brief you provide then ask for a rebate to reflect the fact that in providing a detailed brief you are saving a considerable amount of his or her time and money. After all, if you had not submitted a carefully planned and drafted statement then the consultant would necessarily waste time in clearing up ambiguities. Specify your precise requirements regarding:

- architecture of the premises;
- nearness to support services, raw materials suppliers, trading associates, etc;
- parking space for customers and suppliers;
- nearness of public transport facilities;
- special labour requirements (ie, whether you will require workers possessing particular skills to live within travelling distance of the firm);
- lighting, heating, gas, electricity and water supplies;
- waste disposal facilities; and
- intended rate of growth of the business.

Choosing locations for retail outlets (as opposed to office or factory premises) is a highly specialised activity for which the services of a marketing consultant may be required (see Chapter 10). It involves the detailed analysis of catchment areas, customer travel arrangements, local road traffic, demographic trends in the immediate neighbourhood, activities of local competitors, etc.

Certain local authorities offer property search facilities (which are usually free) in order to attract business into an area. They employ 'business development' or 'industrial liaison' officers to identify and promote suitable premises to firms. These officers may even assist with planning applications, with finding building contractors for property conversion or shopfitting, obtaining fire certificates, licences, and meeting other legal requirements. You can obtain details of these services (if they exist in your area) from your local town hall.

Planning permission

All business premises require local authority planning permission. And any significant change in the purpose for which business premises are used must also be authorised. Applications for planning permission must include details of the premises' existing and proposed use, external appearance and the availability of parking space, how many people the firm will employ and their working hours, the movement of vehicles to and from the premises, and information on waste disposal methods and/or any hazardous materials stored. Permission is not normally refused unless the business would cause a nuisance, a safety or health hazard, or would spoil a neighbourhood (a conservation area for example).

However, marginal situations sometimes occur for which it might be better to engage a consultant to prepare and argue your case. Note moreover that planning permission is itself quite expensive (costing up to £6,000 at current rates) so it is essential that the property be precisely and correctly defined in order to place it in the lowest cost planning category for planning purposes. Consultants specialising in this area know all about planning law, appeals procedures, how to present documents to town hall officials and how to describe the intended project in the most favourable light.

On receipt of a planning application a council official will visit the intended premises and inspect the site. Your consultant will represent you during the inspection, and arrange an appeal if the inspector's report recommends refusal of the application. The decision lies initially with the council planning committee, with provision for appeal to the Department of the Environment.

Property services management

Typical duties for a property services management consultant include advising on possibilities for restructuring leases, negotiating lease surrenders, arranging property maintenance, dealing with rates, and managing service charges.

Some consultants offer property owners a comprehensive property supervision service, including:

- regular inspection of sub-let premises to ensure the tenant's full compliance with the terms of the lease, and the implementation of appropriate remedial measures if the tenant is found to be in breach;
- instructing and overseeing contractors engaged on the maintenance, repair and cleaning of property (note that since

consultants manage the properties of very many clients they are able to place large bulk orders with contractors and hence attract discounts part of which can be passed back to clients);
- computing realistic service charges for imposition on tenants and arranging the collection of the amounts owed; and
- determining appropriate depreciation rates for various types of property.

A consultant will be expert in building methods, costs and materials and thus will know the best supply sources and prices available, the quality of the work of various contractors, substitute materials for particular jobs, and so on. This knowledge of building and maintenance costs can be used to value property accurately for insurance purposes, creating perhaps significant economies on insurance premiums for client firms.

Insurance premiums
Insurance costs are substantial, so it is essential that property be properly valued taking account of likely rebuilding costs, professional fees, loss of rent during the rebuilding period, and other consequential losses. Consultants have the advantage of being able to place many insurances with the same insurance company and so might be able to negotiate better discounts than a business acting alone.

Service charges
A consultant will examine a client's lease in great detail to ascertain precisely the extent of the client's liability for providing services and repairs. He or she will point out alternative interpretations of lease clauses pertaining to these matters, and (importantly) will arrange for a thorough inspection of the premises to establish its exact state of repair prior to the lease being signed. It would not be fair to classify substantial repairs – necessary on account of dilapidation of the building by previous tenants – as routine maintenace to be paid for by the new occupier.

Rating
For new business premises or significant changes of use of existing commercial property a new rate valuation is required. Until now the criteria adopted by Inland Revenue valuation officers when assessing rateable values have been complex, and you would certainly need expert advice if you wished to appeal against the assessment (special land valuation courts and tribunals exist to hear such appeals). The issue was especially complicated for property on

the fringes of government Enterprise Zones (within which businesses paid no rates during their first ten years of operation, hence depressing commercial property prices and market rental values on the outside borders of those areas).

From 1990 however there is to be a uniform business rate for all commercial and industrial property in England and Wales, based on a general revaluation. The revaluation will take into account rentable value, repairs, maintenance and insurance costs and other expenses attached to each property. Disputes arising from revaluations are sure to bolster demand for property management consultancy services.

Planned maintenance

The purpose of planned property maintenance is to conserve land and buildings at a level where no loss of value due to dilapidation is incurred. It involves periodic inspection and the servicing and replacement of items either at prespecified intervals or automatically whenever certain events occur – rather than simply waiting for items to fail. The consultant will forecast the performance and reliability of various aspects of the property, and schedule maintenance activities to occur at predetermined intervals in order to preempt predictable difficulties. This might increase costs in the short run (because guttering, drainage systems, chimneys, etc, will be serviced on a particular date whether they need it or not), but should lead to improved long run efficiency. Maintenance costs depend on:

- the design and quality of construction of the building, its age and life expectancy;
- the extent of the services incorporated into the building (lifts, air-conditioning systems, etc); and
- the tenant's expectations regarding the levels of comfort and amenity the property should provide.

Great care is needed when budgeting for planned maintenance: redecorating every five years imposes a far lower cost when it happens than (say) replacing a roof every 20 years, so appropriate amounts must be set aside and invested each year in order to accumulate the resources needed for major overhauls.

Computerised services

Property consultants hold databases and possess specialist software which enables them to provide their clients with detailed reports on maintenance and other property costs. High cost properties are quickly identified and the causes of additional expense exposed. This enables the consultant to provide comprehensive *performance analyses* of the properties they manage – showing capital and rental growth and rates of return by type of property, geographical location, type of tenant, property use, etc. Other computerised services include:

- continuous monitoring of rents due and monies received;
- automatic issue of rent demands to minimise arrears;
- informing clients of the dates that rents are to be reviewed, lease expiry dates, mortgage repayment and insurance renewal dates, etc;
- reports on when maintenance jobs are due (the computer acts as a diary to remind the user to place orders with contractors and to check that work has been done); and
- statistical forecasts of market rents, property values, building costs, and so on.

Negotiations

Consultants will represent either landlords or tenants in negotiations over rent reviews, lease renewals, submissions to courts or arbitrators, insurance valuations, etc.

Commercial estate agents

Estate agents not only put vendors/buyers and landlords/tenants in touch with each other, but will also supply essential research information and other services to either party. They collate data from local authority planning departments, ratings offices (rateable value is a reasonable guide to the general prosperity of an area), from local buildings inspectorates and from other official sources. The role of the estate agent from the landlord or vendor's point of view is to identify potential occupiers/purchasers and approach them using media most likely to attract their attention. This requires the agent to analyse occupiers' or purchasers' requirements and to assess accurately the rent/price that occupiers/purchasers are willing to pay.

Rent reviews and lease renewals

Once signed, a lease binds the tenant to its terms and conditions for the full period of the contract. Modern leases invariably contain provisions for rent reviews and restrictions on lease renewal. If you accept a lease that embodies unreasonably onerous conditions then not only are you losing out financially but also you will have difficulty in assigning the lease to another party.

Professional advice is frequently desirable in these matters, especially in relation to the following issues.

- Avoiding increased liability on termination of a lease due to the tenant's failure to maintain the property in a satisfactory manner. This could result from not having had a proper survey of the property conducted in order to discover any inherent defects giving rise to such terminal liability (eg, by causing normal routine maintenance to be prohibitively expensive).
- Possible compensation for improvements in the property undertaken by the tenant and/or obligations on the tenant to carry out improvements.
- Uses of the premises (sub-letting for example).
- The extent of services charges.
- Arbitration arrangements for determining rent increases at each rent review and/or the formula to be applied.
- Legal procedures arising from the tenant firm exercising its legal right (under the 1954 Landlord and Tenant Act) to renew a lease.

Sale and leaseback arrangements

Businesses that own their premises can inject much needed capital through 'sale and leaseback' arrangements. The firm sells its land and buildings for a capital sum equal to or just below their market value, but makes the transaction contingent on the purchaser formally agreeing to lease the land and buildings back to the selling firm for a certain period at a predetermined rent. Such a deal is not without costs – there are legal expenses and valuation fees, capital gains tax (possibly) on the disposal, the rent charged may be relatively high, and the firm loses its security of tenure.

Property licences

Landlords in areas where there is a high demand for commercial property sometimes prefer to let premises *via* a licence rather than through a conventional lease. Property licences offer a more flexible means for letting premises; the conditions they embody are similar to those of a lease, but only offer minimal security of tenure because licences do not imply any legal interest in the premises and thus are not covered by the Landlord and Tenant Act. Also, you cannot sell a licence at a premium as you can an orthodox lease.

How property consultants charge

Unlike residential estate agents – who charge vendors a fixed percentage commission on the value of the sale while providing the estate agent's services to buyers entirely free – commercial property consultants derive their incomes from a variety of sources. Obviously, a commercial estate agency will advise you free-of-charge of any properties it happens to have on its books, but if the agent does any investigative work on your behalf you will have to pay the agent a fee (computed perhaps as so many weeks' rent, or as a proportion of a lease premium, or a lump sum remuneration). Consultants who arrange property maintenance normally charge a percentage commission (usually between 15 and 25 per cent) on the value of the repairs and other work undertaken - subject to a minimum amount. For rent collecting, firms might take an agency commission, or buy the entire amount owing in exchange for a lesser amount of cash (perhaps as little as a half the value of the accumulated debt). A consultant engaged to locate premises might charge by the hour or day, or impose an initial lump sum fee to be topped up by a percentage commission on the value of the property eventually rented or purchased.

The problem is that each consultancy you approach may quote an estimate for its services based on quite different formulae for doing the same thing. How, for example, can you compare a lump sum fee quoted by one consultant with a percentage on value of property/ services provided quoted by another when you do not know what the value of the property or service finally selected will be?

Take care to compare like with like when examining competing estimates. Specify *precisely* what you want the consultant to do and the target value of the property or services you are after. If one consultant offers more in his or her bundle of services than others, ask that consultant to provide a separate lower valued invoice excluding the additional services.

Property development consultants

Property development concerns any legitimate major building or property refurbishment work: it is *not* the speculative buying and selling of land. It is undertaken by building firms and by large companies seeking property investments. The role of the property development consultant (as opposed to the owner of the development) is to co-ordinate and generally control the many specialist contractors (builders, demolition firms, architects, etc) involved.

First, the consultant will conduct market research to assess the saleability of the finished development and hence whether the project is financially worthwhile. An important task is to evaluate all the risks attached to the proposal. This requires the preparation of several estimates of costs and revenues covering all likely future events.

Then the consultant will study the characteristics of the intended site and arrange for drawings, costings, valuations and so on, to be completed. He or she will draft the planning application, present it to the local authority and negotiate with council officials. Often, consultants have contracts with banks and other financiers who specialise in funding property development, and hence might be instrumental in arranging finance for the project. The consultant will supervise land purchases and building works, and when the project is completed will liaise with estate agents to find occupiers or purchasers for the finished work.

At the end of a project the consultant will organise independent inspections of contractors' work and will accept or reject this on the client's behalf. Finally the consultant will organise any legal actions against outside contractors arising from slipshod work.

Property conversion

Converting and sub-letting part of your premises may provide a considerable source of income, though certain costs and inconveniences are necessarily involved (separate telephone lines must be installed, office partitions erected, and there is the additional expense of advertising for tenants). Note (importantly) that extra planning permission may be needed prior to the conversion.

Significant economies of scale are available from property conversion – it might be little more expensive to subdivide an entire large building into small lettable units than to undertake all the work necessary just to fit out your own firm. And the rent from sub-letting the units thus created might pay not only for the conversion work itself but also for the essential maintenance and repairs that you would have had to undertake in any event.

Even if your premises are leased and the lease does not permit sub-letting it may still be worth approaching the landlord to ask for special permission to convert the premises and sub-let. After all, you are offering to undertake the conversion into smaller, possibly more marketable units at your own expense, and you would not be doing this if the demand for smaller units did not exist.

If you have recently expanded the business you may feel that you cannot possibly make room to sub-let. But expansion does not inevitably lead to greater space utilisation provided (i) that you have efficient systems for dealing with goods inward, stock control, and finished goods awaiting despatch (so that large areas are not tied up accommodating excessive amounts of idle stock) and (ii) that you take the trouble to reorganise, tidy up the existing premises, and generally conserve the floor space needed for your operations.

Evaluating the work of a property consultant

Property consultancy work is so diverse that is it difficult to establish common criteria for evaluating the calibre of their services. However, some of the following questions might usefully be asked, depending on circumstances.

- Were the costings contained in the consultant's report sufficiently detailed, eg, broken down under separate headings for shopfitting, legal and professional fees, estate agent's fees, obtaining planning permission, etc?
- What proportion of the discounts the consultant negotiated with third party contractors has been passed back to you?
- Are you satisfied that the consultant obtained quotations from enough outside contractors for various aspects of the work?
- If you are letting property, did the consultant fully *justify* the recommended rent? A suitable rent will depend on such factors as:
  — accessibility of the property to customers and suppliers;
  — general prosperity of the area;
  — position of the building, eg, mainstreet or sidestreet, distance from car parks, bus stops, etc;
  — appearance of the building;
  — length of lease and the frequency of rent reviews;
  — rights assigned to tenants under the lease, eg, to sub-let or to make structural alterations.
- How large a contingency allowance did the consultant require be set aside to allow for unforeseen expenditures? In retrospect, was this amount too high (possibly indicating poor forecasting on the consultant's part).
- How comprehensive and detailed was the consultant's analysis of the catchment area of the premises?

Sources of information

Handbook and List of Members of the Chartered Institute of Building
Highwood Publishers Limited
Premier House
150 Southampton Row
London EC1B 65AL
01-833 2124

Royal Institute of British Architects
66 Portland Place
London W1N 4AD
01-580 5333

Royal Institute of Chartered Surveyors
12 Great George Street
London SW1P 3AD
01-222 7000

Chapter 14

1992 Consultants

What will happen in 1992 — European companies — How a consultant might help your firm — Researching European markets — Strategies for market entry — How to enter the European market — Indirect exporting to Europe — Advertising in the European Community — Getting paid — Further implications of 1992 — The consultant's report — Appraisal problems — Sources of information.

After reading this chapter you should:

- understand why so much fuss is being made about 1992;
- recognise the rudiments of the problems attached to selling in the single European market;
- appreciate the roles of the various types of consultant and/or agent active in the field; and
- know where to look for a 1992 consultant and what to expect from his or her report or services.

What will happen in 1992

If all current proposals are implemented, then by 31 December 1992 the European Community will have created a single unified market within which people, goods, services and capital can move without interference. Many trade barriers between member states have already been dismantled; obstacles that remain should be completely eliminated by the end of 1992.*

Important changes will occur in European business methods, notably in firms' purchasing and tendering procedures, transport and distribution systems, branding and advertising, recruitment, financing, and in company administrative and legal structures. To survive and prosper after 1992 a business will need to be productive, innovative and capable of handling change. And (for most UK companies) new linguistic and export marketing skills will be

---

*Nevertheless, frontier controls for drugs, firearms and live animals will continue, and considerable amounts of paperwork to shift goods between Community nations will still be required.

required. A few examples of the major possible effects of 1992 on UK companies are listed below.

Fierce competition from foreign EC based firms for UK public sector contracts.
Until now most European countries have discriminated against foreigners when awarding contracts for the supply of goods and services to their public sectors. Such discrimination must end by 1992, with all public supply contracts over a certain value becoming open for competitive tender from non-UK Community businesses. Moreover, information on all significant national and local government public sector procurement programmes must be circulated throughout the community well in advance of the date of the competitive tender.

The possibility of losing key employees to foreign firms.
Following 1992, workers will be able to seek employment in any member state and reside there with their families for as long as they wish. They will be entitled to receive unemployment benefit in their chosen country of residence and have equal access to public housing and to education for their children in that nation. Individuals may then retire and continue to live in their adopted country.

Currently, member states restrict the right of entry to certain professions (law or accountancy for example) to persons who have qualified within their own national frontiers. Such restrictions are scheduled to end in 1992, by when the training and other requirements for particular professions should have been harmonised across the Community (there are to be 'Higher Education Diplomas' valid and recognised in all member countries). Anyone possessing the appropriate EC recognised diploma (issued only after at least three years' training) will be free to practise his or her profession in any member state.

Changes in insurance
UK firms will be free to purchase insurances from any EC insurance company regardless of where it is based. Equally, EC companies in other Community countries may insure themselves with UK insurance firms.

Direct competition from companies based in other EC countries.
After 1992 any EC company may commence operations in Britain, and British firms will have to compete on equal terms with German, French, Italian and other EC companies for local UK business.

Alterations in the VAT system
The present system of imposing VAT on imports while not charging

VAT on exports is due for abolition (in order to enable goods to pass quickly through national frontiers). This means VAT will be payable on transactions between firms in different member countries in exactly the same way as for internal trade.

Abolition of restrictions on cabotage.
Cabotage means the local transportation of goods within national frontiers – from Liverpool to London for instance – and until now, governments have prevented foreign carriers from engaging in domestic cabotage, restricting this to firms registered within their own countries. These restrictions are scheduled to end by 1992; so that German, French or other Community based haulage firms will be free to compete for business between internal UK destinations. European hauliers will be allowed to pick up and deliver loads between any member states. There are proposals, moreover, for ensuring freedom of shipping between member countries and for opening all European air transport routes to direct competition between airlines.

Ability to raise capital anywhere in the EC.
The Community is insisting that most (but not all) member states abolish all remaining exchange controls against other EC countries by 1 July 1990. Other members have until the end of 1992 to do this (1995 for Greece and Portugal).

Consequently, firms and individuals will be able to borrow money *anywhere* in the EC, while savers may deposit their funds in any Community-based bank or other financial institution. Banks will compete for deposits on the European level and may open branches and/or subsidiaries wherever they wish. Of course, residents of any member country will be able to buy and sell shares in any European company no matter where it is situated.

Changes in the law on intellectual property rights.
The term 'intellectual property' covers patents, trade marks, industrial designs and any other copyright material. Originally, each European country had its own law on intellectual property, so that it was necessary to register trade marks, patents, etc, in every country where protection was required. Today however, it is possible to obtain patent protection throughout Europe with a single application, and member states have further promised to standardise their domestic patent law in order to avoid contradictions regarding what will or will not infringe a patent. Also, a system for registering community wide trade marks will be established to operate in parallel with existing domestic trade mark arrangements.

New technical standards for construction projects.
From now on, specifications quoted for all major European construction projects must use Community standards for structural stability, fire safety, noise and energy protection, and so on. This will enable any European firm to bid for work on any EC based construction project.

Longer term proposals

Important long term EC measures include policies for the harmonisation across countries of laws governing the mass dismissal of labour, and the introduction of new laws to protect workers following the takeover or insolvency of their firms.

The European Commission has drafted three proposals (yet to be accepted by the Council of Ministers) that will significantly affect personnel management in Britain. These cover the following issues.

- Compulsory alterations in the company law of all member states to give workers a say in running their companies.
- Laws that will force a company domiciled in one country to transmit to its subsidiaries in other countries key information about the parent company's current financial position and expected future performance. This information would then be communicated to the employees of the subsidiary firms.
- Regulations to grant temporary workers the same legal rights as permanent employees and to restrict firms' capacities to use large numbers of casual, temporary workers instead of permanent employees.

European companies

Businesses will be able to set-up and operate in any European country and/or sub-contract to any other community firm. At present, limited companies are governed by the company law of their resident country. The EC proposes that although companies will continue to be *established* under domestic law; they should then be allowed to merge with any other European company and/or establish holding companies with other European companies in any EC state. In effect, this means that businesses may form subsidiary companies at will anywhere in the EC. Moreover, the companies so formed are to be governed by a new set of company laws applicable throughout the Community. There will be compulsory worker participation on the boards of such companies, and the accounting systems, auditing requirements and incorporation arrangements (eg, the minimum capital requirement for registering a public company) are to be harmonised for *all* companies operating within the EC. Also, there are draft proposals for establishing Community-wide rules for takeover bids and for the disclosure of shareholding changes in companies.

How a consultant might help your business

1992 will sweep away many bureaucratic restrictions on intra-community trade; but the removal of red tape will not of itself cause you to sell more in the European market. Opportunities will obviously be created for efficient businesses; equally, however, existing deficiencies will be ruthlessly and glaringly exposed. It is not surprising, therefore, that many firms are seeking external advice on how to prepare for 1992.

There are three types of 1992 consultant: some do little more than provide information; others give information and advice; while the third category will undertake specific activities (delivery of goods for example) on your behalf.

Information consultants

Several consultancies have established 1992 databases consisting, usually, of a bank of core information supplemented by weekly or monthly updates on new developments and how these might affect your firm. This saves you having to undertake continuous research in a rapidly changing area, and relevant information is condensed and interpreted by experts in the field. You can find these consultants from the following sources.

- The publications of the Department of Trade and Industry. For example, during 1989 the DTI published a number of editions of a newsletter entitled *Single Market News*, that contained numerous advertisments by consultants concerned with 1992.
- Exporting magazines such as *Export Today* or *Export Direction*. (These also carry the advertisements of various translation agencies; the Institute of Translation and Interpreting for example.)
- The Association of British Chambers of Commerce.

The volume of information available about 1992 can be overwhelming. Thus, information consultants seek to pick out the *important* points: new laws and their implications, tax changes, availability of EC grants and subsidies, information about public procurement contracts available for tender, significant changes in market structures, etc, and relate them directly to client firms.

Provision of satisfactory market research information on target European market sectors and on possible competitors and how they might behave is a crucial concern. You need to establish which EC markets are most likely to buy your products, how to redraft your sales literature to reach these customers, and whether you should redesign products to give them a wider European appeal.

Researching European markets

Unless you possess extensive experience of foreign market research you are well advised to leave this to a market research consultant or agency specialising in the field. Consultants are available for both *market* research and for *marketing* research in European markets. Market research is the investigation of the size and structure of markets – age distribution, socio-economic composition, buying habits, etc. Marketing research, conversely, is research into any aspect of marketing, eg, the effectiveness of local advertising, the consequences of price variations, how local customers respond to different package designs, and so on.

What to expect from a market research consultant
Consultants normally adopt one of two approaches to the location of suitable foreign markets. The first approach is to define the characteristics of the EC consumers most likely to be attracted to the client's product(s) and then select countries and areas most likely to contain consumers of this type. Alternatively, the consultant might advise that you sell only to 'easy' European markets, eg, where most local residents can speak English, where delivery is straightforward, or where local business methods are nearly the same as in the UK.

Next, the consultant will relate your output to each of the following factors.

- Demographic structure; including population size, regional distribution, age structure, average family size, religious groupings, etc.
- Local average incomes and the distribution of wealth; living standards – housing, education, medical and other welfare services.
- Consumer tastes, lifestyles and spending patterns.
- The extent of local competition.
- Growth potential in the local market.

Once this information has been presented you need to consider undertaking further research 'in the field'. You can do this yourself or through a consultant. The advantage of using a research consultancy for field investigations is largely that of cost. To send one of your own executives on an exploratory visit would absorb time (much careful preparation is necessary) and a great deal of money. And you might not really know what you are looking for (eg consumer attitudes towards the product, effectiveness of local advertising media, local methods of doing business, the centre and dispersion of the market, its characteristics, or whatever) in the first place.

Research consultants, conversely, *already* possess a wealth of information on various European markets and know exactly where to look for further data. You can use either a UK-based consultant with direct contacts in the EC country concerned, or a local researcher in the foreign market. The former option involves fewer control and communication problems and is thus more common; but it could prove more expensive and less effective in the long run (local researchers obviously have intimate knowledge of local conditions).

Briefing the research consultant

Tell the consultant the precise objectives of the exercise and your budgetary constraint. Aims might include estimation of market size, measurement of consumer attitudes, analysis of consumer lifestyles, the prediction of the best prices to charge, and so on.

Then the consultant should give you an outline proposal for how he or she will conduct the research: interviews, postal questionnaires, desk research, direct observation, etc, and an estimate of its cost. If you accept the proposal you can expect a report that carefully analyses (i) the structure and growth potential of the market, (ii) the position of your product within the market (see Chapter 3), (iii) the strength of competition, (iv) consumer expectations regarding the product (including credit and after sales service requirements) and (v) available distribution systems. The report should also identify the most lucrative market segments and recommend an appropriate product price. It is essential that the researcher check out competitors' prices, delivery, payment and credit terms. Normally you can expect competitors to quote a local currency price and to specify door-to-door delivery – and you must be able to do the same.

Note how quoting in a foreign currency exposes you to the risk of an appreciation in the sterling exchange rate reducing your sales revenues. (If you quote in French francs, and the franc goes down against sterling you get less pounds for each franc received) so you may wish to contact your bank and arrange a 'forward exchange' deal whereby the bank (for a commission) agrees to buy from you at a fixed, predetermined rate any francs (say) you receive in (say) the next three months.

Evaluating the research consultant's contribution
In order to establish whether a researcher has done a good job, ask yourself the following questions.

- Has the market been properly 'segmented' ie, broken up into smaller units each with its own needs and characteristics and each capable of profitable entry using a slightly different method of approach (presenting the product differently, perhaps even modifying your output in order to satisfy particular demands within various market segments)?
- Does the consultant's report contain an assessment of the reliability of the data upon which recommendations are based? Are you able to check to ensure that *bona fide* research has actually been undertaken and that the information presented has not been made up?
- In following the consultant's advice will you be 'learning by doing', or is the consultant seeking to make you totally dependent on his or her long term services?
- What new things have you learnt about customer tastes and requirements in various EC countries that you couldn't have discovered simply by taking a holiday in the countries concerned?
- Has the cost of the credit you might have to offer to foreign customers been computed and fully explained? Have recommended credit control and debt collection systems been incorporated into the report?

Where to find a research consultant
A list of marketing research agencies and consultants specialising in European work is available from the Market Research Society (see Chapter 10). Also the DTI Statistics and Market Intelligence Library stocks published directories of marketing research organisations and services.

Government assistance for European market research
At the time of writing the DTI will pay up to half the total cost of commissioning a consultant to undertake overseas market research, plus a third of the cost of purchasing published marketing research

data. If you belong to a trade association which does or commissions research on your behalf the DTI will pay up to 75 per cent of the cost. The costs of researching technical standards requirements for certain types of equipment are also repayable. Details are available from the DTI Export Marketing Research Section.

The DTI also provides other useful research services for exporters. It organises exhibitions and collective trade promotions in foreign countries (particulars of which are published quarterly in the DTI journal *British Business*); it operates an enquiry service for individual EC markets (contact the DTI 'Exports to Europe' branch in the first instance); and it provides a computerised intelligence service to exporters. The latter currently costs 50 pence per item of information (eg, overseas enquiries for certain types of product, calls for tender by overseas firms, etc), although the charge is scheduled to increase sharply (to more than £2 per item) soon. Additionally the DTI offers a low cost status report service on EC companies (£25 per report), and possesses an extensive library of statistics and other marketing information about foreign markets.

A number of private export intelligence services have been set up to compete with the DTI scheme. *Export Network*, for example, is a computerised export information and trading service which enables users to call-up news of fresh market opportunities on their computer visual display units from day to day. Details of overseas agents and distributors and background information on foreign markets can also be requisitioned.

Strategies for market entry

If you choose to operate in Europe you need to decide how exactly you will enter various markets. Strategy consultants (see Chapter 3) with European interests can assist you in this respect. The first thing such a consultant will want to know is your attitude towards risk. Are you looking to avoid (or at least disperse) risk *via* licensing, joint ventures or consortia (see below), or would you prefer a full scale (and risky) assault on a certain, albeit carefully researched, European market using just your own company's resources? Most firms go for easy, low-risk (though relatively low-return) options in the early stages, gradually increasing their risk exposure as they proceed. The consultant should tell you:

- *whether* to enter particular European markets (there is no immutable law saying that you must become involved in European sales);

- *where* to enter Europe if you decide to go ahead; in what countries and/or market segments;
- *when* to establish a European presence; and
- *whether* and if so *how* your products and promotional messages need to be modified to make them suitable for the European market.

Product policies for the single market

The cheapest approach to product policy is simply to introduce an existing product to the European market in exactly the same form and with the same (albeit translated) advertisments and other promotional methods as are used at home. Otherwise you will have to alter:

- the product, while keeping the same advertisments, or
- the advertisments, but retaining the same product, or
- both the product and the advertisments.

In deciding how to proceed you need to balance cost against market attraction: the more you relate your product and advertisments to local requirements the more you sacrifice the financial benefits of product standardisation and economies of scale. Also, development and market testing costs, packaging costs, and the costs of after-sales service are usually higher in consequence of modifying products.

Ask your consultant *why* you should bother modifying a product. It may be that significant differences in consumer tastes or incomes do occur between markets; or there could be local legal requirements (although EC policy is to harmonise all product quality and safety standards in time for 1992) or differences in climatic conditions may exist (compare southern Italy with northern Denmark for instance). Otherwise, it is perhaps better to assume that extensive product modification is not worthwhile.

How to enter the European market

Entry to the single market may be direct or indirect. Direct entry involves one or more of the following.

- Exporting to Europe using foreign distributors, foreign branches and possibly foreign agents and/or travelling export sales staff.
- Establishing joint ventures with other European firms to set up production, distribution and other marketing facilities in European markets.
- Investment in foreign based assembly, manufacturing or distribution firms.

Exporting to the single market
To do this you must become familiar with export documentation and financing procedures, and with the various methods for transporting goods (road, rail, air and cross-channel ferry). The more of these responsibilities your firm assumes the less you have to pay, but the procedures can be complex. Could you, for example, single-handedly arrange for the transportation of a lorry load of your goods from your own premises to those of a customer in, say, Dusseldorf or Amsterdam taking care of all customs formalities, booking the necessary space on the ferry, clearing the goods through the destination port and across various national frontiers, insuring the shipment, etc?

In a technical sense, 'exporting' to EC countries should cease in 1992 because procedures for intra-Community trade will by then be essentially the same as for 'domestic' transactions. Nevertheless, certain complex administrative procedures for transporting goods between member states will remain, although some measures for simplifying these have already been implemented.

The single administrative document (SAD)
There is now a single document for clearing goods through the customs and excise departments of Community members, provided that the goods originated in the Community (or have already paid duty on their initial entry). Import duty on goods originating outside the Community is paid just once (although VAT and internal excise duty is still payable as normal). Thereafter the goods are free to move wherever necessary.

Customs 1988
Today, most countries (not just EC members) operate the *Harmonised Commodity Coding System* (HS for short) comprising a series of code numbers which describe goods for customs purposes. For 'exports' to EC countries a variation on HS (known as TARIC) is used.

EC Carnets
A carnet is a document for enabling a firm *temporarily* to import goods into another country (eg, for exhibition or as samples) without paying customs duties. Previously, businesses wishing to show goods to potential customers in several Community countries required a separate carnet for each nation. Now, however, a single document can be used throughout the Community.

Advice on these and other documentation matters is available from your bank (which will probably have produced leaflets covering such procedures), or from a freight forwarder, which is a transport firm specialising in international distribution.

Freight forwarders

As well as actually transporting goods to European (or other) destinations, freight forwarders provide extensive consultancy services including the provision of advice on:

- the most cost-effective means of transport to a destination taking into account the size, weight and nature of the goods and how quickly they must be delivered;
- packaging, and labelling; and
- warehousing in the recipient country.

Often, forwarders can offer attractive freight rates to European centres because of their ability to group together numerous small shipments into one large consignment. Major forwarders also provide container deposit and pick up facilities around the Community.

You have to be careful when selecting a freight forwarder; indeed, one survey revealed that nearly half of all users of forwarding firms were dissatisfied with the service provided! This is perhaps unfair to freight forwarders because exporters do not always appreciate the complexity of the documentation needed to transport goods across national frontiers and of the extent of the administrative red tape and sources of delay that are entirely beyond the forwarder's control. Few air journeys, for example, take more than two hours to EC destinations; yet at least two or three working days may be necessary to clear the goods – perhaps even a couple of weeks!

To find a good forwarder contact the Institute of Freight Forwarders, which is the industry's professional body and which seeks constantly to improve the standard of service that its members provide.

How to evaluate a forwarder's services

In deciding whether a forwarder's performance is satisfactory, ask yourself the following questions.

- Has the forwarder considered *customer* requirements (rather than your own and the forwarder's convenience) when choosing an appropriate transport form? Customer needs vary with respect to how, when and with what urgency goods are required. Also, expensive door-to-door delivery is not always necessary – some customers are willing to pick up deliveries from (say) a local container depot in return for a lower price.

- Were you misled about the forwarder's groupage arrangements? The fact that a forwarder despatches, for example, ten loads per week to West Germany does not mean there will be room for your consignment on any of them! How long must you wait prior to your goods' despatch and how much is the delay costing you?
- Are you fully aware of all the items included in the forwarder's price? Do you know, for example, how much is being charged for insurance, and if so have you compared this with an independent quotation from a local UK insurance firm?
- Have the costs and benefits of various transportation options been properly explained, especially the weight/bulk conversion factors applied by road and rail carriers, ferries and airlines?
- How willing and able is the forwarder to make special arrangements to combine your consignments and other loads in exceptional urgent circumstances?

You can learn more about exporting through reading the excellent free booklets published by the DTI; by joining an 'Export Club' (the addresses of which are available from the DTI) or through a trade association or Chamber of Commerce.

Use of agents

Free access to the wider Community market, coupled with language difficulties and ignorance of business methods in other EC countries is sure to cause many firms to seek agents to represent their interests in European states. Certain private consultants specialise in arranging agency representation for UK firms, and the British Overseas Trade Board offers an agency-finding service. Private agency-finding consultants might be slightly more expensive than the BOTB, but should have the advantage of expert knowledge of particular types of product and/or markets. Also they can dovetail the selection of an agent into a wider EC marketing strategy which could include transport, distribution, warehousing, advertising and sales promotions in target EC markets.

Under the BOTB scheme, information about the exporting company and its products is sent to the commercial department of the appropriate overseas British embassy or consulate which then reports back (normally within eight weeks) with a list of recommended agents. There is a fee (currently up to £500) for the service, but this is refunded if the exporter visits the foreign market on business within six months of receiving the report. A list of potential agents, but containing only their names, addresses and telephone numbers, can be obtained without payment. The essential criteria to apply when choosing an agent are as follows.

- The agent's proven knowledge of local business conditions and practices.
- The agent's ability to conduct local marketing research.
- Whether the agent has contacts with local businesses capable of supplying specialist services to the exporting company (repair and after sales services for example).
- How easily the agent can be contacted.
- Whether the agent will represent competing firms and, if so, the incentives that are needed to encourage the agent to promote the exporter's products enthusiastically.
- How much information and feedback on matters such as consumer responses to the product, the quality of local delivery arrangements, whether local translations of operating instructions are satisfactory, etc, the agent can provide.
- How easily the calibre of the agent's work can be evaluated.
- The agent's track record, how long the firm has existed and its general business reputation.
- How extensively the agent covers the market; how many branch offices it has and their location and whether the agent can genuinely cover an entire EC country?
- Whether the agent possesses sufficient resources for the task: staff, showrooms, technical competence, storage facilities, etc.
- The ease with which the firm can control and motivate the agent? What control and motivational devices (eg, submission of market reports, inspection arrangements, commission and other incentive systems) are built into the deal? Normally the agent will be asked to prepare quarterly sales forecasts and to explain significant deviations of actual sales from these predictions. The agent should keep a record of enquiries received, calls made, customer complaints, etc, and submit details on a monthly basis.
- Will the agent require a large amount of technical training about the product and sales training for promoting it effectively?

Agents operate on a commission basis and may be either *brokers*, who simply bring together buyers and sellers without ever taking physical possession of the goods; or *factors*, who do possess the goods until customers are found and who sometimes sell under their own names at the prices they think best. A *del credere* agent is one who, in return for a higher commission indemnifies the supplying firm against customers' bad debts. Factors (or 'distribution agents' as they are sometimes called) are normally preferred when the product is:

- frequently required at short notice;
- sold in small quantities but has to be transported in bulk;
- one that sells better in showroom surroundings; and
- normally sold after inspection and/or requires a spare parts service.

Note (importantly) that agency law differs markedly between EC countries and that in some countries agents, once appointed, cannot easily be dismissed; and if they are they may be entitled to substantial financial compensation. Details of the law of agency in other EC countries are available (free of charge) from the Department of Trade and Industry.

It is easy to fall out with an agent, so agency agreements must be carefully drafted and if you have no experience of these matters you should consult a solicitor or other specialist before you proceed. Make sure the contract contains full details of:

- the parties to the agreement;
- goods covered (especially whether the agent is to be allowed to repackage or otherwise alter items);
- product sales prices;
- the period of the deal and the territory covered;
- how disputes between the exporter and the agent shall be resolved; which country's law shall apply and whether and in what circumstances the dispute might go to arbitration;
- commission rates and payments for additional services; and
- responsibility for:
  — collecting debts
  — transport of goods to customers
  — breakages and other spoilage
  — local advertising and promotion
  — after sales service.

Piggy-backing
Large firms which already operate in certain foreign markets are sometimes willing to act as agents for other businesses that wish to export to those markets. This enables them to utilise fully their sales representatives, premises, office equipment, etc, in the foreign countries concerned. An example is the 'Tradeway' system operated by ICI, which currently handles the work of 300 UK companies (mostly small businesses) that sell in ICI's 150 markets overseas. The system operates as a conventional agency, using ICI's extensive network of offices and sales organisations in foreign countries, although the company will only offer its services for the marketing of chemical products which complement its own product range.

Sister companies
1992 is causing large numbers of UK businesses to seek 'sister companies' within the EC. Sister companies are foreign firms offering similar products and which are of similar size and structure to the one seeking a partner. They not only act as a foreign agent but will also advise on local conditions, translate documents, and generally provide support and comfort when things go wrong. Your own firm will offer reciprocal facilities to the foreign business: there will be regular meetings and exchanges of information and possibly the exchange of staff for short periods. Ideally the sister company should be engaged in complementary rather than competitive lines of work and face the same sorts of problems as the exporting business. Above all else however, it needs to consist of people with whom you can communicate easily and establish a good rapport. Language might be important here, emphasising again the growing need for training in business language skills. The EC has consistently encouraged sister company arrangements, and offers a clearing house (the Business Co-operation Centre) for this purpose. Details are available from the London office of the EC.

European Economic Interest Groups (EEIG)
These are combinations of European businesses (companies, partnerships or sole traders) which extend over at least two EC states. Their purpose is to pool common research and development or marketing activities, or to manage particular projects. However, the EEIG must not seek to make profits 'in its own right'.

An EEIG has a separate legal identity (established *via* a procedure laid down in an EC regulation of 1985), but individual members have unlimited liability for the debts of the entire Group. EEIGs need not have any capital and are not required to file annual reports or accounts.

Export administration companies
These are specialist export management consultants/agencies which attend to all export documentation, overseas distributions and other export matters on their clients' behalf, operating in clients' names and using clients' letterheads, possibly even working from client's offices. In effect, the export administration company becomes your entire export department as and when you need one; yet you incur no overhead costs! Other advantages are that you retain complete control over how the goods are marketed in foreign countries (you have a one-to-one relationship with the export administrator), and you build up goodwill in overseas markets under your own name.

Normally you will have to pay a small annual retainer plus a commission on sales for the use of an export administrator's services.

Such an arrangement can be highly cost effective for the small and/or occasional exporter. However, make sure the company has an expert knowledge of the target market, and is well represented in that country. A common complaint against export administrators is that because they handle the exports of so many clients they fail to attend properly to the specialised needs of any one of them. Also they are (obviously) more interested in the bigger contracts, perhaps to the detriment of smaller clients' work.

A list of export administrators is available from SITPRO, which is a government agency set up to simplify international trading documents and procedures. Look also in *Yellow Pages* under the heading 'Export managers'.

Indirect exporting to Europe

Indirect exporting is possible through 'export houses', which is a generic title applied to a variety of foreign trade intermediaries. *Export merchants* will buy your goods in the UK and resell them in European markets. They act as principals in export transactions and perform a wholesaling function as far as the exporter is concerned. Some specialise in particular countries, others in certain types of goods. Merchants carry all the risks of failure and you are relieved of all responsibilities for transport, insurance, documentation, etc. In considering whether to use a particular merchant, ask yourself the following questions.

- What is the merchant's track record in your target European markets?
- How many competing products does the merchant handle and why should the merchant promote yours any differently from the rest?
- What is the cost differential between using a merchant and dealing direct?
- How extensive are the merchant's distribution systems (agents, stockists, local branch offices, etc) in various EC countries?
- What are the implications of your loss of control over how your products are presented and sold, especially for your corporate image in foreign markets?

Confirming houses represent, as principals, foreign buyers who are not sufficiently well known in the UK for British firms to supply them on credit. The confirming house guarantees ('confirms') payment for the goods and hence assumes the risk of the buyer's default, charging the buyer a commission for this service.

Lists of export houses are available from the British Export Houses Association. Information on the activities of confirming houses – particularly when they are instructed by foreign buyers to look for certain types of goods – can be obtained from the Export Intelligence Service of the BOTB.

Other means of entry

Joint ownership ventures
Here you join with local investors to create a business which you jointly own and control. Joint ventures are useful for firms that lack the financial, material or managerial resources necessary to enter a new foreign market independently. If you engage a consultant to advise you on the desirability of a joint venture make sure he or she covers the following points.

- Are the working methods of member companies truly compatible, and if not, what problems might this cause?
- Will the establishment of the venture transmit a signal to competitors that they too should be interested in this market?
- How and how often will members communicate and exchange information?
- How and when are the performances of each member to be appraised, and how will underperformance be dealt with?
- How much would it cost to acquire the knowledge, skills and resources necessary to avoid having to participate in a joint venture?
- Is the joint venture suitable only as a short-term measure or could it provide a vehicle for long run expansion in the market concerned? If the latter, then who will finance the expansion in operations, and how (eg, loans, local share issues, introduction of new partners)?
- Will you have to pay compensation if the project is abandoned? Note the conflicts of international laws that might arise in this respect.

Licensing
This method enables you to enter the new market at minimal risk. You offer a foreign firm the right to produce and distribute your branded product (normally protected by a patent or registered

trademark) for a royalty or lump sum fee. No capital investment or exporting know-how are required; but you necessarily sacrifice profits through allowing others to make and sell your goods. A consultant's report on a proposed licensing arrangement should answer the following questions.

- What is to prevent the licensee company setting up in competition once it has learned all your production methods and trade secrets and the licence period has expired?
- How is the licensee to be controlled *vis-à-vis* quality standards, declaration of production levels, and methods of marketing the good?
- How much capital investment would be necessary to establish an independent manufacturing facility in that market?
- Are the terms of the licence completely clear, especially in relation to minimum and/or maximum output levels, territory covered, basis of royalty payments (including the frequency of payment and the currency to be used) and the circumstances under which the agreement might be terminated?
- How many alternative licensees are available if the arrangement fails?
- How frequently is the licensee to report market and other information to the licensor, and what form is the information to take?
- Might franchising be more appropriate than a simple licence? With a franchise the foreign firm adopts your complete business format in the local market – your name, trade marks, business methods, layout of premises, etc. Additionally you provide (in return for a royalty and lump sum fee) a variety of supplementary management services: training, technical advice, stock control systems, perhaps even financial loans. Hence, you retain complete control over how your product is marketed; but the franchisee carries all the risks of failure and your capital commitment is typically low.

Contract manufacturing
This means entering into contracts with local manufacturers to produce goods which you then sell locally.

Direct investment
Outright ownership of foreign-based production/distribution facilities offers many advantages. Transport costs are lower, production decisions can take account of local circumstances, you avoid dealing with troublesome agents or licensees, and can ensure

a steady supply of spare parts and after sales service to your customers.

Advertising in the European Community

Large advertising agencies (see Chapter 10) are substantial multinational corporations in their own right and as such have branch offices throughout Europe. Hence you could brief one of the leading agencies operating in the UK and then simply leave all your European advertising to that agency. Alternatively you might seek out smaller local agencies in target markets. The major criteria to apply when choosing an agency are as follows.

- Does the agency possess an efficient translation service capable of identifying changes in the tone or meaning of an advertisment caused by translation?
- How intimate are the agency's contacts and relations with local media? (Multinationals may be at a disadvantage here.)
- How extensive are the agency's support services such as advertisment pre-testing or access to mailing lists for direct marketing exercises?
- In the case of a branch of a multinational agency, how do local staff compare with the agency's staff in Britain.
- Is the agency capable of devising an entirely new advertising campaign for your product without needing to 'import' ideas about the campaign from the advertisments you use in the UK?
- What is the agency's track record *vis-à-vis* similar products in foreign markets?
- Does the agent offer adequate coverage of target market segments?

If you leave the choice to a consultant, make sure he or she:

- devises an advertising plan for each country that fits in with the company's overall corporate strategy for the European market; and
- puts individual country briefs and recommendations into a common format, so that agency performances in various EC centres can be compared and appraised.

There is no immutable law that you must use an advertising agent for European (or indeed any other) work, and you might choose to devise advertisments for the European market yourself. If so, the DTI will provide you with a list of translation agencies which will rewrite your sales literature in another language.

Getting paid

As trade within the community becomes free of restriction, certain traditional methods of overseas financing (bills of exchange, letters of credit, payment against presentation of shipping documents) will be increasingly unacceptable for settling transactions. In effect, a sale by a firm in (say) London to a firm in Cologne, West Germany, will be the same as a sale by a firm in London to one in Leeds. Local suppliers in Cologne quote their sale prices in West German currency and (importantly) will offer credit terms. To compete with local German suppliers a British firm will have to do the same, ie, quote a local currency full delivered price, and run the risk of the customer defaulting.

Avoiding risk of default

Default risk might be avoided through having the German firm present a post-dated banker's draft on delivery of the shipment; provided the customer is willing to do this (and why should it if there are local businesses willing to supply goods without the inconvenience) and provided the firm's bank is prepared to guarantee the draft. Usually, however, banks insist that funds to the full value of a draft be deposited before the draft is issued, and the German firm may be reluctant to tie up its working capital in this way.

Otherwise, credit insurance is available from a private insurance broker or from the Export Credit Guarantee Department (ECGD). Unfortunately for the exporter, this will only be available if the ECGD (or other insurer) believes there are reasonable grounds for assuming the debt will be settled eg, through the existence of a confirmed irrevocable letter of credit. Thus, cover might be refused and it is essential therefore that exporters conduct comprehensive credit checks – *via* the ECGD, the BOTB, or through a private agency (all of which charge for the service) – prior to assuming such risks.

The Export Credit Guarantee Department

Founded in 1926, this government owned body (due to be privatised shortly) exists to provide UK exporters with low cost insurance against foreign customer default. Additionally it provides much general information and advice on export credit and financing matters. The ECGD is non-profit making, so premiums are low – typically about a quarter of one per cent of the sum insured. About a third of all UK exports to Europe are insured by the ECGD.

Note that it is the *payment* and not the goods that is insured here. Separate insurance is needed for damage to cargo in transit. Details of ECGD services are available from the address quoted at the end of the chapter.

Role of the bank

Without doubt, high street banks are the best source of help and advice on collection of foreign debts. All the UK banks have direct contacts with banks in importing countries, and possess great experience of the financial aspects of international trade. They have divisions and departments dealing exclusively with foreign business and many of them publish excellent free pamphlets explaining various export financing procedures. Only rarely will you be able to improve on your bank's consultancy advice regarding export finance.

Credit factors

Payment difficulties can be overcome – at a price – through using a credit factor, ie, a firm that will purchase at a discount all an exporter's invoices for cash as they are issued. Factors are used not only to avoid default, devaluation and other risks but also because of the high interest cost of the long delays frequently attached to trading overseas. Most high street banks offer a factoring service for EC transactions.

Factoring is convenient, but it can be expensive; you might only get 80–85 per cent of the face value of invoices. Also, a commission on turnover is normally payable to cover the factor's administration costs – issuing statements, reminder letters, legal actions to recover debts – and (since it is the factor that is offering credit and not the supplying firm) the cost of the credit involved. If you are considering using a factor, ask yourself the following questions:

- how does the cost of factoring compare with borrowing on overdraft in order to finance the credit terms that foreign customers demand; and
- might it be worth while employing someone to deal with the clerical work attached to collecting foreign debts rather than paying a factor for this service?

A list of factoring firms is available from the Association of British Factors. Certain consultancies offer a comprehensive credit management service, including factoring and/or collection of accounts, status and market reports, and insurance against credit risk.

Further implications of 1992

Other purposes for which 1992 consultants might be useful include the establishment of warehousing and other distribution arrangements within EC countries, the analysis of changes in operating costs due to new transport procedures, and the identification of better and cheaper sources of supply outside the UK. You may also wish to consider recruiting labour from other EC countries and hence require advice on (i) how to place advertisments in the European press and (ii) the terms and conditions of employment necessary to attract foreign labour. Human resource consultants (see Chapter 9) are increasingly interested in these issues, and might assist in 1992 training (language and export skills, freight and haulage documentation, European business methods, etc).

Legal matters

1992 has important legal implications for many businesses, especially regarding product safety standards and whether the firm's existing sales and purchasing contracts correspond to EC contract law. Note, moreover, that different rules apply to various methods of sales promotion in different EC countries. Did you know, for example, that (at the time of writing) a money-off voucher is legal in Spain but not in West Germany; that a 'lower price for the next purchase offer' is legal in Belgium, illegal in Denmark, and may be illegal in Italy; or that cross-product offers are illegal in Luxembourg, as are free draws in Holland?

The European Federation of Sales Promotion is currently devising common guidelines for these matters with a view to suggesting common laws for promotion throughout the EC. You can obtain details from the Institute of Sales Promotion.

The consultant's report

A 1992 consultant's report might consist of an 'export plan' – specifying the product modifications; changes in marketing methods, advertising and other promotional strategies and new distribution arrangements needed to survive following 1992 – or it might comprise detailed advice on a specific issue such as which companies to target for intended european acquisitions. An export plan should contain the following details.

- Where potential customers are located; what they are like, the kind of service they expect and how the company can reach them.
- Budgets listing anticipated expenditures on selling and distributing within the single market.
- How export documentation and transportation are to be handled.

- Suggestions for modifying, repackaging or redesigning the product to increase its attraction in the wider community, or a statement why product adaptation is not required.
- A European advertising and sales promotion strategy.
- Details of current and anticipated future competitors and how to deal with them.
- Sales and market share targets, plus an assessment of their feasibility and a list of the barriers that might prevent their being achieved.
- Ideas for entirely new products that the firm could offer and which would be particularly suitable for European markets.
- A system for appraising how well the plan is working, including a timetable for achieving objectives.

More general reports might include discussions of:

- takeover targets in key European markets;
- where and how to recruit skilled European labour;
- a scheme for locating public sector spending programmes particularly relevant to the firm (the report should definitely analyse the vulnerability of your business to the loss of local or central government orders to other EC companies); or
- whether to seek business insurances from EC insurance companies outside the UK.

Appraisal problems

It is not generally possible to assess the calibre of a 1992 consultant against the results of his or her recommendations because the consequences of their implementation might not be felt for several years. And by that time it will be too late to complain if the suggestions are unsatisfactory. Rather, you need to appraise such a consultant primarily against the quality of *information* provided and whether this is presented in a suitable form. Is it obvious from the consultant's report what exactly you need to do? If not, should the information have been condensed or formulated differently?

A major difficulty, of course, is that because the measures proposed for 1992 are new and unique, consultants *themselves* are constantly discovering fresh aspects of the subject. Client firms could collect and read 1992 information (new laws and regulations, export intelligence services, tax rate and EC subsidy changes, proposals for further trade liberalisation, etc) for themselves as it emerges – consultants have no monopoly on access to data in the 1992 field. To do all this, however, would absorb enormous amounts of time and effort, and interpretations as well as raw data are required. What you need, therefore, are short, succinct and relevant summaries specifically related to the operational requirements of your firm.

Sources of information

Association of British Chambers of Commerce
212a Shaftesbury Avenue
London WC2H 8EW
01-240 5831

Association of British Factors
147 Fleet Street
London EC4A 3DU
01-353 1213

British Export Houses Association
69 Cannon Street
London EC4N 5AB
01-248 4444

British Exporters' Association
16 Dartmouth Street
London SW1H 9BL
01-222 5419

Chamber of Commerce
See local telephone directory

Department of Trade and Industry
British Overseas Trade Board
1-19 Victoria Street
London SW1H OET
01-215 4919

ECGD Insurance Services
Crown Buildings
Cathays Park
Cardiff CF1 3NH

The BOTB also has regional offices throughout the UK.

The European Commission (London Office)
8 Storey's Gate
London SW1P 3AT
01-222 8122

Export Buying Offices' Association
Elsley House
24-30 Great Titchfield Street
London W1P 8BB
01-493 8141

Export Counselling Service
Export Marketing Research Scheme
Association of British Chambers of Commerce
Sovereign House
212a Shaftesbury Avenue
London WC1H 8EW
01-240 5831/6

Export Credit Guarantee Department
Aldermanbury House
Aldermanbury
London EC2P 2EL
01-382 7000

Export Direction magazine
Swains House
8-15 Aylesbury Street
London EC1R OLR
01-250 1100

Export Intelligence Service
Regency House
1-4 Warwick Street

London W1R 5WA
01-494 4030

Export Market Information Centre
(Formerly the Statistics and Market Intelligence Library)
1 Victoria Street
London SW1H OET
01-215 8444/5

Export Network
Regency House
1-4 Warwick Street
London W1R 5WA
01-494 4030

Export Today magazine
Setform Limited
Europa House
13-17 Ironmongers Row
London EC1V 3QN
01-253 2545

Institute of Freight Forwarders
Suffield House
9 Paradise Road
Richmond
Surrey TW9 1SA
01-948 3141

The Institute of Linguists
24a Highbury Grove
London N5
01-359 7445

The Institute of Sales Promotion
Panstar House
13-15 Swakeleys Road
Ickenham
Middlesex UB10 8DF
0895 74281/2

The Institute of Translation and Interpreting
318 Finchley Road
London NW3 5HT

Market Research Society
15 Belgrave Square
London SW1X 8PF
01-235 4709

SITPRO
Almack House
26-28 King Street
London SW1Y 6QW
01-930 0532

Chapter 15

Using a Consultant to Draft a Business Plan

Introduction — Who to approach — Briefing the consultant — An outline structure for a business plan — Appraising the consultant's contribution

After reading this chapter you should:

- appreciate the difference between a business plan and a business strategy
- know what should be included in a business plan
- be competent to assess the calibre of a business plan drafted by an outside consultant; and
- be able to brief the consultant you hire to prepare your business plan.

Introduction

Firms that require large overdrafts, government or local authority grants, or which seek assistance from trade associations or other outside bodies must normally prepare and submit a business plan in support of their applications. In fact, a 'plan' drafted for these purposes is as much a description of the current activities and general 'state of health' of a business as it is a prescription for intended future projects and policies. In consequence, many owners and senior managers of businesses feel uneasy about writing such a plan: they are not sure what is required, how much detail is expected, or even the format to adopt. Accordingly, some firms (especially small businesses) use external consultants to help draft their business plans.

Who to approach

Banks will not consider an application for a substantial commercial loan unless it is accompanied by a precise statement explaining how the money is to be used. So frequently do firms appeal to their banks for help in drafting business plans that today most banks publish booklets which outline the sorts of information the plan should contain and suggest a model layout for the presentation of data – with recommended headings, sample checklist questions, etc.

Some of these outlines are really very good, and you might need no further assistance. Otherwise, firms may approach their accountants or solicitors for advice in this area. However although solicitors might have extensive experience of business; they will usually have received no business or management training. In particular their knowledge of marketing may be extremely limited. Qualified accountants may or may not have studied non-financial aspects of management, depending on the accountancy body to which they belong (see Chapter 6 for details). Again, the typical accountant's knowledge of sales and marketing management is (to say the least) limited and you will often find that business plans drafted by accountants greatly overemphasise the financial aspects of the firms activities – while ignoring several crucially important marketing issues.

Any of the large consultancy firms will be pleased to prepare your business plan, though using a large consultancy can prove very expensive for the small business. If the plan has a *strategic* aspect you can apply for help through the DTI Enterprise Initiative (see Chapter 1). Note, however, that Enterprise Initiative Business Planning consultancies are available principally for strategic purposes. The DTI scheme states explicitly that a Business Planning grant cannot be used to produce a plan the primary purpose of which is to secure bank funding.

If you obtain DTI assistance you will be matched with a suitable consultant by DTI's independent Scheme Contractor. Otherwise consider approaching the Institute of Management Consultants (see Chapter 1), or look in *Yellow Pages* under the heading 'Management consultants'. In selecting a consultant for this work make sure that he or she:

- has experience of business plan formulation (and perhaps of subsequent negotiations with bank managers and/or grant awarding bodies);
- knows about marketing as well as the financial and legal aspects of business; and
- understands the competitive situation that applies to your industry or line of work.

Benefits of planning
Apart from its usefulness for raising funds; the preparation of a plan offers several other benefits.

- The firm is compelled to confront (perhaps unpleasant) realities and to analyse systematically its strengths and weaknesses.
- The merits of the proposal for which funding is sought will be examined in depth and the project meticulously costed.
- The internal staff who collect and assemble information for the plan should – having invested much time, effort and resources in the exercise – feel fully committed to implementing the plan's proposals.
- Subsequent performance can be monitored against predetermined targets.
- Management becomes aware of what must be done to co-ordinate all the activities necessary to carry out recommendations. This might involve creating or reorganising departments, recruiting new staff or discarding current employees.

Briefing the consultant

Tell the consultant why and how the business began, its development, profitability, your objectives and future aspirations. Offer your own interpretation of the firm's internal situation, and discuss with the consultant *your* perceptions of external opportunities and threats. Specify the alternatives you believe are open to the business and state the short and medium term policies you had in mind for achieving your aims.

Clarify your expectations about how much detail the plan should contain and (particularly if you negotiate a payments by results deal with the consultant) specify the minimum criteria that must be satisfied before it can be regarded as successful, eg, raising a certain amount of money, some stated improvement in market share, or a predetermined increase in the financial return over a certain period. Set the consultant a good example by having comprehensive details of all your financial and other assets, personnel, technical and existing company policies available at the outset of the exercise.

Need for honesty

The tone of a business plan should be sober and reflective. It should be (i) written in simple english, (ii) completely truthful, and (iii) reveal all relevant information. Do not mislead the consultant about, for example, the likely timing of anticipated incomes and expenditures: cash deficits during critical periods can ruin otherwise profitable firms.

If you are hovering on the brink of a cash flow crisis do not conceal the fact. Remember that if you successfully misrepresent your trading position in order to raise a loan you are actually *worsening* your trading situation, because you merely add loan interest and capital repayment requirements to your cash flow difficulties.

Do not accept help from a business planning consultant who promises to 'cook the books' in order to create attractive yet untrue images of your company. The consultant may succeed in raising finance, but will not be around when the firm has to repay the money. Remember also that people who regularly examine business plans (bank managers or local authority enterprise development officers for example) have extensive experience of spotting problems within businesses. Indeed they will be actively *looking* for structural and operational deficiencies as they read the plan: they have seen it all before and are not easily misguided. And even if you can deceive them it is still you who will suffer in the longer period.

An outline structure for a business plan

Below is a draft structure for a business plan which you might adopt for your own company or against which you can compare a consultant's presentation.

Introduction
This should briefly describe the origin and development of the firm and the idea behind the creation of the business. It should then outline:

- the firm's particular strengths and weaknesses; what it is especially good at and the activities it does not perform very well;
- reasons for deficiencies; the measures that have been implemented to overcome them and whether they are working;
- how the firm compares with competitors, how many competitors there are and where they are located;
- the fundamental *purpose* of the business – what the firm exists to do;
- general features of the environments surrounding the firm (eg, the buoyancy of its markets, the tax regime, licensing arrangements, special packaging or labelling regulations); and
- the firm's sensitivity to environmental change.

The product
A 'product' is anything the firm offers for sale, regardless of whether this is a physical good or a service. If you are a manufacturer, briefly describe your production methods and, importantly, the vulnerability of the business to changes in production technology. What have you done to pre-empt the adverse consequences of

possible technical changes? How rapid is the rate of technical change in the industry and how can you predict new developments? Is your manufacturing technology capable of coping with change?

Specify the raw materials your products contain and where you get them. Do your products require particular types of skilled labour? If so, identify the source(s) of your labour supply. Then state:

- the firms general policies and procedures for
  — identifying new product opportunities
  — redesigning or otherwise modifying existing products
  — withdrawing products;
- how each product contributes to the image of the firm;
- special production difficulties attached to the firm's products and how you are dealing with them; and
- after-sales service requirements.

The plan might include proposals (with justifications) for expanding product lines, changing product features, standardising a range of existing products, altering brand images, and perhaps for producing components within the firm rather than buying them from outside.

Constraints on the operations and/or growth of the business
Here you should list and briefly describe the factors that have restricted the firm's ability to achieve its full potential. Constraints might include:

- limited finance, especially lack of working capital;
- lack of availability of skilled labour;
- inability to offer extended credit;
- restricted access to distributors or sources of supply;
- problems with premises, eg, lack of space, shortage of alternative premises in the local area, refusal of local authority planning permission for extensions to existing premises;
- inability to obtain licences, franchises, etc; and
- legal constraints imposed through exclusive dealership arrangements, contracts in restraint of trade, etc.

Then you specify the measures you intend to apply in order to remove these barriers and how much these measures will cost.

The competition
A detailed and comprehensive analysis of competing firms (including possible new competitors, especially those which might emerge after 1992) is an essential part of a business plan. Who are the competitors and what is the quality of their output? What measures are you implementing to ensure you will beat the competition? What

are the sources of other firms' competitive advantage (see Chapter 3) and what are you doing to negate these factors? Your action plan for dealing with competitors might include:

- contingencies for quickly and drastically reducing prices in the event of a new and unwelcome competitor entering the market;
- a statement of whether your firm is or intends being a market leader or market follower, and the implications of this decision; and
- an appraisal of where your business fits into the competitive structure of the market and, where appropriate, plans for altering your position.

Marketing methods

This section should list the means by which you intend achieving your marketing objectives. It is not a strategic analysis (see Chapter 3) or even an audit of your marketing strengths and weaknesses (see Chapter 10). Rather it states *how* you promote and sell your output.

Begin with a brief description of the selling points of your products, who you expect to buy them and why. Then specify:

- how the products compare with those of competitors;
- the sizes and outline structures of existing and intended future markets; and
- customer ordering systems, including arrangements for credit control.

Next, briefly describe a typical customer and his or her buying habits. If the firm is critically dependent on just one or two large customers state the advantages and disadvantages of the situation (steady business, low invoicing and credit control costs, etc).

State and *justify* the firms' pricing policies and relate the prices you charge to your production costs. If you have conducted marketing research (see Chapter 10), outline the major conclusions of the investigation. Distribution must also be considered. Specify the number and characteristics of distribution outlets, their adequacy and the alternatives available if existing outlets fail. Mention any special distribution problems (perishability of output, fragile products, need for special packages, risks of contamination, pilfering, etc) and how they are overcome.

If the firm has purchased its own delivery vehicles, state their type and condition and your garaging and maintenance arrangements. Other matters requiring attention in the marketing section are:

- plans for developing new products;
- seasonal factors affecting demand; leads and lags in sales; and

- marketing 'communications' policies, listed under sub-headings for advertising messages and media, sales promotions activities (coupons, competitions, etc), direct mail, exhibition policies (see Chapter 10), public relations, use of salespeople 'in the field', and so on.

Then you present estimates for the costs of improving various marketing activities, stating the tangible benefits the improvements will create and when you expect them to occur.

Staff and the organisation system

The plan must include brief *curricula vitae* of key employees, summarising their administrative experience and particular management skills. Specify whether you anticipate hiring extra staff and, if so, why. Where can additional employees of the right calibre be recruited and at what cost?

Organisation charts must be provided showing who is in charge of particular functions. Justify the firm's divisional and departmental structures. State, for example, that they were chosen to assist easy appraisal, to increase the specialisation of functions, to create a management development and succession scheme, to provide coverage of a certain market, and so on.

This section should also deal with all legal matters affecting the firm: licences, fire certificates, health and safety requirements, etc.

Short/medium term objectives

Here you specify (i) break-even points for various pricing assumptions, (ii) anticipated profit margins, and (iii) quantitative targets for:

- sales over the next few quarters;
- market shares of various market segments;
- cost cutting programmes;
- plant utilisation;
- returns on capital employed;
- rate of growth of operations;
- cash inflows;
- expansion of working capital;
- introduction or withdrawal of products; and
- improvements in credit control (reducing the average period needed to collect a debt for example).

Premises

State whether your long term strategy is to rent or buy premises, and justify the choice. Relate your existing premises to anticipated future requirements and specify the extensions and property conversions necessary to achieve your aims. Outline the strengths and weaknesses of your premises. Strengths might include such factors as:

- a buoyant demand for the firm's product in the immediate area;
- impressive looking façade;
- no local competition;
- ample local supplies of skilled labour; or
- nearness to raw materials supplies.

Weaknesses could involve:

- insufficient parking space for customers and/or suppliers;
- inadequate gas, electricity or water supplies;
- frequent burglaries; or
- lack of space for expansion.

The business plan should describe how you will build on the premises' strengths and overcome their weaknesses. These matters are discussed further in Chapter 13 above.

Contingency arrangements
The plan should specify alternative arrangements for reorganising various activities if things do not work out. What happens, for example, if:

- a major customer goes out of business;
- supplies fail to arrive on time;
- important raw materials are no longer available;
- distributors' employees call a strike;
- your premises are flooded or catch fire;
- key senior employees leave the firm; or
- bad weather temporarily disrupts your sales?

State the insurances you have taken out, their cost and the extent of their cover.

Financial aspects
You will need to provide profit and loss accounts and balance sheets for the last three years; a detailed cash flow forecast for the next twelve months, plus outline cash flow forecasts for the next couple of years. If yours is a small business you might have to state your personal means (property, insurance policies, etc) that can be used as security against a loan and the extent of your personal investment in the business.

Other items to mention here are key accounting ratios: return on capital employed, liquidity ratio, sales to fixed assets, etc; plus details of major intended expenditures with full justifications. Describe your credit policies and how sensitive your business is to late payment by customers. State also your budgetary control methods and whether they are effective. If they are not effective, specify the alternatives you are considering adopting.

Appraising the consultant's contribution

A good plan is one that is *comprehensive* and *convincing.* Read it through. Has everything been covered, and if you were (say) a bank manager would *you* be prepared to lend a large amount of money to the business? Ask yourself the following questions.

- In preparing the plan, has the consultant revealed resource deficiencies you did not previously realise existed?
- Will existing resources be better utilised in consequence of implementing the plan?
- Is it obvious what you must do in order to implement the plan?
- Is the firm now better equipped to cope with a change in the business environment.
- Does the plan identify things you need to do today in order to influence future events?
- Is the plan sufficiently detailed and does it look far enough into the future? Is it concise and easy to understand? Does it consider a reasonably wide range of alternative possibilities and properly evaluate the implications and side effects of each available option?

Chapter 16

Management Consultants, Professional Negligence and the Law

Introduction — Making a complaint — Causes of inefficiency — Types of complaint — How to sue an incompetent consultant — Agents — Professional negligence — The consultant's personal liability — Supply of goods and services

After reading this chapter you should:

- know the meaning of professional negligence;
- understand the difference between professional negligence and breach of contract;
- be aware of the legal remedies available for unsatisfactory work; and
- know the causes of inadequate performance among consultants and how to complain about this.

Introduction

Consultant/client relations do not always run smoothly. Consultants sometimes expect too much money for too little work; while clients might not appreciate the full extent of the effort needed to complete an assignment. Also, clients can be extraordinarily gullible where consultancy services are concerned. Boards of directors that take enormous care when selecting senior management employees may happily place all their trust in a consultant about whom they actually know very little; and then expect the consultant to perform with perfect efficiency regardless of the particular difficulties of the situation and the resource and other constraints they impose. Clients might not be prepared to accept any kind of disorganisation of existing procedures, and are shocked and angry when the slightest carelessness occurs.

What can you do if the consultant you engage performs badly? The answer to this question mainly depends on two factors: the type of consultant concerned, and the nature of the consultancy contract (see Chapter 1). You have to consider whether the consultant is acting as your or someone else's agent; whether equipment, materials and/or ancillary services are provided as part of the deal, and the causes and consequences of the unsatisfactory work. While not wishing to prejudge the emergence of possible difficulties you do need to look ahead and consider the ease with which you will be able to seek redress for incompetent work, and take this into account when selecting a consultant. For example, a great advantage of using a personnel management consultant rather than a solicitor for anything to do with hiring/firing or other aspects of employment legislation is that while you can use a solicitor to sue an incompetent personnel management consultant, you cannot normally use a consultant to sue a solicitor. In order to take legal action against a solicitor you normally have to employ another solicitor, and although the Law Society does provide a fall-back service for supplying people with solicitors to act on their behalf in actions against other solicitors if all the solicitors initially approached refuse to accept the work, the process can be tedious and complicated and lead to unsatisfactory results. Similar problems apply to complaints against auditors, and indeed to any of the legally protected professions.

Making a complaint

Avoid being a difficult client. Do not follow the consultant around complaining about petty matters, or telephone the consultant's office too frequently, or decline to undertake reasonable amounts of research on the consultant's behalf or overload the consultant with huge quantities of insignificant data. But, if the consultant is undoubtedly incompetent, makes serious mistakes or fails to keep promises, then you have every right to complain.

The first stage in making a complaint is to point out the perceived deficiencies in a clear and precise manner, relating these to the details embodied in the initial brief and consultancy contract. Then insist that the work be redone, withholding payments until satisfactory work is completed. Special difficulties might arise in any matter concerning 'strategy' (and note immediately that much of the consultancy work available through the DTI Enterprise Initiative is obliged to relate to strategy issues) since 'strategy' is such a nebulous concept that one's opinion of whether a consultant's strategy recommendations are adequate has to be subjective. It is essential, therefore, that your expectations regarding the length, depth and content of the consultant's report on strategic aspects of the assignment be unambiguously stated – in writing – at the beginning of the project.

Make sure you complain to the right person (normally the

consultant with whom you initially discussed the proposal and not one of his or her employees) and *justify* all your allegations, quoting specific examples of inadequate performance, producing relevant documents, indicating dates, times, places, etc. Be polite, but firm. State exactly what you want to be done in order to rectify the situation. If the project has been a complete disaster from start to finish and this is entirely and demonstrably due to the consultant's incompetence then you should demand a full refund of all fees already paid.

Minor disputes

For a petty dispute on which the consultant refuses to give way you have to decide whether to continue your relations with that firm for future assignments. Either you give way and accept the consultant's claimed superior knowledge, retaining the consultant for further projects; or you pay off the consultant as quickly as possible and have nothing more to do with that firm. The latter course is usually preferable – there is little point giving your consultant further assignments if you are not entirely satisfied with his or her services.

Causes of inefficiency

Every assignment is to some extent unique, carrying its own peculiarities and difficulties. Consultants must quickly weigh-up troublesome situations, and they sometimes err through not having the time to investigate problems thoroughly. The issues that consultants are brought in to deal with are invariably complicated and demanding – consultancy advice would not otherwise be required. Obviously, the more complex the problem the greater the opportunity for human error. A third source of difficulty is that consultants often need to rely on several sub-contractors whose goods and services may not be up to scratch.

Arguably, moreover, the great expansion in management consultancy that has occurred in recent years (encouraged of course by the DTI Enterprise Initiative) has led to a general lowering of standards. More and more businesses now recognise the efficiency benefits that a consultant might provide; yet there is a desperate skills shortage in several crucial management consultancy areas.

Increasing demand for consultancy services in conjunction with a shortage of suitably qualified people can push up rates and attract incompetent individuals into consultancy. At the same time, existing consultants are encouraged constantly to expand their personal workloads (with resulting diminutions of quality) in order to maximise their reward.

Types of complaint

Complaints about management consultancy services typically concern the time taken to complete the assignment (given that most consultants charge by the day or hour); the quality of the report, service or installation provided; extra unanticipated charges for disbursements; and additional goods or services being provided superfluous to actual need.

Extra charges

Your obligation to pay extra charges depends on the wording of the consultancy contract and (importantly) on whether the original agreed price was an 'estimate' or a 'quotation'. You only have to pay what you agreed to pay, but if the price was an estimate a court will assume you should expect it to vary. (By how much an estimated price may reasonably vary must, ultimately, be determined by litigation.) A 'quote', conversely, is normally to be interpreted as a predetermined fixed price binding on both parties. Quotes become problematic when there is ambiguity regarding what *exactly* the consultant is quoting to do; so spell out your detailed requirements – in writing – when asking for quotations. Simply giving the consultant a broadly defined objective and telling him or her to get on with the job for the price quoted is obviously inviting difficulties.

The best way of dealing with an argument regarding the final bill is to establish what represents a reasonable payment. This you can do by asking other consultants to provide estimates for the same job, or by requesting a trade association or Chamber of Commerce to put you in touch with other firms that have had similar assignments completed.

Time taken

If you ask for a specific number of hours or days work then that is what you will get. But suppose the assignment is unfinished after this period and you have already paid the consultant some money? If the consultant agreed to complete the work in a predetermined period then he or she is obliged to adhere to the agreement.

The consultant must provide any additional work necessary, free of charge, unless (i) unforeseeable circumstances prevented the consultant from working (a strike or other random stoppage in a factory for instance), in which case you must pay the consultant the full rate for time wasted or some lower rate previously agreed, or (ii) the consultant was misled about the amount of work necessary. In general, however, a consultant is to be assumed professionally competent and thus able accurately to predict how long a job will take. And the consultant, not yourself, must bear the financial consequences of his or her faulty judgement.

Quality of work
Under the Supply of Goods and Services Act (1982) you are entitled to services of a 'reasonable' standard. This Act also covers the *installation* of physical goods (computer hardware and software for example). Installations and services supplied with physical goods must be undertaken with reasonable skill and care to ensure that the goods supplied fulfil the purpose for which they were intended, and the services must be completed within a reasonable period.

If you are in dispute with a consultant regarding the quality of his or her services the first thing you must do is to determine what represents a reasonable standard having regard to all aspects of the case. Discuss this with other consultants active in the field, obtain a professional opinion, and if possible, refer the question to a trade association. A reasonable level of service means the type of service provided by an honest, reputable, and genuinely skilled and experienced specialist in the consultant's field. Membership of a relevant professional body or trade association should indicate that the consultant is generally competent (see Chapter 1), although this is not always the case.

The scope for specific complaints about consultancy services is enormous. Some of the commonest accusations are as follows.

- The consultant alters the scope and nature of the assignment without your consent. Obviously, this should not happen, although a consultant might argue that the brief given was so imprecise that he or she had no alternative but to innovate and use personal initiative in determining the extent of the assignment. Either you demand your money back (the consultant is technically in breach of contract) or you accept the amendments under protest and insist there be no further changes. Good consultants avoid this practice because they know how it can infuriate and antagonise clients, so be very suspicious (especially if this is the first time you have used a particular consultant) if it happens.
- The consultant upsets your existing staff. Actually you may be quite happy about this, since your objective in engaging an outsider might have been to shake up moribund workers. But discuss the matter with the consultant and make your intentions clear at the outset of the exercise.
- The consultant takes away confidential information. If you do not wish certain documents, computer files, etc, to leave your

premises you should specify this in the consultancy contract, and identify any information that is not to be revealed to other firms. Loss or damage to important records taken by the consultant must be paid for by the consultant, but only if he or she actually took them. If you sent materials to the consultant unsolicited then the loss falls on you, even if the consultant was careless in losing them after they were received.

- The consultant abandons the assignment half way through. The frequency with which this happens is surprisingly high. A consultant may quote a fixed fee that turns out too low to cover his or her expenses and, realising this, drops the project. Also, consultants sometimes lose interest in assignments that become boring, troublesome or involve excessive amounts of work. Assuming a contract exists the consultant is in breach of contract and must pay damages for the losses you incur – including damages for consequential loss of trade.
- The consultant learns trade secrets and reveals them to competing firms. This is a complicated matter for which specialist legal advice is required. Whether such behaviour is unlawful depends on the following.
  - The nature of the contract between consultant and client. Design consultants, for example, typically insist on contracts whereby they retain the copyright on any creative work done for or through a client's firm.
  - Whether the consultant might reasonably be expected to know about the nature of the client's trade secrets as a normal part of his or her consultancy work. If the assignment is such that discovery of a trade secret might be expected then the consultant will not be able to claim that he or she discovered the secret (a process or ingredient for example) independently and thus will be liable to the client firm.
- The consultant selects expensive sources of materials supply. Point out your concerns, and obtain independent estimates of materials supply prices. Perhaps you and the consultant have contrasting ideas about the quality (and hence the cost) of materials required.
- The consultant becomes overloaded with (more profitable) work and asks to be released from the contract. In this case you are, of course, entitled to compensation, which you may choose to set aside if the consultant can find someone else willing and competent to do the job. This might be better than insisting the consultant go ahead – grudgingly and reluctantly – with the assignment and produce low quality work.

- The consultant wishes to increase the previously agreed fee. This might not be unreasonable in certain circumstances – costs may have risen unexpectedly, more work may be necessary than was initially believed; and it may be better to pay the additional amount than lose the services of a good consultant for future assignments. However, you should ask the consultant to set out the justifications for the request in great detail, including all his or her revised costs and anticipated expenditures.
- You negotiate a contract with a senior consultant, but a junior consultant turns up to do the work. This is one of the most frequent causes of complaint in the management consultancy field, as previous chapters have outlined. If you definitely do not want this to happen you should specify in the original contract that particular consultants are to undertake the assignment. Otherwise you need to be conscious of the possibility of this occurring and take it into account when negotiating the consultant's fee.
- The consultant expects enormous amounts of help and advice from your staff, to the point where you wonder whether you might just as well complete the work in-house. Neither negligence nor incapacity are necessarily involved; rather, you are alleging that the consultant is idle and not doing enough work. Assuming this is true it will normally provide sufficient ground for cancelling the contract and withholding fees. If the consultant objects it is open for him or her to seek redress through the courts.
- Your instructions are not being followed. Are your instructions clear? Why is the consultant not following your commands? Usually the problem results more from misunderstandings and breakdowns in communication rather than from sinister intent.
- You expect the consultant to arrange the supply of ancillary materials and services, but the consultant now insists that your company is responsible for this! A carefully worded contract should avoid such disputes arising.
- The consultant's report is hopelessly inadequate. It is flimsy, superficial and/or delivered late. Such incompetence entitles you to a refund of fees and possibly further damages for consequential loss (see the section on professional negligence below).
- The consultant supplies goods and services in excess of those initially agreed and expects you to pay for them! Invite the consultant to take back any physical goods delivered superfluous to your original agreement. Indeed, even if you do not ask for this to be done you still do not have to pay for excess goods provided they are kept unused in a safe location. After six months,

unsolicited goods become yours. Note however that the situation is entirely different if the consultant acts as an agent (see below), since here your contracts for the supply of goods and services are with third parties and not with the agent him or herself. An agent has authority to bind your firm to contracts with third parties. Such authority may be 'express' (arising from specific instructions given by the principal) or 'implied', ie, arising from activities normally incidental to carrying out express instructions. It is important to realise that, in law, third parties are not expected to know exactly what the principal has authorised the agent to do and may rely on appearances. Hence, if it seems reasonable for the third party to assume that the agent genuinely represents the principal, then the latter is bound by the contracts the agent enters into – even if the agent has disobeyed the principal or has exceeded his or her authority. The principal must then seek damages from the agent for the consequences of his or her breaking or exceeding instructions, though the third parties still have to be paid.

Further causes of complaint
In addition to the really quite serious problems previously outlined, numerous lesser annoyances can occur. These might not be much in themselves, but they cause friction and can easily build up into substantial difficulties. Some examples of these irritations are as follows.

- Consultancies putting insufficiently qualified and inexperienced junior staff to work on clients' accounts.
- Consultant's assuming that *every* client is ignorant of specialist methods and techniques, resulting in an arrogant and condescending manner on the consultant's part.
- Inactivity and long periods of silence from consultants engaged on lengthy projects.
- Failure of the consultant to explain what he or she is doing.
- Offhand and discourteous treatment by the consultant's staff.
- Failure to empathise with client's problems. Consultants typically undertake many projects in the course of a year and sometimes forget that you have spent (at least) several years building up your business.
- Key people in the consultancy organisation not being readily available for important discussions with the client.

How to sue an incompetent consultant

It may be possible to sue a consultant either for breach of contract or under the law of tort.* A breach of contract action would normally involve an allegation that the consultant failed to do something he or she was contractually obliged to do, or that the consultant exceeded his or her authority. All you need to do is prove (i) that a contract existed – with offer, acceptance, consideration, etc, (ii) that the contract was broken, and (iii) that significant damages resulted from the breach. If your consultant does not deliver his or her report on schedule or fails to provide certain goods agreed in the original contract then he or she may be sued for the value of your consequent loss. You have to prove that the loss was actually *caused* by the consultant's breach of contract, and not by some other factor.

Only the parties to a contract can sue on the breach of that contract. Conversely, any interested party can sue under the law of tort. Thus, third parties (eg, investors in the client's business or people who have lent it money) can bring tortious liability claims against a management consultant if the client's acceptance of the consultant's recommendations caused them loss. The commonest tortious liability claim against consultants is for professional negligence (see below).

The legal position

Consultants are legally obliged to apply such care and diligence to their work as is reasonable in all the circumstances. If a consultant professes to possess some special skill, then he or she must demonstrate that degree of care and competence ordinarily expected of a person engaged in the professional specialisation concerned. Also, the consultant must obey your instructions, and should not delegate the duties attached to the assignment to third parties (other consultants for example) without your consent unless:

- the duties are of a secretarial or routine nature, or
- there is an urgent necessity to do so, (equipment breakdown or the need to dispose of perishable goods), or
- it is established trade custom to sub-contract certain duties.

Third parties to whom consultants sub-contract must claim their

---

*Tort means 'civil wrong'. Tortious liability is more general than the liability that arises from breaking a contract. If you are not familiar with the law of contract see the latest edition of Patricia Clayton's book, *Law for the Small Business,* published by Kogan Page.

fees from the original consultant and have no redress against the client firm.

Agents

Special rules apply to *agents* as opposed to consultants who merely give advice and/or supply physical goods or intangible services. An agent is someone you authorise – orally or in writing – to establish legal relationships (usually contracts) between you and third parties. It is extremely important, legally, to know whether someone is acting as your agent or as a supplier of services or goods in his or her own right. A commercial estate agent for example will find a buyer for the owner of a property, but the final contract is between the owner and the purchaser so that if anything goes wrong the owner must sue the purchaser (or *vice versa*) without the agent becoming involved. Conversely, a vehicle fleet maintenance management consultant is typically the *supplier* of vehicle maintenance services (see Chapter 12). If vehicles are not serviced or repaired to your satisfaction you have redress against the consultant, and not the third party garages which actually complete the work or provide physical goods (tyres, car batteries, spark plugs, etc). Property management consultancies which arrange for the repair and maintenance of property may or may not be agents. It all depends on whether the consultant accepts responsibility for the work, or simply agrees to put you in touch with other people who will complete and accept responsibility for the job. The rules of agency are as follows.

- Conflicts of interest between the agent and his or her client are unlawful. Thus an agent commissioned by you to purchase something on your behalf cannot purchase the item for him or her self and then resell it to you at a higher price. The agent is only entitled to recover from you what he or she paid, plus a reasonable administrative commission or fee. Contrast this with a *supplier* of goods or services, who derives much of his or her income from buying and reselling merchandise at a higher price.
- The agent cannot act for a third party as well as yourself (and take commission from both sides) without disclosing the fact to everyone concerned. Consider for instance a commercial estate agent who imposes fees on both landlord and tenant.
- An agent is obliged to maintain strict confidentiality regarding your affairs. Equally, the agent must pass on to you any relevant information. Thus, for example, an agent engaged to sell something on your behalf *must* tell you about every offer received.

If you accept an offer price lower than the highest submitted and the agent concealed the fact that a higher price could be obtained you are legally entitled to recover the difference from the agent.

- If you intend paying a third party *via* an agent but the agent does not pass the money on (eg, if the agent goes bankrupt) you are still liable for the third party debt.
- You are liable for damages to third parties for wrongs committed by an agent 'in the course of his or her authority' eg, if the agent fraudulently misrepresents your firm.
- Agents are not allowed to take bribes from third parties as inducements to recommend that you enter contracts with those third parties.
- You are obliged to indemnify an agent for expenses incurred while reasonably exercising his or her duties. However, agents must demonstrably *earn* their commissions (ie, the events for which they are engaged must occur prior to payment).
- Agents incur no personal liability for contracts between yourself and third parties.

Professional negligence

The roots of contemporary English and Welsh law on professional liability lie in a precedent established in 1964 which determined that liability for negligence extended to statements and advice as well as physical acts. The case in question, *Hedley Byrne v Heller and Partners Ltd,** concerned an advertising agency which asked a bank whether a potential client was creditworthy. In its reply the bank stated that the client was 'trustworthy', but added a qualification that its opinion was given 'without responsibility on our part'. The client then went into liquidation, causing the advertising agency substantial financial loss. Accordingly, the agency sued the bank for having been negligent when giving advice.

In determining the case the House of Lords ruled that a 'duty of care' (see below) giving rise to liability for negligence did exist in these circumstances. The basis of the duty of care lay in *reliance*

---

*[1964] AC 465. An example of the application of the rule established in the Hedley Byrne case is the case of *J E B Fasteners Limited v Marks, Bloom & Co* ([1981] 3 A11 ER 289, in which a chartered accountant who had negligently audited a set of company accounts that showed inflated stock values was held liable to a firm which had taken over the company in reliance on those audited accounts.

on the advice provided. Reliance on advice, the Law Lords decided, creates a special relationship between the parties upon which an action for negligence can be founded. In the particular Hedley Byrne case the bank's disclaimer was held to protect it from financial liability for the agency's loss, but (importantly) the case established the general principles that liability for negligence extends to careless words as well as careless deeds and that damages can be awarded for purely financial loss as well as for physical injury to persons or damage to property.

It followed from this ruling that professional people owe a duty of care not only to their clients, but *also* to third parties who they know are relying on their skill. The key considerations here are whether the advice:

- is given casually without any intention of it being relied upon or in circumstances in which it would be unreasonable for anyone to rely on the advice:
- comes from a person who claims expert knowledge of what he or she is talking about (eg, an insurance consultant who gives bad advice on property investment would probably not be held liable, because the consultant specialises in insurance matters – negotiating claims, assessing losses, finding the lowest premiums, etc. – and not in property investment).

Not surprisingly, therefore, sensible consultants today carry insurance against their possible professional negligence. Indeed, professional indemnity insurance is compulsory for some professions (eg, solicitors) and 'highly recommended' by the governing bodies of others (the Institute of Chartered Accountants of England and Wales for instance).

This necessarily increases the consultant's costs and hence the price of his or her services. But a consultant who has insurance is nearly always a better buy than one who has not. You should regard a consultant's decision to be properly insured as a *strength* and not a weakness of his or her firm. It indicates a responsible attitude and genuine concern for clients, and should not be interpreted as an expectation that the consultant's work will be substandard. If you rely on a consultant's advice and if negligently formulated advice will cause you substantial financial loss then it is perfectly reasonable to enquire whether a consultant is insured against professional negligence.

Professional liability insurance is expensive compared to other types of insurance and some consultancies are not prepared to incur the cost. Think twice before dealing with a non-insured consultant, bearing in mind that *you* could be sued by your own customers for damages resulting from your accepting a consultant's recommendations. You need therefore to be quite sure you can then obtain recompense.

Liability insurance covers only the consultant's acts performed in the course of 'professional work', plus omissions and negligence related (only) to the consultant's area of claimed expertise. Hence, for example, if a computer consultant gives you negligent advice on (say) property management then it is unlikely the consultant's insurance will cover the resulting loss.

Duty of care

To succeed in a professional negligence claim against a consultant you must prove that he or she (i) owed you a legal duty of care, (ii) broke that duty, and (iii) caused you damage as a result. The breach of duty could involve giving bad advice, or not conducting certain necessary investigations, or negligently missing out crucially important information when briefing a client. It must be such that a reasonably prudent professional person specialising in the field would not have committed the breach. In assessing this matter a court will ask the question, 'Has the consultant exercised the skill, foresight and caution as could reasonably be required for an ordinary member of the consultant's profession'?

Carelessness is not of itself sufficient grounds for initiating an action – the consultant must have a clear duty *not* to be careless in the particular situation. Thus, casual conversation does not normally count here, because careless statements during casual conversations are to be expected as a matter of course. A final report, however, should not be carelessly presented.

Two tests might be applied to establish whether a consultant should be liable for bad advice.

- *Causation.*
  Did the bad advice cause financial loss to result directly from its implementation?
- *Foreseeability.*
  Could the consultant reasonably foresee the damages incurred in consequence of the bad advice?

Breach of duty

A consultant will only be adjudged negligent if his or her work was unreasonably careless having regard to all the circumstances of the case, which might include:

- the value of the assignment (less care is expected of jobs involving trivial sums);
- the magnitude of risk attached to the project (the riskier the work the more care is required); and
- the vulnerability of a client's business to bad advice.

Usually it is up to the client to prove that the consultant's behaviour was unreasonable.

Damages

You have to prove you suffered actual financial loss on account of the consultant's advice – which is extremely difficult (indeed almost impossible) where strategy is involved. How do you demonstrate to a court that, say, an incorrect choice of marketing strategy (see Chapters 3 and 10) following implementation of a consultant's recommendations caused a decline in your company's profitability, independent of other considerations?

Exclusion clauses

Although it was held in the 1964 Hedley Byrne case that someone giving advice on condition that it is 'without responsibility' was not liable for resulting damage, the situation was modified by the Unfair Contract Terms Act (1977), which restricts the use of disclaimers and exemption clauses to certain specified circumstances.

Some exemption clauses are legal, provided they are 'fair and reasonable', but it is up to the consultant to demonstrate to a court that any exclusion or exemption clause relating to his or her negligence or possible breach of contract is fair and reasonable in a particular situation. In assessing whether such a clause is 'reasonable' a court will consider:

- the bargaining positions of the parties;
- whether inducements (eg, price reductions) were offered to the customer to accept the condition;
- whether the services were specially designed for the customer;
- trade customs and whether the consumer should reasonably have known of the general existence of exemption clauses in a particular trade.

The consultant's personal liability

Consultants may be individual self-employed business people, (referred to as 'sole traders'), partners in a firm, or employees of a limited company (which in fact they usually own). Sole traders and partners do not have limited liability, which means that if you win a case against them they are personally liable – even to the extent of their houses, cars, furniture and other property – for paying the damages awarded by the court.

The formation of a limited liability company (which can be done off-the-peg *via* registration agents for as little as £100) enables the consultant to separate the consultancy's assets – its premises, equipment, stock, cash in hand, vehicles, etc – from his or her own private property. Effectively the consultant becomes a shareholder in and employee of his or her own firm and is only liable for the firm's debts (including amounts owing on account of being sued for professional negligence) up to the value of his or her holding of shares in the company. (Many limited companies have just £100 of share capital.)

Following a successful court action against a limited liability consultancy you cannot take any of the owner's private goods because, in law, the consultant's company is an entirely different legal 'person' to the consultant him or her self. All you can do is seize the assets of the firm (furniture, word-processors, vehicles, etc).

The disadvantages to a consultant of working through a limited company are the costs of compulsory external auditing and the need to observe all the rules of operation embodied in the Companies Act (1985).

Consultancy partnerships
The costs and inconveniences of forming and running a limited company cause many consultants to operate *via* partnerships of two or more consultants (a consultancy partnership may legally have up to 20 partners). Also, certain professional bodies (notably the three Institutes of Chartered Accountants – see Chapter 6 – and the Law Society) forbid their members to operate as limited liability companies in order to create in potential clients feelings of trust and confidence in the profession. Knowing that someone is liable to the extent of his or her own personal estate if a wrongful act is committed or if negligence occurs can be a powerful selling point for members of a profession.

Note, however, that partners in firms in professions that barred limited liability could and did circumvent the prohibition to some extent through setting up 'service companies' to provide 'ancillary' administrative and supply services under the protection of limited liability. Such a company takes over the partners' premises, staff, equipment and production facilities, leaving partners free to concentrate on professional work. The service company 'charges' a fee to the partnership for its services, which for tax purposes the partnership regards as a normal business expense.

Attitudes are changing, nevertheless, due mainly to the increasing likelihood of law actions against consultants for professional malpractice, and the escalating scale of damages that consultants might face. Accordingly, limited companies are becoming the normal mode of operation for most significant consultancy practices, and the professional bodies are beginning to recognise the realities of the new situation. The Royal Institute of British Architects, for example, removed its prohibition on members forming limited liability companies in 1981.

An advantage of dealing with a consultancy partnership is that if, alas, you do have to sue; partners' liability is 'joint and several', ie, partners are *collectively* responsible for the partnership's debts regardless of which partner ran them up. And if following a partnership's collapse some partners have no assets while others are quite well off, you can go after the wealthier partners for *all* that you are owed.

Supply of goods and services

To the extent that a consultant *not* acting as an agent (see above) actually supplies goods and services (printed materials, computer hardware/software, maintenance work, etc) then he or she is subject to UK consumer protection law just as any other supplier. Thus, for example, under the Consumer Protection Act (1987) the consultant as a supplier must not mislead you about goods prices (eg, by making a quoted low price dependant on facts or circumstances not revealed to you at the time of the order), and all possible additional charges must be disclosed.

Another important piece of legislation is the Sale of Goods Act (1979), by which the seller of goods must:

- sell goods which are of merchantable quality, ie, not defective in any way. If the goods on offer are defective then defects must be pointed out or clearly visible at the time of sale;
- supply goods which are reasonably fit for the purpose for which they are intended; and
- deliver (or make available for collection) goods which correspond to the way in which they have been described or to a sample previously inspected.

Buyers can claim compensation if goods are not delivered, and have the right to reject them on delivery if they do not correspond with the agreed detail of the transaction. Customers are entitled to full compensation if goods prove to be defective or unfit for their purpose.

Under the Act a supplying firm is not lawfully able to impose a condition on a sale saying that the supplier does not accept responsibility for their quality, suitability or delivery. Such a statement is of no effect and the buyer is still entitled to replacement of the goods or a refund.

Defective products

Under the Consumer Protection Act (1987) any supplier is now *generally* liable for defects in products. It is no longer necessary for plaintiffs to prove the supplier's negligence, as was previously the case. The key points of the Act are as follows.

- A 'producer' is not only the manufacturer of a finished article, or its raw materials (or the extractor of raw materials), or the manufacturer of component parts, but may also include any firm or person who imports, processes, distributes or otherwise supplies (eg, by hiring, or lending) the product.
- A 'product' is defined as any good (including electricity) or part of another good, or raw material. Producers are liable for their products, as is any person or firm putting a name, trade mark, or distinguishing mark (such as a business logo) on the product.
- The victim of a defective product must ask the person or firm that supplied it to identify its producer and, if the supplier is unable to do this (ie, if the last known supplier cannot 'pass back' liability for the defect) then the last supplier is fully liable. If more than one producer is involved then all are equally liable and if some are insolvent then the remainder are responsible for meeting the entire claim.

Defences against liability are that:

- the consultant did not supply the good;
- someone else produced it, and is therefore liable; although if the consultancy cannot pass back liability, either because it is in fact the producer or the actual producer has disappeared or is insolvent, then the consultancy is fully responsible for the damage caused;
- the goods are not defective;
- the state of technical knowledge at the moment of supply could not reasonably lead the supplier to suspect the goods were defective; or
- defects arose not within the product supplied but through the way someone else made up or designed the final product into which they were incorporated.

Note, however, that liability cannot be avoided through exclusion clauses in sale agreements or through notices posted around the point of sale denying responsibility. Moreover, the supplying firm must show that it was 'duly diligent' and took all reasonable steps in trying to avoid committing an offence.

Misrepresentation

If the consultancy services actually provided do not correspond to their initial description the consultant may have committed 'misrepresentation', and hence be liable for any damages thus caused. Misrepresentation may occur innocently or fraudulently. The former involves statements that are genuinely believed to be true. Fraudulent misrepresentation, conversely, is false statements which are 'recklessly and knowingly' given. Note however that false statements about merchandise, even if made unknowingly, may be considered by a court as fraudulent misrepresentation since the person selling the goods is assumed to possess expert knowledge about their quality and features.

Many consultancies publish extremely attractive brochures, and have handsomely embellished writing paper, expensive envelopes and other manifestations of a quality firm. Yet the service actually provided might not fit the high quality image which its promotional literature projects. Even so, this is not misrepresentation provided statements made are not actually false. Misrepresentation means a false statement of fact made by one party to a contract to the other before the contract is agreed, with the intention of inducing the other party to enter the contract. Bragging and blowing one's own trumpet are not normally regarded in law as statements of fact and cannot therefore constitute grounds for misrepresentation! Conversely, a consultant who promised something which he or she could not possibly deliver is guilty of deliberate deception and can be sued for damages. What you need to do is ensure that all the consultant's promises are *actually embodied in the contract*, since it is then much easier to sue.

Other grounds on which you can sue management consultants include:

- the consultant having received a commission from an equipment manufacturer to recommend that you purchase a certain type of equipment and not disclosing this, with the consultant wrongly, claiming that he or she was providing independent advice (you are entitled to sue for the value of the consultant's commission plus any resulting loss);
- disclosure of confidential information, especially to competing firms; and

- incompetence or negligence on the part of sub-contractors for which the consultant is responsible.

Once they realise that a problem exists most consultants will do their best to make amends, either by completing unfinished work or by refunding fees. Occasionally, however, a consultant might challenge your allegations by claiming that you were the cause of the difficulty or that he or she was wrongly or inadequately briefed. In this case you should complain to the consultant's trade association if he or she belongs to one (eg, the Management Consultancies Association, the Institute of Management Consultants, or the Association of Independent Computer Consultants, etc – see Chapters 1 and 8) and ask it to intervene. Often, such bodies will arbitrate in such disputes. Ultimately, however, you might need to take the consultant to court.

If the amount involved is less than £500 then unless the case involves complex matters of law or if fraud is alleged, you must use the county court 'small claims' procedure. This, in comparison with standard county court proceedings, reduces the formality and inconvenience involved, though all court appearances are harrowing to some degree. County courts themselves can currently handle cases involving sums of up to £5,000 for each alleged breach of contract. The High Court of Justice deals with cases involving larger sums.*

The cost of using the small claims procedure is only a few pounds, and solicitor's costs cannot be awarded against the losing side. Actions in higher courts are much more expensive.

Nevertheless, regard legal action only as a last resort. Much time, effort and energy have to be devoted to preparing a case, and you are not guaranteed your money even if you win. If a large sum is involved the consultant may choose simply to liquidate his or her firm, and it is *your* responsibility – not that of the court – to enforce payment of the judgement. Enforcement can be tedious and expensive, so think carefully before embarking along this road: there is absolutely no point in proceeding if the debtor has no money or assets to sell (bankruptcy of the debtor might be a better option in this case, since when bankruptcy proceedings are threatened, previously undisclosed assets sometimes suddenly appear). However, enforcement costs are recoverable from the debtor if you do eventually succeed.

---

*For details of how to take someone to court see Chapter five of my book *Small Business Survival*, Pitman Publishers, 1989.

Index

1992, 65, 93, 212
1992 consultants, 242–67

ACAS, 157, 178
accountants, 108, 269
accounting bodies, 109
accounting firms, 10
ACORN, 200
acquisition strategies, 64
Administration of Justice Act 1970, 114
Advertisers' Annual, 204, 206
advertising, above the line, 202
advertising agents, 201
Advertising Association, 195, 204, 206
advertising in the European Community, 261
advertising staff, in-house, 13
agency agreements, 256
agency representation, 254
agents, 22–3, 286
APACS, 67
appraisal, 49
appraisal, employee, 172
architects, 231
Association of British Chambers of Commerce, 246, 266
Association of British Factors, 263, 266
Association of Independent Computer Specialists, 135, 154, 295
Association of Media Independents Limited, 206
audit trail, 139
auditing, 110
auditing, management, 24
auditor's fees, 111

BACIE, 182
brainstorming, 216
breach of contract, 285
British Direct Marketing Association, 191, 206
British Exporters' Association, 266

British Institute of Management, 32, 195, 206
British Psychological Society, 156, 182
British Standards Institute, 90, 106
BS 5750, 90–91
business plans, 268

cabotage, 244
CACI, 200, 206
CADCAM, 150
CAM Foundation, 206
Campaign magazine, 206
capital structures of companies, 115
Chartered Association of Certified Accountants, 120
Chartered Institute of Building, 125, 129, 230, 241
    Handbook and List of Members, 129, 241
Chartered Institute of Public Accountants, 120
Chartered Institute of Transport, 221, 228
City Directory, The, 113, 120
Collection Agencies Association, 120
collection of foreign debts, 263
commercial estate agents, 236
commercial software, 147
Commission for Racial Equality, 179, 182
commission versus fixed fee payment systems, 41
Communication, Advertising and Marketing Foundation, (CAM), 184
competitive strategy, 62
computer aided design, 215
computer bureau, use in direct marketing, 190
computer consultants, 130
computer installation costs, 137
computerisation, 131
computerised accounts, 138

Computer Services Association, 135, 154
Computer Users Year Book, 154
Confederation of British Industry, 28, 32, 127, 129
confirming houses, 258
consultancy partnerships, 291
consultancy styles, 21
consultant project managers, 123
Consumer Protection Act 1987, 292–3
contingency allowances, 41
contract hire, 224
contract manufacturing, 260
contract purchase of vehicles, 224
contracts, consultancy, 45
copyright, 47
core workers, 85
corporate imaging, 197
corporate planning, 54
cost reduction, 118
costing a consultancy project, 45
county court small claims procedure, 295
Creative Handbook, The, 206
creative processes, 216
creativity within large consultancies, 15
credit factors, 263
credit management, 113
crisis (disaster) consultancy, 198
culture within organisations, 75
Customs 1988, 252

data processing, 132
debt collection, 114–15
decentralisation, 81
defects in products, 293
demand for consultancy services, 19
departmentation, 80
Department of Trade and Industry, 32, 266
design consultants, 208
Design Council, 195, 214, 219
Design magazine, 219
design strategy, 209
designer software, 148
diagnostic methods, 20
directive consultancy, 21
direct marketing consultancies, 189
Direct Marketing Guide, 207
Direct Marketing World magazine, 192, 207
Directory of Management Consultants in the UK, 28
Direct Response magazine, 192, 207

disbursements, 40
disclaimers, 290
dismissal of employees, 176
distribution agents, 255
distributors, 186
divisionalisation, 82
DPA, 68
DTI 'Exports to Europe' branch, 250
duty of care, 289

EC Carnets, 252
EC contract law, 264
employee remuneration consultants, 169
employee share schemes, 170
Employment Protection (Consolidation) Act 1978, 86, 176
EN 29000, 90
Engineering magazine, 219
Enterprise Initiative, 29, 31, 94, 100, 133, 184, 214, 269
environmental change, 53
Equal Opportunities Commission, 179, 182
equal opportunities legislation, 179
equipment and service suppliers, 22
estate agents, 230
estimates for consultancy services, 35, 280
European Commission, 245, 266
European companies, 64, 245
European Economic Interest Groups, 257
European markets, 247, 251
exclusion clauses, 294
executive leasing, 126
executive search consultants, 163
exemption clauses, 290
exhibiting, 194
exhibition stand planning, 195
expert systems, 152
export administration companies, 257
Export Buying Offices' Association 266
Export Credit Guarantee Department, 262, 266
Export Direction magazine, 246, 266
export houses, 259
Export Houses Association, 266
Export Intelligence Service, 266
Export Marketing Information Centre, 267
Export Network magazine, 267
export plans, 264
Export Today magazine, 246, 267

exporting, indirect, 258
exporting to the single European
 market, 252
Exports to Europe branch of DTI, 102,
 106

facilities management, 25, 143
factoring, 113
FEACO, 29, 32
feasibility studies, 144
fee structures, 43
fees, 38
financial management consultancy,
 107, 113
financial management support services,
 138
fixed fees, 39, 43
Fleet News magazine, 223, 228
fleet vehicle maintenance, 221
flexible manufacturing systems, 103
flexible versus formal structures, 79
flexible workforces, 84
franchising, 260
Fraser plan, 161
freight forwarders, 253
fulfilment houses, 189–90
full-service consultancies, 14, 35

genuine occupational qualifications,
 179
grievance procedure, 171
groupage, 25

headhunters, 163
Higher Education Diplomas, 243
honeycomb organisations, 16
human resource planning, 181
human resources management
 consultants, 155

industrial relations, 179
Industrial Society, The, 156, 182
information technology, 130
in-house services, 12
Institute of Chartered Accountants, 120
Institute of Directors, 32
Institute of Freight Forwarders, 221,
 253, 267
Institute of Internal Auditors, 121
Institute of Linguists, 267
Institute of Management Consultants,
 28, 32, 269, 295
Institute of Marketing, 195, 207

Institute of Personnel Management,
 156, 182
Institute of Practitioners in Advertising,
 204, 207
Institute of Public Relations, 207
Institute of Sales Promotion, 188, 195,
 207, 267
Institute of Training and Development,
 156, 182
Institute of Translation and
 Interpreting, 267
insurance, 15
 against professional negligence, 288
intellectual property, 244
investment appraisal, 118
investor relations, 194
invoice discounters, 114
invoicing procedures, 44
ISO 9000, 90
IT consultants, 133

job design, 171–2
job evaluation, 179
joint ventures, 259
just-in-time stock control, 104

Keynote Reports, 207

labour turnover, 181
large consultancies, 11
lease renewals, 236
leasing vehicles, 224
licensing, 259
limited liability, 291
line and staff organisation systems, 79
list broking, 191
locating management consultants, 26
locum management, 126
logical systems design, 146

mailing agencies, 190
mailing lists, preparation of, 191
make or buy decisions, 96
management accountants, 118
management by objectives, 83
Management Consultancies
 Association, 27, 32, 39, 295
management consultancy, 11
 development of, 10
Management Consultancy Information
 Service, 28, 32
management information systems, 140
management of sub-contract labour, 124

manufacturing automation protocol, 103
manufacturing management consultants, 100
Market Research Society, 200, 207, 249, 267
market segmentation, 186
marketing, 183
marketing audit, 185
Marketing, Chartered Institute of, 184
marketing communications consultants, 193
marketing consultants, 183
evaluation of, 187
marketing mix, 184
marketing plans, 68
marketing qualifications, 184
marketing research agencies, 249
marketing research consultants, 199
Marketing Week magazine, 207
matrix organisation, 79
media independents, 203
media relations, 193, 202
misconduct, 177
misrepresentation, 294
Money for Business Magazine, 121
monitoring the project, 48
morphological analysis, 216
motherhood consultancies, 16

objectives, 56, 66, 274
objectivity, 20
ODD consultants, 73
optimised production technology, 104
organisation design, 73

payments by results, 39, 188
performance appraisal, 172
peripheral workers, 85
person specifications, 161
piggy-backing, 256
planned property maintenance, 235
planning permission, 233
plans, marketing, 68
POISE, 67
Porter, Michael, 62
portfolio analysis, 60
positioning, product, 57
premises, 274
process consultancy, 22
product design, 212
product policy, 251
product ranges, 185
product standards, harmonisation of, 212

Production Engineering Research Association, 100, 106
productivity audits, 101
productivity consultants, 101
professional indemnity insurance, 288
professional negligence, 15, 26, 111, 287
professionally qualified staff, 124
management of, 86
project management, 122–3
project planning and control, 124
promotional strategies, 188
property conversion, 239
property development consultants, 238
property licences, 237
property management consultants, 229
property search consultants, 232
property services management, 233
proposals, consultants', 36
public relations consultancies, 192, 207
public sector contracts, 243

quality assurance, 90
Quality Circles, 96
quality management, 89
quality management consultants, 93
quality performance measurement indices, 94
quotations for consultancy services, 280

raising finance, 115
recognition agreements, 174
recruitment algorithms, 160
recruitment consultants, 158
redundancy, 177
redundancy planning, 180
rent reviews, 236
resource consultancy, 22
retainer, 43
risk analysis, 140
Road Haulage Association, 228
road hauliers, 221
robotics, 103
routing system, 227
Royal Institute of British Architects, 241, 292
Royal Institute of Chartered Surveyors, 230, 241

salary structures, 169
sale and leaseback, 237
Sale of Goods Act 1979, 292
sales force, effectiveness of, 185
sales letters, 191

sales promotion consultants, 188
selecting a consultant, 38
selection tests, 164
service companies, 291
single administrative document (SAD), 252
single European market, 242, 251
sister companies, 257
SITPRO, 258, 267
small consultancies, 16
software designers, 148
solicitors, 175
spans of control, 77
specialist consultancies, 10, 16, 34
standardisation, 210
strategy consultant, 51
strikers, dismissal of, 178
suppliers, 22
Supply of Goods and Services Act 1982, 281
surveyors, 230
SWOTS, 67
system design, 148
systems analysis, 145
systems plans, 146

takeovers, 64
TARIC, 252
tax and VAT relief on motor vehicles, 225
team rate for consultancy services, 44
Technical Help for Exporters (THE), 102, 106
technical standards, 102, 245
telemarketing agencies, 190
Television Audience Research Bureau, 200
tests of personality, 164
time based systems, 39
tortious liability, 285
trade secrets, 282
training consultants, 167
Training Officer magazine, 156, 182
training specifications, 168
Transition magazine, 156, 182
transport consultants, 220

Unfair Contract Terms Act 1977, 290
unfair dismissal, 176
unity of command, 78
used vehicle agreement, 225

value analysis, 210
vehicle operations, 226
vehicle purchasing and leasing, 223
vehicle security, 226
venture capital, 117
Venture Capital Report, 121

White Book, The, 207
Work Research Unit of ACAS, 158
writing down allowances, 224
wrongful dismissal, 176–7

Index of Advertisers

DBI Associates Limited   134
Doctus Management Consultancy Limited   93
Drake Beam Morin Limited   157
Remit Consultants Limited   187